Fishing Michigan

Eric Sharp

Detroit Free Press

Credits

Editor: Owen Davis

Designer: Robert Huschka

Artist: Martha Thierry

Photo editor: Craig Porter

Chief copy editor: Tim Marcinkoski

Copy editors: Tom Panzenhagen,
Steve Schrader, Shelly Solon

Design and graphics director: Steve Dorsey

Project coordinator: Dave Robinson

Cover photo: Craig Porter

Photographers: Alan R. Kamuda, Craig Porter, Eric Sharp,
Susan Sharp, David P. Gilkey, Paul Warner

Special thanks: Laurie Delves, Gene Myers

Printed in the United States of America
ISBN 0-937247-40-5

=====

To my wife, Susan,
who in 34 years of marriage
has never insisted that I grow up.

=====

Fishing Michigan

Table of Contents

Introduction vii
Chapter 1: Bass 1
Chapter 2: Walleyes 15
Chapter 3: Salmon 27
Chapter 4: Trout 45
Chapter 5: Perch 61
Chapter 6: Northern pike 65
Chapter 7: Sunfish 73
Chapter 8: Muskies 79
Chapter 9: Sturgeon 89
Chapter 10: Catfish 95
Chapter 11: Suckers 101
Chapter 12: Carp 105
Chapter 13: Ice fishing 115
Chapter 14: Hand-lining 121
Chapter 15: Lures 125
Chapter 16: Tackle 135
Chapter 17: Gadgets 149
Chapter 18: Exotics 159
Chapter 19: Lake St. Clair 165
Chapter 20: Great Lakes 175
Chapter 21: Fishing books 187
Epilogue 195

Introduction

Fishing isn't a spectator sport

FISHING IS AN UNUSUAL SPORT. YOU CAN HAVE LITTLE TANGIBLE success — and still have a great time. As proof, let me tell you about a trip I made back when my mustache was still red and a friend asked me to join him and another buddy on a fishing expedition to the Dead Stream Swamp near Houghton Lake.

The guy who proposed the trip had arranged for a guide to take us and our gear upstream 20 miles, help us set up camp and then leave us on our own with the canoes and a rowboat with a three-horsepower engine, which we would use to come back down four days later.

I should have had second thoughts when we stopped at a grocery store and my friend, who shall remain nameless because he is still alive, but whose initials are retired Detroit Free Press photographer Al Kamuda, announced that all we needed to buy were canned vegetables and butter to cook the fish we would catch. The other fisherman and I insisted on throwing in some bread, peanut butter and bologna, and after loading the groceries into the car, we headed off to meet our guide.

The guide was friendly but seemed a bit frenetic. While getting away from the landing, he managed to shove a heavily loaded, 18-foot boat onto my right hand. I later found I had two broken fingers, but fortunately they didn't inconvenience a southpaw like me as much as I feared.

The next red flag should have gone up as we were motoring up the headwaters of the Muskegon River in the guide's boat with two canoes and the rowboat lashed alongside or towing behind. It had begun raining, and as I huddled in my poncho next to the guide, I realized that some of the moisture on his face wasn't rain but tears.

When I asked what was wrong, he blurted out that he would never forget us for our willingness to take a chance on someone like him. As you might have guessed, my next query was a gentle probe aimed at learning why we would entertain any doubts.

He answered that it wasn't everyone who would hire a guy so recently released from Northville, then a hospital that housed the criminally insane. (I never did learn what he had done to earn residence.)

The rest of that day proved that while the sojourn in Northville might have eliminated his criminal tendencies, he still would have set alarms ringing after an ink-blot test. Perhaps his most interesting accomplishment was setting fire to a five-gallon can filled with gasoline, but space does not allow for a recitation of all his quirks.

We set up camp, eventually convinced the guide we would be fine on our own and breathed sighs of relief as we waved him off downstream (though I must admit that after the sound of his motor died away, I lay in my tent that night listening for faint putt-putts that would indicate he was returning).

It was getting dark and still raining. We fished for a couple of hours without catching anything and went to bed after dining on canned corn and peanut butter and bologna sandwiches and talking about how we would tear up the pike the next day.

When we got up, it was still raining, and the usually clear river looked like a cup of yesterday's coffee. The three of us got into the boat and canoes and spread out upstream over several miles of river, but no one caught anything. We returned to camp just before dark, and as one of the others got the fire going, I stood on the bank casting a red-and-white spoon into the river.

Bang! I got a hit, and though it turned out to be an undersized northern pike, it was a fish. After I released it, we stood in the rain eating canned peas and soggy bologna and peanut butter sandwiches and talking about how the next day we would fish the good-looking, deeper water only a few minutes downstream.

The next morning the rain stopped just long enough for us to remove our ponchos, then get soaked when a hard squall came through as we were eating our breakfast of peanut butter and bologna sandwiches. We pulled on our raingear again, got into the boats and went downstream to one of the likeliest-looking pike and bass spots I had seen in my life. We fished it for 10 hours with half the lures and baits known to man without a bite.

That evening, over our repast of canned mixed vegetables and toasted peanut butter and bologna sandwiches, we formulated a plan for the next day. Rather than concentrating on the river, we would head up some of the side creeks and catch the brook trout that lived in the ponds behind numerous beaver dams. I had fished some of those ponds with great success, and we sat in the rain around a hissing, spitting fire and talked about the chances of catching a 16-inch wallhanger.

The next morning, the engine on the rowboat wouldn't start. Since there seemed to be little point in pulling the engine cover and trying to fix it in the steady rain, we downed our breakfast of peanut butter sandwiches and fried bologna, and I rowed the boat upstream and up a creek while the others paddled the canoes to other tributaries.

I dragged that boat over a dozen beaver dams before I came to one that looked absolutely perfect. Tying off the boat below the dam, I kept my silhouette low and cast a small spinner into the deep, dark pool above.

That pool didn't produce so much as a nip. Nor did the myriad of others, and when I returned to camp that evening I found the other two fishermen had been equally unsuccessful. I must admit there was more than a little solace in that fact, and as we sat in the rain and dined on canned baby carrots and fried peanut butter and bologna sandwiches, we decided to call it a trip the next morning and head for home.

I spent two hours trying to get the outboard going without success, so we headed downstream under paddle power. Thanks to three days of nearly non-stop rain, the river was swollen over its banks and flowing at about five knots. The water was the color of manure and looked like the pioneers' descriptions of some Western streams: "Too thin to plow, too thick to drink."

When we reached the wide waters above Reedsburg Dam, about a mile from our takeout, we came across an elderly man in a 12-foot boat who was trolling for northerns in the rain. When I asked how he was doing, he grinned and lifted up a stringer of hammer-handle pike, none of which would have been within three inches of the legal size limit.

I started to tell him his fish were all undersized, but he was far enough away that I would have had to yell, the rain was falling in earnest, and I decided to let him work it out with the game warden.

Three hours later I was back at our then-home in the Detroit suburb of Harper Woods. We hadn't caught a thing, my tent and sleeping bag were still sitting soggily in the car trunk, and my stomach was upset from the effects of downing four big, greasy cheeseburgers at the first fast-food joint we encountered after leaving the river.

So when my wife, Susan, asked how the trip went, I pondered for a moment, then grinned and said, "Great," and regaled her with our misadventures. And 25 years later, I still grin whenever I think of that trip.

But I have to admit one thing. As an immigrant from Scotland, I never did develop the taste for peanut butter that American kids do while they're still in diapers. And after that trip to the Dead Stream Swamp, I never ate the stuff again unless it was a case of absolute desperation.

The adage says that a bad day of fishing is better than a good day at work. As someone who has had the good fortune to spend many of his working days fishing, I've had the best of both worlds.

Something I've learned during all those thousands of hours of trying to catch fish is that unlike football, baseball and hockey, angling isn't a spectator sport. True, I watch fishing shows on television and read fishing magazines like every other angler when I can't get out, but fishing is still something you do rather than watch.

I've also learned why we call it "fishing" and not "catching," and that the important thing is the process rather than the result. What makes fishing fun isn't putting fish in the boat but figuring out how to put them there.

For more than 20 years I've been a full-time outdoors writer who gets to fish for all kinds of species in many of the best waters in the world, from smallmouth bass on Lake Erie to striped marlin off New Zealand's Bay of Islands, from Arctic char in northern Canada to huge, transplanted brook trout at the tip of South America.

I've been in the best places at the best times, and I've had some success, but there still are days that end with the scoreboard reading: Fish 20, Outdoors Writer 0.

And it's not always the size of the fish that counts. I've had just as much fun and finished the day just as happy after catching a mess of panfish as a day when I caught a 500-pound marlin. Taking pleasure in the fishing rather than the catching is a trait I've noticed in most of the good anglers I've been lucky enough to meet.

Mark Martin lives in Twin Lake, Mich. One of the country's top walleye pros, he routinely gets to fish on Lake Erie, Saginaw Bay, Little Bay de Noc and Lake Michigan for walleyes so big that one weighs as much as the average daily limit of five or six fish in most parts of the country.

Yet I've watched Martin break into an ear-to-ear grin as he pulls a 10-inch perch through the ice and adds it to a bucket load that will be dinner in a couple of hours.

Flip Pallot does an excellent television show called "The Walker's Cay Chronicles" and spends most of his time roaming salt water to catch everything from bonefish to tuna. But his favorite pastime when he's at home in north Florida is taking his airboat onto the headwaters of the beautiful St. Johns River to throw poppers at bluegills with a fly rod.

For further proof that the species you seek isn't all that important, consider the lifetime quest of a nice guy named George Von Schrader, who introduced me to fly-fishing for carp on the Great Lakes. Originally from Wisconsin, he started fly-fishing for carp in Green Bay in the 1970s. After moving to Arkansas, he came back to the Great Lakes for a month every summer to continue his search for giant carp on the fly.

George eventually became the best and most knowledgeable American carp angler I've known, and he spent much of his too-brief life trying to convince others that this usually reviled species was truly a remarkable game fish.

Like most American anglers, I held carp in contempt, a sentiment that lasted about a half-dozen fly casts. While I spooked some huge carp (probably the smartest and wariest fish in the world), Von Schrader caught and released three.

Once I landed my first 20-pounder, I was hooked harder than the fish, and it wasn't long before I expanded my horizons beyond George's sight-casting techniques with fly and spinning rods. I've fished for carp with 12-foot English bait rods, electronic bite indicators and other specialized European tackle in the murky waters of southern Michigan.

And how many of you have experienced a great sucker run, when you can catch 50, 60, maybe 100 fish a day if you use light tackle and apply finesse techniques usually used for steelhead? After a day like that, you will never think of suckers as trash fish again.

I've also found fishing to be balm for a troubled mind.

Rick Jameson, the former director of Michigan United Conservation Clubs, died of cancer at age 49. A few days before he died, he called and asked if I would take him fishing. We went to a little private lake he had access to and spent a few lazy, peaceful hours throwing flies and lures at bluegills until Rick's thin, weakened body was racked by the terrible after-effects of chemotherapy.

As we drove home that afternoon on back roads, Rick, who had no illusions about what was to come, drank in the beautiful Michigan summer day and said that he would like to make one more fishing trip the next weekend. On Friday, his wife, Robbie, called to say she had found him dead in his bed, and it helps me to think that he died imagining the beautiful lake we would visit and the fish we would catch the next morning.

MICHIGAN FISHING

Michiganders are fortunate to live in a state that might have the best freshwater fishing in the nation. We have a couple of things going for us that allows me to make that statement.

First, we have a climate that, while cold in the winter, still supports a much bigger variety of game fish than found in most other states. The Michigan Department of Natural Resources gives master angler awards for 52 types of fish. The National Fresh Water Hall of Fame in Hayward, Wis., recognizes records for 58 Michigan species, ranging from warm-water critters like largemouth bass, longnose gar and warmouth to near-Arctic species like lake trout, brook trout, burbot and northern pike. Only seven states have more species in the record book.

Second, Michigan offers anglers tremendous access to fishing. You can drive along some of the great trout steams out West or past famed bass lakes in the South, and in many areas all you can do is look, because the land around those streams is locked up in private hands and there are few places where anglers can get to the water.

But Michigan anglers can find boat-launching sites, wading access and bank-fishing spots along much of the state's 36,000 miles of creeks, brooks and rivers, 11,000 inland lakes and more than 3,000 miles of Great Lakes shoreline.

More than 1.3-million adults buy fishing licenses in Michigan every year, spending $18 million on licenses and more than $1 billion on tackle and trips. The only states where people spend more are California and Florida, which not only have two to four times our population but also draw far greater numbers of visitors who go to those places to fish. That's hard to understand when our Great Lakes fishing is so good, accessible and relatively cheap.

Michigan truly has some amazing fishing. During the fall, the St. Marys River at Sault St. Marie, the Pere Marquette in the northwestern Lower Peninsula, the St. Joseph in the southwest and the Au Sable on the eastern side offer the finest fishing for chinook and coho salmon outside of Alaska, and they would give many Alaskan streams a run for their money in numbers of fish and average size.

The St. Marys also is developing an excellent summer fishery for Atlantic salmon. Anglers can drive to the parking lot at the local electrical generating plant and begin casting for fish they would pay $500 to $1,000 a day to catch on the famed salmon rivers of Canada and Europe.

As for steelhead, anglers on more than a dozen Michigan rivers routinely catch as many fish in a day as most California, Oregon and Washington anglers could expect to catch in a season. And when it comes to trolling, I was in a boat on Lake Erie where four anglers caught and released 54 steelies that averaged 10 pounds in a five-hour afternoon.

While walleyes are found in lakes throughout the state, Little Bay de Noc on Lake Michigan, Saginaw Bay on Lake Huron and the western end of Lake Erie offer the finest walleye fishing in the world in terms of numbers and size.

The Professional Walleye Trail and Wal-Mart RCL Walleye Circuit annually schedule events on these waters because they know the people who see these tournaments on television will be agog as they watch anglers cull eight-pound fish for bigger ones. During a recent walleye tournament in western lake Erie, anglers were required to put up a 10-fish bag that weighed 85 pounds to make the top-10 cutoff for the final day.

Do you like bass fishing? Lake St. Clair and Lake Erie are without question the best smallmouth lakes in the country and among the top five all-around bass waters.

It's not unusual for anglers to catch 50 to 100 smallmouth a day on these waters, fish that average two to three pounds and occasionally exceed five. But there are a host of other rivers and lakes where smallmouth and largemouth bass can be fished with fly, spinning and casting tackle.

And if you like solitude as much as bass, try a midweek trip to Craig Lakes State park in the central Upper Peninsula. The only access is by foot or boat, with no motors allowed, so most lakes in the system have only a couple of anglers who portage in a canoe or an inflatable.

Huge areas of the Lake Michigan shoreline have superb smallmouth fishing that is ignored because everyone is farther offshore fishing for trout and salmon.

Speaking of trout, the Manistee and Au Sable are two of the best-known streams in eastern America, and they are regaining their former glory after a couple of decades of decline. Fly-fishing is what draws most anglers, but there are tons of opportunities for spin and bait fishermen in these and hundreds of lesser-known but not necessarily lesser streams.

One thing I can't do in a book, and wouldn't dream of trying, is to teach anyone how to fish. That's not to say you can't learn a lot from fishing books, and there is extensive literature that will make you a better angler if you read it.

But all a book can do is provide information about things the writer has learned and that you can try. It's still up to you to go out and try to put those suggestions into practice.

In most cases you'll find that the suggestions work, at least some of the time. But this is when an angler must really put to use the most important piece of tackle he owns — the brain that lets him observe what's happening and mark down those observations in his mind for future use.

If you go to a lake or river and catch fish on a day when the air temperature is 80 degrees, the water is 60, the sky is sunny and the water is clear, that's no guarantee you can catch fish from the same lake or river on a day when the air is 60, the water is 40, the sky is overcast and the water is murky.

Observation should tell you that it might be time to try something different, and I've seen days when something different has meant going home and watching the end of a baseball game on television.

I hope you will find things within these pages that will help you catch more and bigger fish, or perhaps species you haven't caught before. But mostly I hope to encourage you to get out and fish more, and in places you've never been. Because in the long run, fishing isn't so much about what or how much you catch as it is about being out there trying to catch something.

Chapter 1

Bass

T HE BIGGEST LARGEMOUTH BASS I ALMOST CAUGHT DOESN'T
hang on a wall but in my memory, as huge and luminous as a full moon
rising over Lake Huron.

I only need to close my eyes to see that immense body — like a watermelon
with fins — and feel its incredible weight bending the rod, then experience
again the stunned disbelief as I watched it swim away.

It's not my warmest and cuddliest memory, yet it's one I wouldn't give up for
memories of 10,000 smaller fish I landed.

Bass — largemouth and smallmouth — are by far the most important sport
fish in the United States, although not as popular as their smaller relatives, the
sunfish. Paul Young, a Scottish friend who hosts a wonderful European television program called "Hooked on Fishing," once introduced a show about bass
fishing on Lake St. Clair by saying, "We're going to try to learn why 20–million
American anglers spend so much time and money pursuing a fish that rarely
grows bigger than five pounds."

The reason is that bass have a lot going for them. They are ubiquitous, with
largemouths dominating in the South, smallmouths north of 42 degrees latitude, and both species available to anglers in most places east of the Rockies.
The only state that doesn't have a bass population is Alaska.

In 2001, 44 percent of the American angling population fished for the several closely related species lumped under the term black bass. A total of 191-mil-
lion angler days were spent in pursuit of smallmouths, largemouths, Kentucky
(spotted), redeye, Suwannee, Flint River and Apalachicola bass, and a couple
of in-between versions like the Neosho smallmouth.

Bass anglers spend at least $15 billion a year on their angling activities, including more than $1.75 billion on licenses and $9 billion on tackle. That works out to an average of about $750 for every man, woman and child who tries to catch a bass. But many of those anglers were casual types who probably spent less than $50 on a handful of fishing days all season.

The bulk of the bass-fishing money is spent by intense specialists who own $35,000 bass boats they replace more often than their cars, $2,000 worth of rods and reels, and at least that much in artificial lures and other tackle (not hard to spend in a day when bass plugs sell for $5 to $15).

Bass are remarkably aggressive and can be caught in huge numbers on all kinds of tackle when conditions are right. Gerry Gostenik, a professional bass angler and guide from Dearborn, and I once caught and released more than 80 smallmouths that averaged more than three pounds in four hours on a gorgeous November afternoon on Lake Erie.

We caught those fish in 17 to 23 feet of water by doing the Erie drag, twitching tube lures in such elegant colors as snot across the sand.

I remember another glassy summer morning on Lake St. Clair when I fished with Kim Stricker, a paint manufacturer who also fishes the national tournament circuit as a pro. In two hours we caught 40 big smallies that smashed surface plugs, one of the most exciting forms of angling I know.

But my older son Cameron still talks about a week on Peninsula Lake in Ontario, when he was eight. He caught 105 smallmouths up to five pounds on worms and leeches in five days. Cameron is 31 now, but what he remembers most is that it was the first time he fished mostly on his own, without the old man helping and telling him what to do.

Before we get deeper into this discussion of Michigan bass fishing, I just have to tell you about that monster largemouth I almost caught. As you might have guessed, it was in Florida, home of a subspecies of Micropterus salmoides that grows so large that the Florida-strain bass has a separate section in the International Game Fish Association record books. (Most of the world line-class records now come from a couple of California lakes where Florida largemouths were transplanted 20 years ago.)

I was driving from Ft. Myers to Miami on Alligator Alley in the days before it became I-75, when there was no fence to stop anglers from fishing in the canals that line much of that road as it slices through the Everglades.

There was a wide spot in a canal about 15 miles east of the toll gate at the Naples end, and I often had caught bass up to five pounds there by casting spoons and plastics from shore. Since I had a couple of hours to spare before I had to be home for dinner, I decided to stop and fish.

I had caught and released some two-pounders on a Johnson silver minnow spoon when I noticed an alligator a ways up the canal that had edged to within about 10 feet of an oblivious mallard duck. "Hmm," I thought, "this might get interesting," and watched to see if the gator got his lunch.

I was continuing to reel the spoon in slowly while staring at the unfolding tooth-and-claw tableau when I felt a slowly growing resistance. It brought my attention back to the lure, which I figured had hung up on some vegetation. It wasn't until I had stared into the water for several seconds that I realized the large, dark object about three feet down in the water a few feet from my toes was the back of a huge bass. And the reason I couldn't see my spoon was that it was in the bass' mouth.

When I say that bass was huge, I mean HUGE. I was then the outdoors writer for the Miami Herald, a sister paper to the Free Press, and regularly got the opportunity to fish for big bass in some of the South's best waters. I had landed several bigger than 10 pounds, and this one made them look like bluegills. I tell people it was at least 15 pounds, but in my heart of hearts I know it was closer to 20.

Now you have to realize that all this took place in a few seconds, and when I realized what was going on, I struck upward with the seven-foot bass rod and hit that sucker with all the power I thought the 20-pound line could handle.

Friends, that was a powerful rod, made to convince bass that burrowed into dense weeds that they could either leave voluntarily or leave significant bits of their anatomy behind. On many occasions, the rod boated five-pound bass that would have beaten George Perry's 80-year-old world record of 22 pounds, four ounces if I had been allowed to weigh the weeds I hauled in with the fish.

As I struck, there was a tremendous weight on the line, like trying to lift a concrete block with a rod, and I could see the bass jerk upward about a foot and then roll right over until it showed its snow-white belly. While it was still upside down, the fish shook its head frantically, opened a mouth as big around as a five-gallon bucket and then . . . nothing. The rod straightened, the bass swam away, and I stood staring stupidly at an empty canal.

For a second I thought I had broken the line. Then I saw that the spoon was still in the water. I reeled in and stared in disbelief. The hook was missing. I examined the lure closely and saw that the hook shank had broken off where a rivet, which held it to the spoon, had rusted.

I had used that spoon for years in fresh water and salt, had seen the rust and done nothing about it, and paid the price for my carelessness.

Species

There are at least seven species of closely related freshwater fish in the United States that we call bass but which aren't, and three others that aren't closely related to the first group but which really are bass. This illustrates why biologists use scientific names when they talk about fish.

Smallmouths (Micropterus dolomieui), largemouths (Micropterus salmoides) and several of their close cousins are among the non-true-bass species. They really are oversized members of the sunfish family, the black basses, and the only black bass that live in Michigan. (Smaller species like the Kentucky, Apalachicola, Flint River and redeye bass all live farther south.)

White bass, which also live in Michigan, are true basses, members of the temperate bass family. That family includes the striped bass, yellow bass and white perch (which is not a perch), and we'll get back to them later.

But when you say "bass" in Michigan (and most of the United States, for that matter), you're talking smallmouths and largemouths. Some people have trouble telling them apart, but it really isn't hard. In smallmouths, the rear corner of the jaw extends only to the center of the eye, and there is often (but not always) some red in the eye itself. In largemouths, the rear corner of the mouth extends behind the eye. All you have to do is close the fish's mouth and look.

In addition, most anglers soon recognize the distinct color differences in each species. While there is no single color pattern for largemouths or smallmouths, largemouths almost always have a darker back, well-delineated marks (blotches or diamonds) along the lateral line on their sides, and light bellies.

Smallmouths tend to be more uniformly colored and usually have red eyes. Those caught over sandy bottoms are often pale green on top, shading to paler green on the sides to white on the bellies. Those taken from dark bottoms are usually dark bronze to almost black on top, with mottled green or bronze vertically striped sides and dingy bellies.

Fred Mather, a 19th Century fisheries biologist who helped establish America's hatchery systems, wrote a poem about the differences:

The little mouth has little scales, there's red in his handsome eye.
The scales extend on his vertical fins, and his forehead is round and high.
His forehead is full and high, my boys, and he sleeps the winter through.
He likes the rocks in summertime, Micropterus dolomieui.
The bigmouth has the biggest scales, and a pit scooped in his head.
His mouth is cut beyond his eye, in which is nary a red.
In his eye is nary a red, my boys, but keen and well he sees.
He has a dark stripe on his sides, Micropterus salmoides.

Smallmouths and largemouths overlap through most of their ranges, largely because smallmouths have been transplanted to many southern waters, but they have decidedly different preferences in habitat.

At the extreme northern end, many waters will hold nothing but smallmouths. At the extreme southern end, you will find only largemouths. In between, one species usually will dominate, depending on which gets the most advantage from the habitat.

Smallmouths

More than 100 years ago, in "The Book of the Black Bass," Dr. James Henshall wrote the famous line: "The black bass is, inch for inch and pound for pound, the gamest fish that swims."

You can argue all you want in favor of other species, but even people who disagree with Henshall admit that the smallie is right up there. I've never been able to select a single favorite species of fish the way some friends do, but the smallmouth is always among my top three (at the moment the others are bonefish and steelhead). Bronzebacks don't bite a lure, they attack it, and once they're hooked, they fight all the way to the boat.

Henshall said he originally considered the smallmouth to be the better game species of the two biggest American bass but eventually changed his mind, arguing that if all things are equal (water temperature, size, etc.), the largemouth is just as hard a fighter.

I have to disagree. I've found that largemouths from northern waters do fight harder than those in the South, but lactic acids build up quickly in the muscles of even the most northern largemouths, and their general pattern is to fight hard for a couple of minutes, then quit.

That's why pro bass anglers developed techniques for derricking largemouth bass into their boats within seconds of hooking them, and why some of those same pros dislike the new tournaments on northern smallmouth waters, where the bass fight so hard and long that there is a much greater chance of losing the fish before it can be boated.

Nationally, the biggest smallmouths don't get as large as the biggest large-mouths, but in Michigan the smallies on average are as big or even a little bigger than largemouths. Three-pound, 17-inch smallmouths are commonplace here, and 18-inch, four-pounders aren't unusual. But most of those five- to six-pound, 20- to 22-inch fish that people claim to catch would shrink dramatically if they were weighed or measured.

Smallmouths in northern waters can live more than 15 years, although few probably make it past 10. (It takes that long to reach 20 inches, and there aren't that many 20-inchers.) At the southern end of their range, they grow a lot faster but live only about half as long.

The world-record smallmouth of 11 pounds, 15 ounces came out of Dale Hollow Reservoir in Tennessee, and the only other smallie bigger than 10 pounds in the International Game Fish Association record book came from Kentucky.

Randy VanDam, owner of D&R Sports in Kalamazoo and the older brother of renowned bass pro Kevin VanDam, caught an Ohio-record smallmouth of nine pounds, eight ounces in Lake Erie in 1993. As the Erie smallmouth population continues to grow and the winters get milder, there is a good possibility that a 10-pound-plus smallmouth will come from its waters.

The Michigan-record smallmouth is nine pounds, four ounces, caught in 1906.

Smallmouth bass feed much more heavily on crayfish than their largemouth cousins, so my tackle box is loaded with lures in crayfish colors (olive and dark orange). But the truth is that a hungry smallmouth will try to eat just about anything that doesn't look dangerous, and an angry smallmouth (like one guarding a nest) will attack anything, period.

Smallmouths eat smaller fish, but they also feed much more heavily than largemouths on small invertebrates like stone-fly nymphs, hellgrammites (dobsonfly nymphs), leeches and dragonfly larvae, making them excellent targets for the fly rod in shallow water. Smallmouths also take flying insects that land on the water, and in the Great Lakes region they will gorge themselves on mayflies during the annual hatches of the Hexagenia species.

I have caught smallmouths in late June so full of mayflies that when we lifted them out of the water, a fist-sized mass of brown sludge poured from their mouths onto the deck.

Largely because of what they like to eat, smallmouths prefer clear, cool water (55 to 70 degrees is ideal), and they love moderate current, which is why you find so many in places like the Huron and St. Clair rivers. They also like deep water, which serves as a winter refuge, so they're not often found in smaller lakes and ponds where largemouths thrive.

Smallmouths prefer rocky areas where they can find a lot of crayfish and insect larvae, but they also will roam in packs over sand flats in lakes in pursuit of schools of minnows.

Smallmouths in lakes and big rivers usually hang out in shallow water in spring, then disperse after spawning. Smaller fish often stay in the shallow areas, but larger smallmouths usually move into deeper water, eight feet or more. In the heat of summer and depths of winter, they can be found loafing in schools in 20 to 40 feet of water, where the oxygen levels are highest, and where the temperature is lower in summer and higher in winter.

Minnesota recently allowed a bass season through the winter, and ice fishermen there report that they are catching smallmouth bass at depths of 60 to 70 feet on inland lakes.

Smallmouths are notorious wanderers. Bass pros say the problem with locating a good pocket of smallmouths before a tournament is that they might not be there when it comes time to fish for money. But that seems to change in fall and winter, when the fish congregate on a reef or other area with good underwater contours and settle in for months at a time.

Smallmouths usually spawn in late spring in two to six feet of water when the water temperature reaches about 60 degrees. They like to build their nests by a rock or chunk of downed timber, but in places like Lake St. Clair, which has an almost featureless bottom, they will spawn in last year's weed beds and on small rubble.

The male guards the nest for a couple of weeks after the female lays the eggs. Smallmouths at this time are as irritable as an elephant with a sore nose and as aggressive as a starving grizzly bear.

The nests usually appear as light, round patches on the bottom, two to four feet across, where the parent fish have carried away the debris to provide a clean base to lay eggs. In parts of Lake St. Clair and other places with muck-bottomed bays, the nests sometimes appear as black circles on a lighter background.

Just about any lure thrown anywhere near the nest will trigger a defensive attack, and there is a lot of argument about whether it is ethical to fish for smallmouths on beds, even if they are released immediately.

Some anglers and biologists say that removing the fish from the nest, even for a few minutes, allows sunfish and other raiders to dart in and eat many of the eggs. But other anglers and biologists point to places like Lake St. Clair, where there has been extensive — though illegal — catch-and-release fishing during the spawning period in recent years, yet the smallmouth population keeps growing.

PLACES TO FISH

Michigan residents are fortunate in having access to some of the finest bass waters, and perhaps the two best smallmouth waters, in the world — lakes St. Clair and Erie.

Until the mid-1980s, both were good bass lakes but not exceptional. Then came the zebra mussel, a dime-sized, filter-feeding, clam-like organism from Europe. They individually filtered the nutrients out of a few quarts of water a day, and collectively sucked so much water through billions and zillions of feeding tubes that the clarity of St. Clair and Erie more than trebled.

The result was a bonanza for sight-feeders like smallmouths, northern pike and muskellunge, whose numbers skyrocketed, while the walleye population decreased about 50 to 70 percent.

Kent Lake, in Kensington Metropark about 30 minutes from downtown Detroit, provided the most dramatic example I have seen of the way zebra mussels can change a bass fishery.

When I returned to the Free Press in 1990 after a 10-year sojourn in Florida, Kent Lake was a good largemouth fishery where you caught the odd smallmouth. Then the zebra mussels arrived, probably hitchhiking on a boat trailer or the engine cooling water of a boat that had been in the Great Lakes.

In late spring of 2002, we caught 16 smallmouths and one largemouth one morning on Kent Lake. The water has become so much clearer that it favors sight-feeders like smallmouths, which spot prey a distance off and chase it, over ambush-feeders like largemouths, which lie in wait in murkier water and pounce on anything that gets close.

Some other superb smallmouth bass waters are the Detroit River, St. Clair River, Huron River, Shiawassee River, Grand River, Lake Margrethe, the east arm of Grand Traverse Bay, and Waugoshance Point at Wilderness State Park in the Lower Peninsula, and Little Bay de Noc, Craig Lake State Park and Drummond Island in the Upper Peninsula. A ton of other rivers, inland lakes and Great Lakes bays offer excellent numbers of smallmouths, but most don't produce the numbers of four- to six-pound fish the above-named waters do.

Michigan has excellent numbers of largemouth bass and places to fish for them, but relatively few anglers bother in a state where the salmon are king and walleyes and smallmouths the royal court.

That's changing in southern Michigan, which is not only home to most of the largemouths but to the people who join bass clubs and go tournament fishing.

Our bass are the northern largemouth subspecies. Two things differentiate them from the Florida subspecies — a few more scales along the lateral line, which even experts have a hard time spotting, and size, which is obvious to anyone.

A three-year-old Michigan largemouth will average about 12 inches long and one pound. A three-year-old Florida fish will be 15 inches and two pounds. As time goes on, the difference becomes more dramatic, with eight-year-old Michigan largemouth averaging about 20 inches and five pounds, and Florida fish of the same age nearly double that weight.

The difference between northern and southern fish isn't merely a longer growing season, because if you move northern-strain largemouths to the South, they don't grow much faster than they do north of the Mason-Dixon line.

But when we compare peaches to nectarines, or Michigan smallmouths to Michigan largemouths, the picture changes. Largemouths still gain length a little faster than smallmouths in Michigan, but they don't weigh more than our chunky smallies.

Smallmouth and largemouth reach five pounds at about 20 inches in length, something to keep in mind the next time someone holds up a 16-inch fish and announces it's a five-pounder. (You can see all of those you want on the Saturday morning TV fishing shows.)

Largemouths

What does a largemouth bass eat? Anything he can fit inside that bucket mouth.

Among the creatures I have found when examining the stomach contents of largemouths from around the country are fish of numerous species (including smaller bass), crayfish, mud puppies, small lampreys, a young muskrat, sludges of indeterminate insect larvae, baby alligators, leeches, frogs and toads, snakes, dragonflies, small turtles, mice and one unidentifiable, sparrow-sized bird.

In Michigan, largemouths eat any of the above they can find, but their primary prey are fish like gizzard shad, alewives, gobies and sunfish, and they also eat a lot of crayfish.

Slow streams that often silt up, thick vegetation, downed trees and sunken abandoned cars are largemouth palaces. When you think largemouth, think "places to hide," and you'll find fish.

Lakes, docks, anchored boats and raised boathouses are excellent places to look, especially in the morning and evening. But it's important to develop flipping and pitching techniques that let you skip or bounce lures far up into the shadows under these objects, because a lot of bass simply won't come out for food.

Though largemouths usually are turned off by water that looks like three-day-old hot chocolate, moderately murky water is a good place to throw spinner baits, rattling plugs and big plastics. They move a lot of water and tell the fish that even though it can't see the lure, there's something moving through that might be edible.

The toughest place to fish for largemouths is probably in thick vegetation. These fish will live in places that can't be believed unless seen. I have fished largemouths in southern lakes that lived in hydrilla and duckweed so thick that it took the fish three or four tries to break through the surface and grab the weedless rubber frog I had landed on top.

We would cast the lures up there and stand in disbelief as the green mat bulged up several inches, hit from below by bass that apparently could see the silhouette of the lure or hear it skittering over the pads.

PLACES TO FISH

For big largemouths (and some nice smallies), try the lower reaches of the Grand, Kalamazoo and Huron rivers; Cass Lake; weeded shorelines in Lake St. Clair and Lake Erie; Sleepy Hollow State Park near St. Johns and Wakeley Lake near Grayling. The Upper Peninsula also has some decent largemouth fishing, but it's a lot more hit-and-miss, and the fish generally run smaller in a place where the climate has been described as nine months of winter and three months of poor sledding.

TECHNIQUES

The same techniques that catch smallmouth bass also will take largemouths, and vice versa. But there are subtle differences that work better for one species than the other.

The best part about bass fishing is that you can do it so many ways. My favorite is wading a river and casting streamers or poppers with a fly rod for smallmouths. But I also love to drift along the shallow, weedy shorelines of lakes in a belly boat or a cataraft and throw big, weedless surface bugs for largemouths.

Of course, it's tough to beat a 50-fish day doing the Erie drag with a spinning rod and tube bait for open-water smallmouths, or the open-mouthed excitement of teasing a largemouth out of heavy cover with a finesse worm on a bait-casting outfit. Come to think of it, there probably isn't a legal way to catch bass that wouldn't be fun.

Fly-fishing for bass is fun, and it is best done in shallow waters, whether in rivers or lakes.

A good all-around bass rod is an eight-weight, nine to 10 feet long. Most trout fishing is done with four- to six-weight lines, but the heavier line is needed for bass fishing because the lures tend to be heavier and more air-resistant than trout flies. That makes the lures a lot harder to cast on light trout rods.

A relatively inexpensive reel can be used when fly-fishing for bass because bass rarely run more than a few yards, and bass anglers rarely use leader tippets under six pounds, which makes a high-quality drag unnecessary.

You also can get away with a level fly line, which costs about a quarter or a third as much as a weight-forward line or the double-taper lines used for trout fishing. Double-taper lines are unnecessary because they are designed to land a fly and leader delicately, and there isn't a whole lot that's delicate about fly-fishing for bass. The angler often deliberately makes a splat with the line and lure on the surface to get the bass' attention.

A weight-forward line — often sold as a bass bug taper — makes it easier to cast a big lure, but if your budget is tight and you have to make a choice between an expensive line and more poppers, buy a weight-level line and go for the poppers.

I've found that river bass choose the same kinds of lies in swift current that rainbow trout do in colder waters — behind standing sticks or in back-eddies ahead of boulders.

Undercut banks can be highly productive. One afternoon I took about 20 smallmouths ranging from 10 to 14 inches from a 50-yard undercut on an outside bend in the Shiawassee River downstream from Owosso. They must have been lined up under there almost nose to tail.

I also love warm, summer evenings when I can drift a shoreline in a float tube, cataraft or canoe and toss surface poppers with a fly rod. By the way, when it comes to the proper popper color, Jack (Bass) Allen, who was Florida's most famous fly rod bass guide, used to drawl to his clients, "Any color is OK — as long as it's yellow."

My experience is that yellow is the best all-around color for largemouths in lakes, but you better have other colors from green to red to black on hand for those days when the bass decide to make Allen a liar.

For smallmouths, especially in rivers, I prefer poppers in more natural colors — minnow black-and-white, frog green and crayfish olive-and-orange. But smallmouths are also much more likely to take big dry flies, so your box should include humpies, brown drakes, Michigan caddis (Hexagenia limbata) and hopper patterns.

Streamer patterns like the black-nose dace, thunder-creek minnows, woolly bugger, rabbit strip leech, imuddler minnow and zonker work well in streams shallow enough to be waded. But when people ask me what streamers to use to dredge bass out of deep lakes with sinking lines, my answer never wavers — get a spinning rod.

I don't understand what people think they are accomplishing when they drag a fully sinking fly line across the bottom in 10 to 20 feet of water. Other than the fact they are holding a fly rod, I don't see that it has much to do with fly-fishing.

I did develop one fairly effective streamer for dredge fishing about 20 years ago. It's simple, with a black sparkle-yarn body and six-inch black saddle hackles and strips of silver mylar for the tail. I tied it to imitate the most effective single bass bait I know — a black plastic worm.

Spinning and bait-casting anglers have their choice of a whole host of effective baits and techniques that can be varied not just with the seasons but with changing conditions throughout a single day.

After fly-fishing, my second favorite bass technique is used on still mornings or evenings when the sky has a slight haze and the water lies as flat, still and gleaming as a bath of molten lead.

That's when I love to cast surface plugs like a Smithwick River horse, floating Rapala, Pop-R, or even a relative antique like a jitterbug. Nothing in angling is as exciting as that split second when a bass, trout, snook, tarpon or any other fish explodes through the surface to take a lure.

The smallmouths in lakes St. Clair and Erie have figured out that exotic round gobies are tasty and abundant, so anglers are using tube lures the general shape and color of gobies, which probably arrived in the ballast of ocean-going ships.

Anglers also have found floating plastics like flukes and floating worms to be effective bass lures, especially in spring. And for fishing around structure, little beats a weedless jig with a two- to three-inch rubber tail.

But bass also will smack spinner baits, and the second-most exciting kind of fishing might be watching a smallie come rocketing up like a little submarine missile through 15 feet of clear water and drive himself and the lure two feet above the surface.

Surface plugs for bass apparently started in Michigan in the late 1800s when James Heddon whittled a small, fish-shaped object out of a piece of wood, threw it into the water and saw a bass come up and eat it. He whittled some more shapes, fitted them with hooks and an eye to tie the fishing line to, and, *voila,* the Heddon Lure Co. of Dowagiac was born and still turns out such popular plugs as the Torpedo and Zara Spook.

Then there's the Erie drag, one of the simplest and most effective bass fishing techniques I know. It was developed after bass began keying on the round gobies whose population exploded in lakes Erie and St. Clair in the late 1990s. Maximizing its potential involves mastering a few subtleties. The best example I've seen came on a beautiful day in November, when bass pro Gerry Gostenik and I hammered the smallmouths on a reef on the Ontario side of Lake Erie about 30 miles southeast of Windsor.

In its most basic form, the drag involves casting a tube bait and letting it skid across the bottom as the wind pushes the boat. It's a no-brainer technique that almost always will produce fish.

On the day Gostenik and I did so well, another boat was fishing within 50 yards of us, even moving in 50 yards upwind to drift over the same places we did. But we could see we were catching five bass to every one caught by the three anglers in the other boat.

The difference was that they cast out the tube lures and then put their rods in rod holders on the gunwale of the boat. As the boat drifted along, the other anglers sat in the boat seats or stood with their hands in their coat pockets and watched the rod tips. One grabbed a rod whenever he saw the tip jerk to signal a strike.

But Gostenik and I continued to hold our rods in our hands after we cast, and we added a little more action to the lures by twitching them gently as the boat moved with the wind.

I noticed that a lot of our strikes came just after one of those twitches, and we were especially likely to get a hit moments after the bait hung up on a weed or piece of rock and then popped free. With the rod in hand, we were able to set the hook faster, and I'm sure the anglers in the other boat missed a lot of fish because they couldn't pick up the rod in time.

Because they are ambush-feeders, largemouths prefer heavy cover like dense weeds and downed timber, and they also feed more aggressively in murky water. I don't think it is an accident that largemouths have a highly visible, deeply curved lateral line running along their sides, while the lateral line of smallmouths is straighter and less evident. The lateral line is an organ that senses pulsations moving through the water (much as our ears sense sound). The largemouth's lateral line probably is better suited for tracking down things that can be felt moving through the water but not seen.

Fishing for largemouths often involves using much heavier tackle than for smallmouths. One reason is the thick cover largemouths prefer. It sometimes takes 17- or even 30-pound line to land a fish that has wrapped the line around lily pad stalks, dense weed or even the branches of a downed tree. And largemouth anglers usually can get away with heavier line because the water tends to be murkier.

Largemouth anglers in the South think of 10-pound line as ultralight. But 10-pound is probably the most common line for Northern smallmouth anglers, and they sometimes go down to eight- and even six-pound because these fish have eyes like a hawk and can be line shy in clear lakes.

I've saved a discussion of bait fishing until last. That's because most dedicated bass anglers won't use it. They rarely or never kill a fish. But there's no question that a shad drifted under a float or a crayfish cast into a pool at the end of a riffle will catch a lot of bass.

One of the best examples I've seen of the effectiveness of live bait came a couple of years ago when I was fishing for perch on Lake St. Clair with Joe Belanger, a charter skipper from Tilbury, Ontario; Bert Cummings, a Michigan angler who founded Bert's Custom Tackle, and Free Press photographer Craig Porter and his daughter, Rekha, then 10, and son Devin, then 13.

We had caught a stack of big perch, and Rekha had moved up to the bow to fish with Joe when something hit her minnow and bent her rod nearly double. She yelled to Belanger for help, but Joe just coached her, and a few minutes later she landed a four-pound smallmouth that had inhaled a perch minnow.

While Rekha was landing her fish, Devin hooked up with another big smallie. Seeing what was happening, I quit trying to interest perch in the miniature crank bait I was experimenting with and threw it toward the front of the boat.

I hadn't turned the reel handle five times before a smallmouth grabbed the bright-orange, one-inch lure, and for the next half-hour we often had three or four smallmouths on at one time before the school moved off. The fish went three to five pounds.

Last year, I experimented with casting live shad or drifting them under a float in weedy bays at the western end of Lake Erie and caught some impressive largemouths, the biggest nearly six pounds.

The problem with live bait is that a fair proportion of the fish take the bait so deep that trying to retrieve the hook will almost certainly kill them, if not at that moment, then later.

A good rule would be to fish with live bait only if you intend to keep fish to eat. Otherwise, stick with artificials. You'll get about as many fish, once you learn the techniques, and you'll be doing the bass a favor.

CATCH-AND-RELEASE

Dedicated bass anglers like to think that because they practice catch-and-release, they don't kill fish, or at least not many. That assumption must be qualified by noting that the time of year and how the angler handles the fish are key factors.

Some biologists say they see a lot of dead bass floating on Lake St. Clair on Mondays in spring after a weekend when dozens of bass boats are on the waters. The bass season is supposed to be closed then, but anglers go out to practice catch-and-release fishing, mostly for bass that are spawning or preparing to spawn.

Conservation officers haven't made too big an issue out of this practice because walleye and pike seasons are open then, and the bass fishermen can argue in court that the lures they use are just as likely to attract one of those species.

Some biologists say spawning bass are under enormous physical stress, and that fishing for them increases the number that don't survive to spawn the next year.

But other biologists and anglers point out that bass numbers and sizes in Lake St. Clair have increased dramatically in the past 10 years, when the spring catch-and-release fishing became more popular. If the point of fishing regulations is to preserve the species, they say, then keeping the season closed in spring is pointless.

As for those dead-fish Mondays, proponents of opening the bass season in spring argue that some fish die from the stress of spawning whether or not they are hooked by a fisherman. And they say there's no proof that catch-and-release fishing significantly affects bass mortality.

Catch-and-release is the practice of the vast majority of Michigan's dedicated bass anglers all year. My observations have convinced me that most bass taken home for the pot are caught by casual anglers who aren't targeting bass but will happily keep any legal-sized fish they can hook.

I've also made day-after visits to sites where thousands of fish were released after being weighed at major bass tournaments, and I have never seen more than a handful of dead bass floating on the surface.

The tournament fish probably are treated far more carefully than most. Anglers lose ounces, and potentially thousands of dollars, for any fish brought in dead. The tournament pros put sedatives in the live wells to keep the fish quiet, and they also use ice in the wells and aerate the big troughs at weigh-in sites to improve oxygen levels in the water and lactic-acid levels in the fish.

Most fish caught by bass anglers not in tournaments are dropped back in the water as soon as the hook is removed. And when the water is warm, most anglers take pains to revive the bass by the side of the boat before letting it go.

But many anglers could improve their technique when they lift fish out of the water by their lower jaw, called "lipping." Rather than simply holding the bottom of the bass' mouth between their thumb and forefinger and lifting straight up, many anglers bend the front of the jaw down as they turn the fish sideways for a picture or to show a companion.

This can easily break the fish's jaw and open it to a fatal infection.

FOOD VALUE

There are a lot of recipes for largemouth and smallmouth bass, but my favorite is one of the oldest — planked bass.

Scale and fillet the fish and pin it flesh-side out to a pine board a foot wide and two feet long. Rub the fillets with butter, then salt and pepper them liberally.

Stand the plank at an angle about six inches away from a campfire and let it cook for two hours. Check the fish often to make sure it isn't too close to the fire that the edges of the fillets burn, or so far away that they don't cook.

Next, take the fish off the board, throw it away and eat the plank.

Catch-and-release bass fishing is easy for me because I don't think bass taste all that great. (I'm not all that nuts about trout, either, having a decided preference for whitefish and walleye.)

Some people love bass, and I admit that the quality of bass as table fare varies enormously with the water from which they are caught. Fish from turbid waters tend to have a muddy taste, and failing to remove the lateral line from any bass from any waters is a guarantee that I won't like it.

Most people who eat bass fry it, but the best recipes I've tasted require baking the fish.

White bass

This freshwater member of the sea bass family is far removed from the sunfish family. It's more closely related to its bigger relative, the striped bass, than largemouth are to smallmouths.

White bass and striped bass have been cross-bred to produce offspring called wipers or whiterock bass, which have been introduced in many lakes around the country, but not in Michigan or the Great Lakes.

White bass are a lot smaller than stripers (or black bass, for that matter). A big one goes three pounds, and the world record (from Saginaw Bay) is six pounds, seven ounces. They are found throughout the Great Lakes, where they are native, but the best fishing for them probably is in western Lake Erie and the Detroit River, where they show up in early summer after wintering in the deeper waters at mid-lake.

White bass are minnow eaters that travel in schools, so if an angler catches one, he and his companions should cast right back to the same area because there will be more. This is one fish that can be spotted by watching for bird activity on the surface.

White bass pin a school of bait fish against the surface, where diving terns and gulls are waiting to pick them off. Another good sign is a sudden spray of bait fish that leap from the water. Anglers can often load up on white bass by running quickly to these commotions, letting the boat stop and casting into the area where the bait fish were seen or the birds were diving.

I've never understood why white bass aren't held in higher regard. It might be because of their relatively small size (a four-year-old will go about 13 inches and a pound). But a two-pound, 16-incher fights about as hard as any fish of its size. Unfortunately, few white bass live long enough to reach that size.

FOOD VALUE

Very good. The meat is firm, with big white flakes, and it responds well to baking. For reasons of taste and toxic chemicals, be sure to remove the strip of red-brown fat that parallels the lateral line under the skin.

Chapter 2

Walleyes

A FRIEND GOES TO NORTHERN ONTARIO EVERY SUMMER WITH three buddies. They spend a week, fishing every day for walleyes, or pickerel, as they say in Canada, and sit around a campfire each evening to watch the sun go down over the lake.

For years the locals had been telling my friend, "I bet you wish you had pickerel fishing like this at home." My friend never said anything, but last year he took a picture with him. It showed a walleye he had caught a few weeks earlier on Lake Erie.

When he showed it to the boys hanging around the cracker barrel in the local store, there was stunned silence. The 12-pounder my friend was holding was bigger than six of the local walleyes put together. And when my friend told them, truthfully, that the 12-pounder was one of five walleyes bigger than eight pounds he had caught that day, he said you could hear the unspoken "liar" as clearly as if someone were roaring it through a loudspeaker.

Michigan walleye fishing is, bar none, the best in the world. Can you name anyplace else where someone could enter a major walleye tournament, come to the final-day weigh-in with five fish larger than seven pounds each, and finish second?

That happened to Mark Martin of Twin Lake, one of the country's top walleye pros, when he fished a Wal-Mart RCL tournament on Saginaw Bay. Martin led entering the final day, and he came to the last, winner-take-all weigh-in with five fish that went 36 pounds, five ounces. But he was topped by another pro, Todd Riley of Amery, Wis., whose five fish weighed 38 pounds, one ounce.

A few miles down the Ohio shoreline from Michigan, Ted Takasaki, president of Lindy/Little Joe Tackle Co. and a touring pro, posted a one-day limit of five walleyes that weighed 53.2 pounds in a spring Professional Walleye Trail event. It was a record for any tournament.

That same week, two Michigan anglers I know caught and released 17 walleyes bigger than nine pounds in one day. (The biggest went 11 pounds, four ounces on a digital hand scale.) They were fishing a place in Michigan's Lake Erie waters they had never tried before and where they had never seen other boats. When they showed me pictures of the fish, they swore me to secrecy about the location because they think the big fish will concentrate over that small spot again next spring.

Ironically, it might be because our walleye fishing is so good that we Michiganders are far from the best walleye fishermen. A lot of us are accustomed to going out on big water like Lake Erie, Saginaw Bay or Little Bay de Noc and filling a five-fish limit in a couple of hours by trolling. We also think a five-pound walleye is a nice fish but nothing exceptional.

The national tournaments are dominated by people from little towns in Wisconsin, Minnesota, Nebraska and Iowa who think it's normal to spend a whole day vertical jigging and trying to scratch a few two-pounders from some overfished inland lake.

There have always been some walleyes in the Great Lakes system, especially Lake Erie and Lake St. Clair. But until a generation ago, inland lake fishing for Michiganders mostly meant bass, northern pike, trout and sunfish. Most of our inland lakes didn't have walleyes, or not many, and before the 1970s relatively few people owned boats big enough to fish comfortably on the big lakes.

When you read stories about Michigan fishing in the early 1900s, the emphasis is on largemouth and smallmouth bass. Lake Erie had lots of walleyes, and there was a fair population in Lake St. Clair, a short swim up the Detroit River from Lake Erie.

Writers in national magazines talked about the walleye fishing in Minnesota and Wisconsin, and in Lake Erie. But when it came to inland lakes in Michigan and the three other Great Lakes on which we have shoreline, the fishing was for bass, perch, pike, muskellunge, lake trout and whitefish.

But Michigan has enjoyed a walleye explosion in the past 30 years, primarily from the efforts of walleye clubs. They took over the job of raising walleyes from the state Department of Natural Resources and planted fish throughout Michigan.

Houghton Lake is an excellent walleye fishery, and while I hesitate to mention it, so is Lake Margrethe in Crawford County, the lake I live on.

I've caught a fair number of walleyes in the Huron River between Portage and Base Line lakes in Washtenaw County, but most of those were taken when I was drifting leeches for bass.

The Grand River is another stream that produces walleyes all summer, and it's one of the few places where I have consistently taken them on a streamer fly. Again, the walleyes hit when I was fishing streamers for bass in pools at the end of fast riffles.

Muskegon Lake, a drowned river mouth just inside Lake Michigan, is a superb walleye fishery, although many anglers who live there fish only at dusk or after dark. They're usually trolling, although I've caught walleyes there by casting crank baits in the shallows along the docks and seawalls.

In northern Michigan, Lake Leelanau north of Traverse City has long been a good place to catch big walleyes, and I've caught a lot of walleyes slow-trolling crawler harnesses in Burt Lake in Cheboygan County. Many of the fish in that lake were under the legal keeper size of 15 inches, but I suspect they've grown a lot in the three years since I fished there last.

In the Upper Peninsula, some of the best walleye fishing is on the St. Marys River and lakes Gogebic, Michigamme and Chicagon. Most of the fish from the inland lakes will barely surpass the minimum legal size, but the St. Marys is big-fish water, routinely producing walleyes bigger than five pounds.

Some of the DNR's earliest stocking records are for lakes in the UP, and it's interesting to note that walleye probably were not native to most of the lakes there, even though the UP is contiguous to Wisconsin, where walleyes were as common as mosquitoes.

Walleyes are an important part of Michigan's sport fishery today, both in terms of economics and angling benefit. That's especially true in the densely populated, southeastern corner of the state.

The state does a creel census at various ports and uses this information to estimate the number of species caught by anglers each year.

The figures for Lake Michigan in 2000, the latest year available, were: perch, 393,140; chinook salmon, 133,415; coho salmon, 62,700, and walleyes, 37,047 (also behind lake and brown trout). For Lake Erie the numbers were: perch, 223,455; and walleyes, 205,215; with another 97,000 walleyes coming from the contiguous waters of the Detroit River. All the salmonids combined accounted for just a few thousand.

Walleyes are popular because there are a lot of them, they have been plant-ed all over the state, they taste wonderful — baked, broiled or deep-fried — and they are easily accessible to anglers with small boats. If lakes Erie or St. Clair are too rough for a 16-footer, there are always more walleye waters within an hour's drive.

I admit that I'm among those who occasionally disparage the fighting pow-ers of walleyes and say that if they didn't taste so delicious, far fewer people would fish for them. And it's true that the average two- to four-pound walleye caught on an inland lake wouldn't last kissing time in a sparring match with a one-pound smallmouth bass.

But there are three instances when I find that walleyes do fight well — in rivers with a good current, in northern Canadian lakes, and sometimes when they weigh more than about six pounds. But no matter where you're fishing, you'll still get a lot of argument on the question of sporting value.

I consulted a couple of fishing books to see what they said about the wall-eye's sporting qualities. "Freshwater Game Fish of North America" said: "Strong fighters, walleyes stay deep and wage a determined battle." Ken Schultz's massive "Fishing Encyclopedia and Worldwide Angling Guide" said: "As a food fish, the walleye has few peers in fresh water, which helps counter-balance its reputation as a sluggish battler when hooked."

So you pay your money and take your choice.

Walleyes are abundant, but they aren't always easy to catch. That difficulty attracts some excellent anglers who aren't interested in the fight as much as they are in fooling the fish. But I should also say that in 2002 I've traveled to northern Manitoba, northern Ontario and the Boundary Waters Canoe Area Wilderness on the border of Canada and Minnesota, and in all three places I caught walleyes that fought admirably, even though most were only about two pounds.

One reason walleyes probably have earned a reputation as sluggards in Michigan is that we fish for them with relatively heavy trolling tackle and often in fairly deep water.

When I fished the northern regions, we used light spinning rods with four-pound line, which can turn a two-pound walleye into a real battler. We caught a lot of the fish in rivers at the outlets to lakes, where they could use the current to their advantage and bend the rod almost as much as the pike did.

By contrast, on a recent trip on Saginaw Bay we caught walleyes by trolling for them in 25 to 30 feet of water. Most of the fish headed immediately for the bottom, as is the walleye's wont, and we dragged them back to the surface.

Every single one had a distended swim bladder, the result of being pulled up from a region of much greater pressure (about 30 pounds per square inch at 33 feet) to one of lesser pressure (about 15 p.s.i. at the surface).

All of the fish immediately went belly-up when they reached the surface, and we had to fizz them to return them to a right-side-up orientation. (In fizzing, a hollow hypodermic needle is inserted through the skin into the swim bladder to let the excess pressure escape.)

Once they were fizzed, the fish were fine. But even I'm smart enough to know that a walleye with an over-inflated swim bladder probably will be about as active as a scuba diver with the bends.

Walleyes are among the most predatory fish in North America. A big walleye's diet is mostly minnows, smelt and alewives, but they also eat a lot of perch and smaller walleyes if the opportunity presents itself. The exception comes in June and July, when they gorge themselves on hatching brown drake and Hexagenia mayflies.

Walleyes are large members of the perch family, another group that, like pike and salmonids, circles the northern hemisphere in sub-Arctic waters. The family includes darters, small fish that run two to six inches; North American yellow perch and European perch (which has a slightly different color and runs a bit bigger than our perch); sauger, which look a lot like walleyes but are smaller; and zander, the European walleye that looks almost exactly like our fish but averages slightly larger (although the Volga zander of Eurasia is about the size of a sauger).

Biologists apparently can differentiate between zander and walleyes, but I've caught zander in France and they looked just like walleyes to me. One of the American anglers in our group thought they seemed a bit darker, but he was from North Dakota, where the river walleyes are usually quite pale. And I've seen walleyes in the clear, tea-colored waters of Canadian lakes that were just as dusky.

Walleyes come in a wide variety of color variations, mostly a product of the tint of the water and the lake bottom. Our Great Lakes walleyes tend to have dark olive to black backs with pale sides and white bellies.

But catch a walleye from a lake in northern Ontario, Quebec or Manitoba and you'll understand why the early French settlers named them dore, a variation of the French d'or, or "the gold fish." Those walleye usually have sides that are a bright brassy color, shading to bronze on the lower portions. They are beautiful, but I suspect that if you put a few of them over a featureless, light sand bottom in Lake Erie they would soon be as pale as the natives.

The easiest way to differentiate a walleye from a sauger is to look at the dorsal fin (the big front fin on their backs). A sauger's dorsal is spotted; a walleye's is not. In addition, the lower lobe of a walleye's caudal fin (tail) has a white tip; the sauger's does not.

Saugers are thinner and run a bit smaller than walleyes, with few exceeding 20 inches in Michigan. That's mostly because they live half as long. The world-record sauger is eight pounds, 12 ounces, the Michigan record six pounds, nine ounces. The state-record walleye is 17 pounds, three ounces.

Biologists figure that roughly 50 percent of any fish population dies each year from predation, disease, commercial and sport fishing, spawning stress or old age. Since it takes about 10 years for a fish to reach eight pounds, how come Lake Erie, Saginaw Bay and Lake Michigan have so many huge walleyes? The first answer is: Because they have so many walleyes.

If you start with 1,000 walleyes in an inland lake, the odds are that 10 years later only two to four of those fish will be alive. An angler's chances of running across one of those graybeards are slim.

But even in the lean years, millions of walleyes spawn in Lake Erie's western basin each spring, with the females producing about 30,000 eggs for every pound they weigh.

That's an amazing amount of biomass dropped on the bottom, so if you start with, say, 30-billion walleye fry from a single year-class (a conservative estimate, by the way), 10 years later you'll still have tens of thousands around from that year-class.

The second factor is the huge forage base of the Great Lakes. Where fish in inland lakes must rely on insects and other invertebrates, walleyes in the big waters of the Great Lakes have a much richer smorgasbord of alewives, smelt, yellow perch, white perch, white bass, salmon and bass fry, other walleyes and, more recently, round gobies, which I have found in the stomachs of many Lake Erie walleyes.

Walleyes in most waters spawn in March or April just after the ice goes out, when the water is about 45 degrees. (They might spawn as late as May in northern Canada.) The males are usually four years old and the females about six when they make their first spawning run.

In most places, they spawn in the shallows of lakes and rivers, anywhere from one to six feet deep, where the wind action or current will keep the eggs supplied with freshly aerated water.

Many Great Lakes walleyes run up rivers like the Thames and Grand in Ontario and the Maumee in Ohio (which with a run of more than 10-million fish is the world's largest walleye production site). But biologists have learned that many other walleyes spawn on rock reefs 20 to 30 feet down in the big lakes themselves.

Walleye eggs hatch in about three weeks, and the fry soon leave the rocks and gravel where they were born and migrate to the upper layers of the water, where they form part of the prey base for fish like white bass that feed near the surface. A lot of those minnows you see exploding from the surface to escape a bigger predator are probably juvenile walleyes.

At about five months old, the young walleyes return to the bottom, where they are fair game for everything from crayfish to sturgeon, and they also begin to prey on the fry and larvae of other fish.

The survival rate of walleye year-classes can vary wildly. A bumper crop of fish might be followed by a year in which reproduction nearly fails entirely, and the primary reason is the weather.

A sudden cold snap that drops water temperatures just before or when the walleye fry hatch won't have much effect on the fish, but it will kill the minuscule crustaceans that feed walleye fry or even the things eaten by the things walleye fry eat. The collapse of a year-class usually means that something happened to the fish in the fry state, not as adults. Not even commercial fishing can affect walleye populations as much as nature can.

Northern walleyes grow to about four inches their first year. By the second year they are about seven inches and weigh only three or four ounces. They don't reach one foot and one pound until their fourth year, and a 20-inch fish that goes three to four pounds is probably about eight years old.

The eight-pound fish so prevalent in Lake Erie and Saginaw Bay are about 12 years old (and 24 inches long), and a 12- to 13-pound walleye is a graybeard approaching the maximum life span of 20 to 25 years.

Walleyes like water temperatures in the mid-70s. They have been transplanted extensively to waters in the mid-South, especially Arkansas, Tennessee and Kentucky.

Those southern fish don't live as long as northern walleyes, about 13 years at the outside, but they grow much faster, and many anglers think the place to go for a realistic chance at taking a 13- to 15-pound walleye is not Michigan but Greer's Ferry Lake, Ark., which produced the world-record fish of 22 pounds, 11 ounces in 1982.

I should probably say here that every spring I get a call from someone who has heard about a new state-record walleye. Last spring, it was a guy who went into Bottom Line Bait and Tackle on Jefferson in Brownstown Township, the closest bait and tackle store to the busy Lake Erie Metropark launching ramp and the clearinghouse for all of the walleye gossip.

The man's fish was supposedly 17 pounds, 11 ounces, but he never brought it to Bottom Line for weighing on the store's certified scale. And there were a couple of discrepancies in his story.

The first story he told Bill Dougherty, the owner at Bottom Line, was that he kept the fish in his live well for a day but let it go because he was afraid it would die. Then a few days later he said the fish had died, so he tossed it.

What seemed even stranger was that the same guy showed up at Bottom Line a few days later, all excited because he had an eight- or nine-pound walleye he was going to donate to the huge aquarium at the Cabela's store in Dundee. (The man also had called Cabela's to say he was bringing in the 17-pounder for an official measurement, but he never showed up.)

The clerks at Bottom Line thought it was strange that the guy would rush an eight-pounder to the aquarium but never think to donate a state-record fish. I tried to contact the angler several times, but he never returned my calls, and the big fish soon melted away as mysteriously as it had appeared.

The state record remains 17 pounds, three ounces, caught in 1951.

Michigan's walleye are rivaled in size by those in the Columbia River in Washington and the Winnipeg River in Manitoba, which some locals are convinced will produce the next world record.

Walleyes move into the rivers in spring and run upstream to spawn. After spawning, they drop back downstream and recover their strength in bays near the spawning areas. Walleyes usually aren't aggressive biters, and they are even more lethargic than usual in this post-spawning phase, gradually gaining strength and energy.

Their occasional lack of interest in feeding is demonstrated wonderfully in western Lake Erie, where millions of walleyes can be found recuperating in 15 to 25 feet of water through late April and much of May.

Sometimes the fish-finder screen is literally black with walleyes, fish so thick the sonar can't see bottom, and yet anglers might troll for 30 minutes or longer without a bite. The key is to put the lures in front of thousands of walleyes looking for the few in the mood to eat.

By the way, although Lake Erie has a walleye population estimated at 30 million to 35 million, that's only a third to a quarter of the 100 million to 120 million that roamed these waters when the walleye population peaked 10 years ago.

We probably won't see those numbers again. When walleyes peaked, Lake Erie's shad, alewife and smelt populations were high, but there were few big predators other than walleyes. Since then, the populations of salmon, steelhead and smallmouth bass have increased sharply as the zebra mussels cleared the waters and created conditions that improved the breeding success, adult survival and growth rate of these aggressive sight-feeders.

The purchase of an underwater television camera a few years ago has shown me that walleyes can be very finicky feeders. I've used the camera a lot while ice-fishing, and several times I've watched walleyes swim slowly around a bait or lure for up to 30 minutes without touching it.

Once on Little Bay de Noc I saw a 10-pound walleye put its nose an inch from a jigging spoon and watch as the spoon and attached minnow bounced around a few inches from its nose.

I tried jigging the lure, letting it sit still, allowing it to settle to the bottom, bringing it up slowly and bringing it up quickly. The fish would follow it everywhere, but nothing I tried could induce a strike. I tried dropping minnows down to the fish without a hook in them. (The water was so clear that at 23 feet, I could almost count the scales on the walleye's sides.) The fish looked them over and let them fall unmolested.

I even tried lowering a second lure through the same hole to increase the temptation level. As you might guess, all I succeeded in doing was tangling the lines.

By the end of May, walleyes usually are back to feeding normally, but now the big schools start to break up and the fish scatter around whatever body of water they live in. The trick now is to find underwater breaks and points that attract minnows, which in turn will concentrate the walleyes.

Walleyes often move into the shallows after they've recuperated from the stress of spawning, especially in more turbid lakes. The water warms there first, so bait fish are attracted to these areas and the walleyes follow.

On evenings in late spring, I've caught a lot of walleyes by casting crank baits in four to eight feet of water. In inland lakes at this time I usually concentrate on points where the wind-driven walleye chop churns up the water and stirs up a lot of feeding activity. But in Lake Erie and Lake St. Clair, the fish are often on shallow flats far from any visible structure.

You'll hear a lot of people talk about a walleye chop, a one- to two-foot sea that's easily handled by small boats but breaks up the water's surface and stirs up the bottom in feeding areas. A lot of tiny organisms dislodge from the bottom sediments, and slightly larger organisms start feeding on them. The activity moves up the food chain and draws in the bait fish that are the primary food of walleyes.

But just as important, the walleye chop reduces light penetration and underwater visibility. Most experienced anglers can tell you about times they trolled over water that was far too deep for the surface waves to have any effect on the bottom sediments. When the water was smooth, they got few or no bites. When the wind built a good chop, the walleyes started hitting their lures.

If you had talked to a Michigan walleye angler 50 years ago, maybe even 30 years ago, he probably would have assured you that walleyes bit only at night, and those caught during the day were mostly flukes. (There's a pun there somewhere for anyone knowledgeable about fish nomenclature, but I can't figure it out.)

That was before the professional walleye tournaments forced anglers to fish between 7 a.m. and 4 p.m. Suddenly, fish that supposedly wouldn't bite in daylight were landed in large numbers and sizes all day.

Walleyes do tend to feed more actively in low light and at night. They're designed for it. Walleyes get their common name (which was accepted officially by the American Fisheries Society in 1932) from the tapetum lucidum, a membrane at the back of the eye that gathers incoming light and intensifies it much as a night-vision scope does for a human.

It's similar to the membrane found in the eyes of deer, cats and other animals that hunt at night or must avoid nighttime predators.

This built-in night scope, which they share with sauger and zander, lets walleyes hunt efficiently after dark and in turbid water. But a lot of walleyes live in clear lakes, especially in northern Michigan and Canada, and in those conditions the fish usually seek deeper water or the densest weeds during the day.

I suspect a lot of the walleyes-bite-only-at-night myth arose in places like eastern Canada, Minnesota and Wisconsin, where walleyes have long been the most-sought food and sport fish and often inhabit very clear lakes.

In those conditions, it's common to find walleyes on the bottom during the day, conserving their energy by not doing much of anything. Daytime fishing in these waters was often so unproductive that many anglers wouldn't even try to catch walleyes until a couple of hours before dark or in the first light of dawn.

But to dispel that myth, all you had to do was go to Lake St. Clair, which until the 1980s was a turbid lake with underwater visibility that averaged about three feet. (Today, thanks to zebra mussels and pollution control, that figure exceeds 10 feet.)

Detroit-area anglers routinely caught lots of walleyes in daylight, mostly by trolling. They could troll effectively because the turbid water limited the growth of underwater vegetation.

That had changed dramatically by 1990. The clearing water allowed sunlight to penetrate deeper and caused a huge increase in the subsurface greenery. The walleyes disappeared from places where they had been common, and it took awhile for anglers to figure out they could still catch the fish at midday in clear water by vertical jigging in the weeds or working crawler harnesses slowly across the bottom in deeper water.

But in most lakes the night hours are when an angler is more likely to catch the biggest fish, outside of the spring spawning periods. (Places like Lake Erie and Saginaw Bay don't count because you can catch big walleyes there at any time of the day, or year.)

TECHNIQUES

Mark Martin has qualified for the Professional Walleye Trail national championship for 14 straight years, and he is one of the top all-time money winners in the sport.

When he fishes in tournaments, he has to follow the rules of launching at dawn and returning to the dock for a weigh-in around 3 or 4 p.m. But when he fishes for fun at home, he usually doesn't back his boat trailer out of the driveway until about 9 p.m., when he heads for a launching ramp on Muskegon Lake just inside the channel entrance that leads to Lake Michigan.

"There's a population of huge walleyes that only leave the big lake to spawn," Martin said. "The rest of the year, they roam up and down the coast, and you can usually find them hanging off the mouths of the rivers, waiting for the current to bring them food.

"These are huge fish, big killers that will eat a one-pound walleye. I spend a lot of time out here, and you almost never mark these fish in the daytime. But if you come out and troll up and down the shore off the river mouths after dark, they'll be there."

On a warm summer night, Martin and I sat in his big Lund walleye boat as the electric trolling motor on the bow pulled us along parallel to the Muskegon Harbor breakwaters at about 1.5 miles an hour. We were in about 20 feet of water just outside the harbor, and a light breeze raised only a ripple on the dark water.

On the lighted screen of the fish finder, we could see an occasional large, hook-shaped mark that was a fish.

"They're there. Look at those big killers," Martin said as he clipped a No. 9 Rapala crank bait, black with a white belly, onto a spinning rod rigged with 10-pound line. He fastened another Rapala onto a second rod, this one with a dark-blue back, and we flipped them over the side, where they dived to about eight or 10 feet.

We hadn't gone 100 yards when the rod on my side of the boat jerked back. (OK, it was my side because I got to it first.) I lifted it and felt the strong head shake of a big fish.

The one I was fighting that night proved to be a nine-pounder, and we had hardly put it over the side when another rod went and Martin landed a fish that could have been the twin of the one I caught. We hooked and lost another big fish a few minutes later, then the propeller shaft failed on Martin's trolling motor and we decided to call it a night.

"You can't fish these big guys without a trolling motor," he said. "You can go slow enough with your kicker, but it just makes too much noise. You have to use stealth techniques to fish these big walleyes at night."

That's a far cry from the annual floating funfest that forms each spring on Saginaw Bay and Lake Erie as hundreds of boats troll noisily over the heads of millions of big walleyes that for some reason will ignore the chaos and continue to feed.

But even when there are a ton of fish under you, I've learned from veteran charter skippers that the best way to catch fish is to troll around the edges of the mob, or even move off a mile or so and look for a smaller school of fish you can have to yourself.

Spring is a good time to use crank baits on big water like the Great Lakes or Lake St. Clair. But by the time summer starts, most trolling anglers switch to spoons, often in the same colors as those used for salmon but a bit smaller.

A good tactic on a day when the spoon bite is slow is to downsize the spoon. Walleyes can be surprisingly fussy about the size of the lures they take, and picking a spoon that matches the size of the bait fish is equivalent to the fly angler who picks a fly that matches the hatch.

In Lake Erie, some fish, especially the bigger ones, migrate 200 miles east to spend the late summer, fall and early winter off Pennsylvania and New York before heading back toward the western basin in late winter to prepare for the next spawning run. Walleyes tagged in Lake Erie have been caught in Lake Huron and Ontario's Thames River as far as 175 miles from the tagging site.

The fish that stay in the western basin year-round usually break into small schools that roam constantly in search of prey fish, and the trick for anglers is to find a school and work it carefully.

Running the boat directly over the school three or four times with the big motor roaring wide open is a great way to break up the fish and end the bite. Smart anglers circle well around the school until they are upwind, then move through with an electric motor or drift to the fish while jigging for them.

Once the fish start their summer pattern, the plug and spoon trolling bite usually changes to a slower trolling bite with crawler harnesses, a jigging bite or even a drifting bite with harnesses or blade baits like Erie Dearies.

Walleyes are often spread through the water from top to bottom at this time of year, and the trick to catching them is figuring out where in the water they are feeding.

I saw an example of this during a recent walleye tournament on Saginaw Bay. Three days before the event, anglers were catching fish by pulling crawler harnesses on planer boards about 50 feet behind the boat. Snap weights were fastened to the lines about 10 feet above the bait, and most anglers experimented with one- and two-ounce weights that got the baits down about 15 to 25 feet.

This technique produced fish for three days, but on the final day of the event many anglers who didn't change their presentation came in with far smaller catches. Several anglers who had limits on the last day told me they had changed the presentation from midwater to the bottom, either by slowing the boat to a crawl (0.5 miles an hour) or switching to a bottom-bouncer rig that dragged through the mud.

In smaller lakes, jigging off rocky points and over reefs is usually the best way to catch walleyes, especially in midsummer when the fish go deep as the sun comes up. Using a technique called back-trolling, the angler runs the motor in reverse just fast enough to hold the boat back against the current and keep the line from the rod to the jig as close to vertical as possible.

By lifting the rod slowly a few inches and letting it down, the angler gives the jig some action and can also feel a subtle walleye bite, which often is simply increased pressure on the line rather than a well-defined tap or tug.

Walleyes usually don't like big outboard motors roaring over their heads, but they don't seem to mind small ones. I've caught a lot of walleyes trolling inland lakes in northern Michigan with a five-horsepower outboard putt-putting just fast enough to move me at about two miles an hour.

Not long ago, I was with a group that fished a lake in northern Manitoba where we sometimes caught walleyes in water as shallow as three feet, with the motor idling just above their heads. This lake gets little fishing pressure compared to lakes in Michigan, but I think the key was the dark water, with visibility of about two feet.

Blue pike

We should mention the blue pike, a clearly defined walleye subspecies that once flourished in lakes Erie and Ontario and sustained a huge commercial fishery. Until the 1960s, science recognized two walleye subspecies — the yellow walleye, the fish we catch today all over Michigan, and the blue variety.

The blue pike got its name because it had a gunmetal-blue cast, compared to the yellow or olive wash on the other subspecies, and because one of the walleye's popular names was the walleyed pike or pike-perch. The blue pike numbers in Lake Erie alone were estimated at more than 100 million at their peak.

But starting about the time of World War I, commercial fishing, steadily increasing amounts of pollution, and exotic invaders like smelt and alewives began to tip the ecological balance in the lake.

By the mid-1960s, the food chain had been so disrupted that the blue pike had disappeared, and by the early 1970s it was declared extinct. Every now and then someone would catch a fish in Lake Erie that he thought was a blue pike, but scientists were always doubtful.

Then in 1999 an angler from Conneaut, Ohio, Jim Anthony, came forward with a fish he had kept in his family's home freezer for 37 years. It was a blue pike he caught in 1962, when they were already so rare that he decided to try to preserve one.

In late 1998, Anthony read about the efforts of Carol Stepien, a biology researcher at Case Western Reserve University who was trying to learn if the blue pike was truly extinct or if some might still survive in Lake Erie or in lakes in Canada.

Anthony's remarkable effort gave her the DNA samples she needed to compare to fish brought in by people who were sure they had caught blue pike. Unfortunately, the DNA showed that while some of these fish were bluish and had bigger eyes than a stock walleye (another defining sign), their DNA was not the same as in Anthony's fish.

The evidence now is that the blue pike had gone the way of the passenger pigeon and the Michigan grayling by about 1970. But maybe we shouldn't give up hope entirely. I spoke last year to a 75-year-old former commercial fisherman from Canada who said he caught blue pike in Lake Erie into the 1970s.

He would get one every three or four years, and he was convinced that a few might still be around. Since this is a man who started as a commercial fisherman in the late 1930s, when blue pike were abundant, and who had handled tens of thousands of blue pike before they became rare, I have to figure he knew whereof he spoke.

But I also realize that any species, whether it be walleyes or elephants, must maintain a minimum population to ensure its survival. Drop below that level and the species produces too few new members to overcome losses from disease, predation and old age. It also begins to suffer severe genetic defects that result from inbreeding.

Lake Erie today is home to perhaps 30-million walleyes of the yellow sub-species, and the genes from a handful of blue pike would soon be diluted to invisibility. While someone might catch the occasional walleye in Lake Erie that looks like a blue pike, we might be seeing a color phase that's a ghostly reminder of a world gone forever.

Chapter 3

Salmon

N O MATTER WHAT HAPPENED, I WAS GOING TO HANG ON TO THAT rod. Even if I didn't make it, they would find it locked in my cold, dead fingers — assuming they ever found me.

I was fly-fishing for salmon at Carmichael Flats on the Muskegon River just downstream from Newaygo on a warm, fall day after a weekend of rain. The water was high and stained, and big chinooks were jumping like trained dolphins.

Carmichael is always big water, but on this day it seemed a little bigger than usual as I edged out from the bank and into casting distance of a pod of fish about 50 feet across and downstream.

This was back years ago when we were still throwing western flies like the Skykomish sunrise, Alaska Mary Ann and the two-egg sperm, before we had learned about the deadly effectiveness of finesse salmon flies like Spring's wiggler, the P-M blonde and the black stone nymph.

I had spent $200 on an eight-weight carbon fiber rod from Scott, a nine-foot black cannon that with a little practice would hurl those big, ugly streamers 70 feet. The truth was that $200 wasn't in the family budget in 1976, but what the heck, I had nearly a month to think up something before my wife, Susan, saw the credit card bill.

Slowly, carefully, I waded into the faster water and began laying out a long, lazy loop of bright-orange line. It's amazing how dumb we were then. Today, all of my salmon lines are gray or green, muted colors that blend into the water and the trees. The fashion then was for colors as bright as the wig on that guy who used to hold up the John 3:16 signs for the television cameras at every major sporting event.

Dick Pobst, who owned the Orvis shop in Ada, had turned me on to Carmichael Flats the year before, saying it was a place to hunt really big salmon, 30- to 40-pounders that would make your arms ache like you had spent a weekend splitting oak rounds for firewood. Dick was trying to set a state record on fly there, and if it was good enough for him, I figured it was more than good enough for me.

I was dropping the fly about 20 feet upstream from the fish and letting it sweep down and through them, shaking out line through the guides to keep the line slack and the fly as deep as possible. This was also back when we were using traditional floating fly lines rather than the light-line-nymphing techniques developed 10 years later.

On the fourth or fifth cast, I hooked a 12-pounder, played it down through the fast water and landed and released it on a shallow gravel bar about 100 feet downriver. It took me only a couple of minutes to walk back upstream in the slow water against the bank, sidle out to my spot and begin casting again. Nothing happened for quite a while, and I was casting almost mechanically when a solid jolt on the rod took me by surprise.

Friends, that was unquestionably the biggest salmon I have ever hooked on a fly, until then or since. I slammed the fly home with an automatic up-and-sideways lift on the rod, and the fish ripped downstream on a tight line, thrashing into the air three feet above the water when it came to the gravel bar where I landed the previous one.

All I could do was palm the reel spool with my right hand to try to slow the run, because it was obvious this fish was way more than 30 pounds, maybe even touching 40. It jumped and landed twice, with an immense sploosh that exploded most of the water off the gravel, a male with a nasty-looking hooked jaw and a body that looked as big around as my waist.

The fish headed downstream again at a smart clip, and 35 yards of fly line and 50 yards of 20-pound Dacron backing melted off the reel, a Scientific Anglers No. 7 model that never was meant for this kind of abuse. Realizing I had better do something quickly if I didn't want the fish to take the last 100 yards of backing, I decided to follow the fish downstream, as I had the last one.

I never figured out what happened. All of a sudden I went tail over teacup into the fast water, and the next thing I knew I was bouncing downstream off the rocks while the salmon pulled me farther toward the middle.

Normally, getting dunked isn't much of a problem. I manage it several times a year and usually bounce back to my feet before my pants get wet inside my waders. But this time I inhaled a mouthful of water and started choking and gagging so hard I couldn't get my feet under me.

The next couple of minutes were grim. Every few seconds I would manage to get my head above water and suck in a little air, but it was impossible to coordinate the moments my head was above the waves with the moments I wasn't coughing explosively. I finally wedged against a rock and was able to crawl, mostly underwater, into the shallows, where I collapsed over another rock, still clinging grimly to the rod.

I would like to write that I felt a tug on the line, found the fish was still there and landed it. But it had long since buggered off, as my New Zealand friends say, and I was happy to leave the river still in possession of my rod, not to mention my life.

Michigan is home to six kinds of salmon — four from the Pacific, one from the Atlantic and one that was sort of homegrown. And a discussion of salmon should also include a seventh species, the lake trout, which isn't a salmon but acts like one and is fished for like one.

Chinook

Chinooks are the bruisers of the Oncorhynchus genus, which includes all North American Pacific salmon, and the biggest salmon known. The world record is a 97-pound, four-ounce fish caught in Alaska's Kenai River, and the Michigan record is 46 pounds, one ounce (taken in 1978, when the lakes were chock full of the alewives that the salmon were introduced to control). But I also should note that the average chinook from Michigan is about 12 pounds, and that's about the average for most Alaskan waters, too.

The Kenai and a couple of other streams in Alaska and British Columbia are home to subspecies or races of chinooks that grow incredibly large. I've never caught one bigger than 50 pounds, but I have been drift-fishing on the Kenai when I saw fish jump that weighed at least 70. These giants spend more time in the ocean before returning to spawn than other chinook populations.

Most chinooks don't spawn until their fourth year, and some races on the Pacific Coast stay out feeding in the big water until they are six or seven (which explains why they get so big).

Our Great Lakes fish mostly are fourth-year spawners, which means we see a lot of fish caught in the 20- to 30-pound range but relatively few bigger than 30. If you fish streams, you also will encounter a few tiny, first-year males running with the older fish, jacks about the size of a 14-inch brown trout. They look more like a meal than a mate for a big, ripe four-year-old female.

No one knows why some yearlings make the spawning run. It could be something wrong with the small male's genetic wiring, but my guess is that it's another example of the way nature hedges its bets. If something happens to the rest of that little male's year-class out in the ocean or the big lakes, at least some of his group's genes will stay in the species' pool.

Biologists also have tried genetic manipulation to create triploid fish, which are sterile and presumably would spend a fifth year feeding in the Great Lakes, when some would reach the 50-pound mark. So far, it hasn't worked, but we can hope.

A ripe female usually is accompanied by one big male and a few smaller ones as she makes her nest (redd) in the gravel stream bottom. After brushing away the top layers to reach the clean, loose gravel underneath, she spills her eggs onto the redd while the big male ejects white clouds of milt that fertilize them. The smaller males also take turns darting in from the edges to dump some of their sperm on the redd.

The eggs fall into the gravel, where they spend the winter. The little fish hatch in early spring, spend a few months feeding like the juvenile trout that live there and after a few months head downstream in search of an ocean. In Michigan, they encounter one of the Great Lakes, but that seems to be fine with the salmon as long as there is enough to eat.

In some ways, it's remarkable that chinooks and other Pacific salmon have established themselves in the Great Lakes, and not because of the switch from salt water to fresh. In their native waters, these fish prefer a temperature range of about 50 to 55 degrees, yet come winter in the Great Lakes, they must survive for months in water 33 to 40 degrees.

Like all Pacific salmon, chinooks are short-lived and fast-growing, and all the members of a year-class die after spawning, males and females.

If you want a melancholy experience, put on a pair of waders and walk along one of the salmon streams on a rainy mid-October day as the run is coming to an end.

The carcasses of dead fish are everywhere, their eyes pecked out by birds and their once-silver skins black where they aren't covered with patches of light, furry fungus.

In the gravel shallows, you see the living dead, the last spawners, who sport fins worn to ragged nubs by the effort of moving gravel, and whose bodies already show signs of the fungus that eventually will consume their flesh.

By now the handful of remaining salmon are piscatorial zombies, automatons still driven by the genetic imperative that brought them there but so weak and uncaring that they often make no effort to move when you touch them with a booted foot.

A big female, probably 25 pounds in her prime, struggles weakly to hold her place over the eggs she laid 10 days ago and has protected from trout, suckers, stone rollers and other potential predators.

She gives one final hard tail thrust against the current, then lies on her side, shaking and moving her gills weakly as the river pushes her downstream and under an overhanging bank, where she dies a few minutes later.

But she has done her job, giving her unborn offspring time to settle down deep into the gravel, where they are protected from the predators and washed by water rich in life-giving oxygen. And when the baby salmon hatch and eventually wriggle up through the gravel to begin the cycle anew, some of the insects they eat will have fed on the carcass of their mother.

I enjoy trolling for chinooks on the big lakes, where the crank baits and spoons are the standard lures. Most charter captains will tell you that once the lakes begin to warm in June, the key is to find the warmest surface water.

Warm can be a relative term. Fishing out of Ludington one spring day, we found the water uniformly 39 to 40 degrees from shore out to about three miles. Then we passed through a mile-wide patch where the temperature climbed rapidly to 43.

The screen of the fish finder, which had been blank for two hours, began showing the big hooks that mark salmon, mostly about 40 feet down, and we usually would get a strike within a minute after passing over the fish.

Later in the year the trick is to find colder water, the 50- to 55-degree stuff the salmon and their primary prey, the alewives, find the most comfortable.

April, May and early June find salmon close to shore, sometimes in less than 20 feet of water a couple of hundred yards off the beach. The shallows warm faster, and the tributary streams pour in water that is warmer than the lakes at this time of year. It also is clouded by suspended matter that absorbs the sun's rays and increases the warming potential.

As inshore waters climb into the 60s in early summer, the salmon move farther offshore. They show a penchant for feeding in the upper layers of the lake in the early morning and evening but go deeper, sometimes well below 100 feet, as the sun climbs and its rays penetrate deeper into the water.

The advent of underwater television systems, combined with underwater visibility that often exceeds 30 feet (thanks to zebra mussels), has shown that salmon will sometimes follow a lure for amazingly long distances. One charter captain told me that he watched one salmon swim behind a lure for more than an hour. He said the fish obviously was attracted to the lure but showed no inclination to strike, even though the skipper tried tricks like turning the boat, which made the spoon flutter down, and varying his speed.

The anglers were still watching the TV screen and discussing the reasons the fish wouldn't hit when, for no reason they could see, it swam a few feet off to one side, turned and darted in to grab the spoon.

My favorite way to fish for salmon is in a stream, going eyeball to eyeball with the big buggers as you try to stop them from taking your line under a snag and they try to pull your arms out of their sockets.

Early in the salmon run, late August to early September (depending on the river and rainfall), anglers who fish the pier heads in places like Oscoda and Ludington catch a lot of salmon with spinning and bait-casting tackle. I usually cast spoons or spawn sacks from the piers, and I've found that fishing at night is often better than in daylight, mostly because the angling pressure is lighter.

If you fish at night, it's tough to beat a fluorescent spoon that has been hit two or three times with a small electronic flash (the kind used for photography) or exposed to the bright beam of a flashlight for 30 seconds.

Another popular and effective stream technique is pulling plugs. The anglers anchor their boat above a good hole where salmon hold in their migrations, or the anglers hold their position with the oars of a drift boat that is drifted slowly through the hole.

Plugs like Hot 'n' Tots and Wiggle Warts are allowed to drift off the stern of the boat into the holes, where the big lips on the front of the plugs make them dive deep and dart around and vibrate in the current.

When the angler uses the boat's anchor line or the oars, the lures can be made to move back and forth through the holding area. But most strikes come soon after the lures drop into the dark water or as the boat works down through the hole and the fish are forced toward the downriver end of it.

This is one of the most effective and exciting ways to fish for salmon. Most strikes occur when the lure is only a few yards behind the boat, and if the fish doesn't take off on a blazing run, the first thing it usually does is get airborne.

But my favorite way to fish for salmon is wading with a fly rod because there is no more effective lure than something that looks like the nymphal stage of a trout-stream insect.

No one knows why this is. Some benighted souls apparently still believe the myth that a salmon won't eat once it heads upstream to spawn, and that any fish caught are actually snagged, even if it's in the mouth.

But experienced salmon anglers know that isn't true because we have stood a rod-length away in ankle-deep water and watched fish turn and chase a fly 10 feet before biting it. We still don't know whether the fish strikes because it wants to get the fly out of its nest, or because it's angry, or because the fly triggers a response from the days when it fed on insects as a juvenile. Whatever the reason, salmon in a stream will bite a lure or fly.

Most fly anglers use the light-line-nymphing technique developed in Michigan. The normal floating or sinking tip fly line is replaced with the thin, plastic-coated running line normally used as backing.

A four-foot, 20-pound monofilament butt section is attached to the end of the fly line with a three-way swivel at the end. The key to a lot of hookups with salmon is to get the fly to pass the fish's head at eye level, and there are two easy ways to do that.

One is to attach a slinky weight (split shots inside a cloth tube) to one of the free swivels. Or you can tie a four-inch dropper line to one of the swivel eyes and clamp split shots to the dropper.

I usually tie a six-foot leader of eight-pound fluorocarbon line to the third eye of the swivel. Tie a nymph to the end of the leader, then tie another 18-inch chunk of leader to the eye of the first nymph. Tie on a second nymph and you are ready to cast, or to flop and drop, to be honest about it.

Using slinkies or split shots allows the angler to change the weight quickly as he moves along the river and the water depth changes. He might want four "A" shots to fish a six-foot-deep, dark pool with a strong current, and three BB shots to cast to a spooky fish lying on a clear, shallow flat.

I've always used an eight-weight rod for salmon, but I've noticed that 10-weights are becoming more popular, no doubt a product of the bulky, unwieldy light-line rig that, if truth be told, can be cast with a spinning rod.

Fishing to visible salmon on shallow redds, or nests, is the easiest way to catch fish, but a lot of anglers don't like to do that. They say it disturbs the female, and hooking and playing her uses up valuable energy she needs for nest-building and spawning.

It's possible to put the fly in front of the accompanying males with a little practice, and there usually are so many salmon holding in the deeper pools that it isn't necessary to disturb hens on their nests.

I have fished some pools where salmon were piled up so thickly that even though I rarely saw one, I got a hookup on almost every cast. Polaroid sunglasses help here, and novice anglers soon learn to spot the flickers of movement deep in the dark, tannin-stained waters that mark a restless salmon.

Another trend in Michigan is spey rods, the 13- to 16-foot fly rods developed on the Spey River in Scotland and designed to let an angler pick up 60 to 70 feet of line with a single lift and lay it back up at the top of a drift.

Once again, Michigan anglers didn't let tradition stand in the way of catching fish. They simply put a double-nymph setup on a six-foot leader below a float and found that the big rods were not only easier to cast, they allowed the fisherman a lot more line control.

I've heard a number of anglers disparage light-line-nymphing and Michigan spey techniques, arguing that they aren't fly-fishing. I agree that they don't have much to do with fly-fishing in the traditional sense, but so what? They are still legal and sporting ways to catch salmon in a stream.

It's amusing that some people I've heard running down these salmon techniques won't hesitate to fish for trout with a sunken nymph under a strike indicator. The only real difference between a strike indicator and a bobber is that you can buy a bobber in any outdoors store for 98 cents, but a strike indicator will cost you $2.98 at a fly shop.

I've gone back to fishing salmon with a traditional floating fly line about 75 percent of the time. I don't get as many strikes, but when the fish are in thick, I'm just as happy with 30 hookups a day as 90.

Coho

The coho, or silver salmon, was the species Howard Tanner chose to introduce to the Platte River in Lake Michigan in the 1960s when he was the state Department of Natural Resources fisheries chief. Numerous skeptics said this saltwater fish never would survive in the sweet-water seas of the Great Lakes, and if by some miracle a few did live, they would never reproduce.

But Tanner knew Pacific salmon had been planted, albeit on a far more limited basis, in lakes in Wyoming and other Western states, and they had done pretty well. And those salmon didn't have the benefit of an immense ecosystem that was stuffed to the brim with prey fish but lacked a top-level predator.

The result was a salmon explosion as the cohos gorged themselves on alewives, smelt and other prey fish. Their numbers skyrocketed in the big lakes following the decimation of the lake trout and walleyes that had been the top predators. (Those out-of-control alewives and smelt were exotic species introduced in the previous century.)

The cohos in Lake Michigan follow a migratory route that takes them south along the shoreline to Indiana, where they provide a spectacular spring fishery, and then north on the other side of the lake to Wisconsin waters, where they probably spend most of their lives.

The fish make a beeline across Lake Michigan in their third summer, usually reaching the Michigan coast south of Platte Bay in July. (A few of the males make this return in their second year.)

The fish spend the rest of the summer roaming and fattening up in the waters offshore, and in late August they begin their spawning runs up Michigan rivers, with the Platte run the most notable.

Great Lakes cohos typically are about six inches long and four or five ounces in weight at the end of their first season, and 28 inches long and eight pounds when they return to the rivers to spawn. But that growth is dependent on the food supply, and the variations can be dramatic.

Alewives, the fish cohos were brought in to control, are another species that likes warmer waters in the 50-degree range, and they die of exposure in cold water a lot faster than the bigger, more thermally efficient cohos.

For several years in the early 1990s, the states around Lake Michigan were planting so many salmon that the alewives were hammered. When that predation rate was combined with a particularly hard winter, alewife numbers declined dramatically.

Naturally, so did the numbers of the fish that preyed on alewives. And not only did the number of salmon decrease with the alewife decline, so did their size. The states agreed to reduce the annual plantings of all salmon by 20 percent, and a fortuitous weather pattern produced a couple of mild winters. The salmon numbers came back, although they probably never will reach the levels of the 1970s and early 1980s, when the alewives were out of control.

The effects of the food supply on salmon never were more dramatically illustrated than a couple of years ago, when salmon numbers were relatively low and alewives rebounded quickly after an extremely mild winter.

In an average year, the Michigan DNR receives a half-dozen applications for master angler awards for cohos, which must weigh 12 pounds. But in 2000, after the alewife boom, the DNR issued more than 700 master angler certificates for cohos, and skippers in southern Lake Michigan sometimes returned to dock with limit catches of fish that were all bigger than the master angler weight.

Cohos spawn a bit later than other Pacific salmon, and there usually is an excellent run in the St. Marys River at Sault Ste. Marie just before Christmas. Like other Pacific salmon, cohos spawn only once and die after spawning.

Another little-known and less-pressured coho fishery is in western Lake Erie, centered on Erieau, Ontario, about 50 miles southeast of Detroit. This was once one of the continent's finest walleye spawning grounds, but for reasons yet to be explained satisfactorily, most of the walleyes moved out about 1999 and were replaced by huge schools of steelhead and a nice mix of coho (along with a few chinooks).

Cohos in the big lakes are caught by trolling, with crank baits the choice in spring and spoons through the summer. They are wonderfully acrobatic fish, often jumping four feet out of the water as they try to throw the hook. And anyone who has seen the sun reflecting off the scales of a mirror-bright coho knows why they are called silver salmon.

While eight pounds is the Great Lakes average, the state-record fish on rod and reel is 30 pounds, nine ounces. In 1973, when Lake Michigan had far too many alewives, DNR workers netted a 39-pound, two-ounce coho from the Manistee River, nearly six pounds bigger than the 33-pound, four-ounce rod-and-reel world record.

Cohos are wonderful to catch on light tackle with a spinning rod or fly rod when they run up rivers to spawn. The problem in Michigan is that there are far fewer coho spawning rivers than chinook streams. Unlike cohos, chinooks have established strong natural spawning runs in many rivers around the Great Lakes.

Pink salmon

You have a choice of stories when it comes to how pink salmon got to the Great Lakes from a hatchery in Thunder Bay, Ontario.

The one I've heard that makes the most sense is that when the American states bordering the lakes voted against introducing the smallest Pacific salmon species in 1956, technicians at the Ontario hatchery decided to release the few thousand fingerlings in their tanks, figuring they would be eaten along with other prey fish.

But in the words of that great philosopher Gomer Pyle, "Surprise, surprise, surprise!" The little salmon not only survived, they established spawning runs in streams along the Lake Superior shoreline, and today they are established in lakes Michigan and Huron, too.

The world-record pink is a 12-pound, nine-ounce fish from Alaska, but the biggest caught in Michigan was eight pounds, nine ounces, and a typical Great Lakes pink is one to two pounds. (A three-pounder will earn you a master angler award.)

Pinks also are called humpies for the massive humped back the males develop during the breeding season. Combine that with their hooked jaws and you have something that looks like an escapee from a science fiction movie.

The biggest and best pink run occurs in the St. Marys River at Sault Ste. Marie, usually starting about three weeks before the fall chinook run. Theoretically, pinks spawn every other year, and since the Great Lakes pink salmon all started with the same year-class, the St. Marys should get a run of fish one year and none the next. But either through mutation or genetic drift, a few pinks started spawning in off-years, and they did very well.

The result is that the St. Marys now gets ridiculous numbers of pinks in one year and merely massive numbers the next. They happily hit flies (of just about any color), spawn, spinners, spoons or even bits of colored yarn tied to a hook.

I once stood on the seawall on the Canadian side of the St. Marys catching a pink salmon on every cast. It was easy because in the marvelously clear water I could see dozens to hundreds of them at any moment.

Another day I stood in the same place staring hungrily at a dozen big chinooks holding in the deep water of the old navigation canal on the other side of the seawall. They were far below practical fly-fishing depth but could be reached with a spoon.

The problem was that every time I cast the spoon, I saw the smaller form of a pink salmon dart out to intercept it before it could get down to the bigger fish. After an hour, with about 20 pinks landed and released, I gave up.

I like to fish pinks with a four-weight fly rod or a 10-foot European-style spinning rod designed for four-pound line. The problem with these fish (and the reason states didn't plant them nearly 50 years ago) is that their flesh deteriorates within days, perhaps hours of entering the river. Unless you catch a newly arrived fish, the flesh is soft and an unappealing gray.

But they are a wonderful light-tackle game fish and a great way to introduce kids to salmon fishing in a stream. And at the rate they are colonizing streams, don't be surprised if there's a pink run in your area before long.

Hybrids

About 10 years ago, DNR fisheries chief John Robertson was fishing the St. Marys River and landed what seemed to be a world-record pink salmon. Then in the next week he saw or heard of a dozen fish the same size or bigger and decided an investigation was in order.

An examination proved that the giant pinks were really a hybrid, a cross between pinks and chinooks that the National Fresh Water Fishing Hall of Fame soon recognized as pinooks.

Pinooks look exactly like pink salmon, although oversized ones, from the outside. They have the same big spots on the upper body and both lobes of the tail (chinooks have spots only on the upper tail lobe), and they lack the chinook's black gums.

They fight as hard as a chinook (some anglers say harder), and most are caught by the same trolling methods used for chinooks and coho salmon.

If you look in the National Fresh Water Fishing Hall of Fame record book, you will see that all of the fly records come from the Garden River in Ontario north of the Soo (they run from Lake Superior). All of the others come from the St. Marys system at the Soo or south of there (fish from Lake Huron).

The world record is a 19-pound, eight-ounce fish caught on a fly in the Garden in 1997. The Michigan record, caught by a troller in Lake Huron, was 14 pounds, one ounce.

Steelhead

For years I wondered why steelhead were: A) put in the genus salmo, whose other members were Old World species like the brown trout and Atlantic salmon, and B) were listed as trout. It was obvious that anadromous steelhead — those that swim upriver to spawn — were about as different from stream-resident rainbows as Atlantic salmon were from brown trout.

I was glad to see the fisheries biologists change their minds a few years ago and move the steelhead from salmo to the genus Oncorhynchus. This is the same close-knit group that includes cohos and chinooks, which also originated in North America and are native of the Pacific drainages.

Like the other Pacifics, steelhead are born in a stream and after two or three years migrate down the river to the ocean or a big lake, where they live for three years before returning to their birth stream and spawning for the first time.

But unlike other Pacifics, there are three subspecies of steelhead — perhaps races would be a better name — that have different habits.

One is the common, garden-variety rainbow trout that is born, lives and dies in the same river. Most people think of the steelhead as an anadromous version of the rainbow trout. I've come to think of the rainbow trout as a non-anadromous form of steelhead. A typical stream rainbow is about a foot long and weighs a pound at three years and is 17 inches and two pounds at six years. It rarely lives longer.

Coastal rainbows, the ones with the steel-gray backs that earned steelhead their nickname, have the most developed migratory gene. Tagged steelhead have been netted more than 2,000 miles from the rivers where they were tagged.

Many of the original steelhead released in the Great Lakes starting about 140 years ago were coastal rainbows, which typically are about 22 inches and four pounds at age three and can reach 36 inches and 20 pounds by age eight, although few make it.

Then there's the Kamloops rainbow, a migratory fish that developed a routine of spawning in freshwater streams and then growing up in huge Kamloops Lake in British Columbia, thousands of years before man came up with the same idea. A Kamloops rainbow is usually about 16 inches and one pound at age three, and 26 inches and six pounds at age five, slotting in perfectly between its coastal and stay-at-home relatives.

The world-record steelhead is a 42-pound, two-ounce fish caught in Alaska (although a 52-pounder was netted in British Columbia), and the Michigan record is a 26-pound, eight-ouncer from Lake Michigan. The inland world record is 37 pounds.

But steelhead were also one of the earliest trout to be raised in hatcheries because they were abundant, relatively hardy for salmonids and traveled well on trains. As a result, man has so mixed up the genetics of these fish that most of the Great Lakes steelhead are probably amalgams of gene pools from a dozen populations, if not more.

Rainbows were named for the rose-colored stripe that is usually clear on the sides of river-resident fish, less so on Kamloops fish and often non-existent on an ocean or lake-run steelhead.

But after a steelhead has been back in a stream for a couple of weeks, it often develops a metallic red stripe that contrasts strongly with a body that can turn almost black.

Today, all of the Great Lakes have steelhead populations, some of which enter the rivers in fall, some in winter, some in spring and some in summer. The St. Joseph River, which flows into the southeast corner of Lake Michigan, might be the most prolific steelhead river in the Great Lakes, and perhaps the country, with runs in all seasons of the year.

A lot of the St. Joseph fish are skamanias, a race (maybe a subspecies) that's easy to raise in hatcheries and grows quickly. Indiana began releasing large numbers of skamanias in Lake Michigan a few years ago, and they provide more angling for Michigan fishermen than for Indianians.

But no matter how you categorize them, steelhead are deservedly considered the hardest-fighting and most-acrobatic fish in fresh water. And probably the most admired, too.

It doesn't matter what kind of tackle or technique you use to hook a steelhead, the odds on your losing the fish before landing it are probably higher than with any other freshwater species.

Michigan is fortunate in having steelhead that run year-round in some rivers and can be taken from spring until fall in the Great Lakes. Steelhead fishing is far better in Michigan than in the great majority of Pacific Coast streams that once had runs of these magnificent fish but saw them wiped out by dams, pollution and commercial fishing.

One spring I fished the Huron River spillway in Flat Rock, about 20 miles from downtown Detroit as the crow flies and one of the most urbanized places in the world. Everyone was hooking fish every few minutes (although the landing rate seemed to be about 20 percent). Fishing next to me were two anglers from southern California who couldn't believe that we could have this kind of fishing in the heart of a metropolitan area.

They told me steelhead had all but disappeared from the northern California streams they used to fish, and that in many areas an angler was considered successful if he caught a couple of fish in a week, not several in one day.

Western Lake Erie's walleye fishing has fallen off some (although in spring it's still probably the best there is), but the walleyes have been replaced by a glut of steelhead.

A couple of years ago I took some Scottish friends on Lake Erie with Joe Belanger, a charter skipper from Tilbury, Ontario, who has fished the lake for 40 years. Fishing the same spoons used for salmon, we caught and released 54 steelhead that mostly ran eight to 10 pounds but included a couple of beautiful 14-pounders.

Lake Michigan has the most unusual steelhead fishery, an estimated one-million-plus fish from rivers all around the lake that spend the summer hanging around the scum lines that form in the middle of the huge lake 20 to 30 miles offshore.

These fish are a living testament to the complexity of our natural systems. If you open the belly of a mid-lake steelhead, rarely will you find bait fish in it. Mostly what you will find are ants, beetles, grasshoppers and other terrestrial insects.

This weird offshore diet is the product of a coastal weather pattern called a sea breeze. Each summer day, the land heats up in the morning, and the warm air over the land is driven high into the atmosphere.

This reduces pressure over the land, and cooler, low-altitude air from over the lake flows in to compensate. This is the sea breeze beloved by sailors and overheated beach-goers. (The opposite often happens on nights when the land gets colder than the water.)

But as the cool air flows onto the land, it lowers the pressure over the lake. Something has to fill that partial vacuum, and that's the warm air from the land that has risen, flowed outward at high altitude and then descended as it cooled and became denser.

Riding the outbound leg of that thermal roller coaster are enormous numbers of land bugs, most of which are dropped down onto the lake. Wind patterns on the lake surface concentrate the bugs (and other debris) in long slicks called scum lines, where the steelhead mass to feed.

On calm days, you often can see the steelhead bodies flashing as they cruise just under the surface, and I've also seen lake herring, alewives and whitefish sucking bugs off the surface 25 miles from land.

One of these days I'm going to catch a steelhead in the scum line on a dry fly by riding out in a big boat and then drifting around in a belly boat (an overgrown inner tube.) We've tried it twice, but both times the wind kicked up too big to spot the fish.

In spring, I've found that my European carp tackle is ideal for catching steelies off piers. In addition to 11- to 13-foot rods that will cast a two-ounce bait or lure more than 100 yards, the key to the Euro system is a rod pod and a couple of electronic bite alarms.

The rod pod is a frame on which the rods rest while the angler waits for a bite. The rod pod has adjustable feet to compensate for uneven ground along the riverbanks where Europeans usually fish.

The alarm is a black box, about the size of a cigarette pack, which screws into the top of the front rod support. After I cast out the bait (usually spawn), I lay down the rod on the pod so the line runs through a small slit in the top of the black box.

If a fish picks up the bait and runs with it, the bite alarm sounds off like a little siren, and the tone can be varied so you know which rod has the take. There's even a little flashing light for night fishing.

Trolling and pier fishing are fun, but as in fishing for salmon, my favorite way to catch steelhead is to wade. Sometimes this is done in mid-winter, in temperatures so cold you spend the long waits between bites dreaming up electrical testicle warmers for waders.

But if you have a good day, when you get four or five strikes and land three fish, or a spectacular day, when you get a dozen takes and land nine, the rush of playing that leaping, line-melting fish is so incredible you will be hooked for life.

A spey rod is ideal for steelhead fishing, assuming the stream is wide enough to let you maneuver a 14-foot rod. But you won't need room for casting. With a spey rod, the angler usually can reach over and lay the bait, fly or lure above the fish and drift it past the steelie's head with little or no line touching the water.

Most of the spey rods sold in this country are real monsters, 14- to 16-footers designed for 10- to 12-weight fly lines. I think a much better rig would be a 12-foot rod designed for an eight-weight line. In Michigan, we never have to cast far to the fish, and an eight-weight would be light enough that most anglers could fish with one all day and not feel tired.

Steelhead are ideal fish for spinning tackle, and in the past four years I've noticed a tremendous increase in the number of anglers who fish steelies with nine- to 10-foot spinning rods designed for four- to eight-pound lines.

These aren't the same as the noodle rods that Michigan's Dick Swann popularized about three decades ago. Noodles are usually 10 to 12 feet long and have a limber tip that will protect two-pound monofilament from the lunges of a steelhead.

Noodles work well, but I prefer a slightly shorter and stiffer rod on which I can use four- to six-pound line, cast better and land the fish faster. I release nearly every steelhead I catch, so I think the shorter the fight, the better the chance the fish will survive.

I've heard anglers say steelhead are obviously quite different from Pacific salmon because steelhead spawn more than once. But that's misleading.

Of all the young steelhead that reach the sea or the Great Lakes, only five to 10 percent live long enough to return to their birth streams and spawn. More than half die after spawning for the first time, and the numbers that survive to spawn again are whittled down by about the same percentage every year.

Any Great Lakes steelhead larger than 24 inches and six pounds is undoubtedly a repeat spawner and at least six years old. An eight-year-old, fourth-time spawner is probably the last of several million smolts in its age-class that were born or stocked in that river eight or nine years before.

Atlantic salmon

OK, we want to fish for Atlantic salmon. So let's see, we could spend a bundle to fly to Scotland or Iceland or Norway and pay $1,000 a day for a spot on a good river where we might catch a dozen fish in a good week. Or we could drive to Sault Ste. Marie, park by the power plant and fish for the Atlantic run in the St. Marys, the one in which anglers sometimes hook double-digit numbers per day.

Let's stipulate here that Atlantic salmon, and Pacifics for that matter, don't feed after they enter a stream. (People used to believe they stopped feeding when they reached fresh water, but the salmon gobbled up alewives in the Great Lakes and put the kibosh on that idea.)

But salmon will strike at a lure. Whether they do so from memory, habit, reflex or anger, no one knows. We do know that most of a fish brain is given over to the senses of sight, smell, hearing and feeling vibrations (through the ears and lateral line on the sides). There probably are just enough brain cells left to manage the muscles and internal organs and take care of reproduction.

Trying to understand why fish do things on the basis of our understanding of why people do things is probably a great mistake. Suffice it to say that we do know salmon will often take a lure even when they no longer are eating.

In Michigan, Lake Superior State University has been quietly raising Atlantics in some unused pen stocks in the power plant and releasing them into the St. Marys. For the past couple of years the return has been excellent, especially in July.

The university fish weren't the first Atlantic salmon in the Great Lakes. When white settlers reached the shores of Lake Ontario, they found Atlantic salmon so thick that some men in a small boat caught 2,000 pounds of fish in one night.

In the 1840s, a farmer reported stopping his wagon beside a stream where he saw the salmon running, and he pitch-forked up a wagon load of Atlantic salmon in a couple of hours before heading home.

These were probably the landlocked form of the Atlantic, the kind still found in lakes from Maine through the Canadian Maritimes. But some Atlantic salmon might have entered Lake Ontario from the sea through the 800-mile St. Lawrence River, although Atlantics in other parts of the world don't make river runs much longer than 300 miles.

There are many reports that these fish left Lake Ontario and ran up rivers to spawn, which would make them landlocks. But the same reports said the Lake Ontario salmon commonly exceeded 40 pounds, and since the world-record landlocked is 22 pounds, 11 ounces, it's possible that sea-run giants came up the St. Lawrence. The world record for a sea-run fish is 79 pounds, two ounces, taken in Norway more than 70 years ago.

If we had better scientific descriptions of those long-gone Lake Ontario fish, we might be able to say for sure if they were landlocks or sea-runs. Landlocks usually have larger spots than sea-run fish, and the landlocks usually have a blue or brown cast. The sea-run fish are as silver as a new dime.

One thing we know is that while salmon can make some prodigious leaps to ascend falls in their upstream migration, Niagara Falls provided a cork that kept the Atlantics out of the four upper Great Lakes for millennia.

The salmon raised and released at Sault Ste. Marie are sea-run stock. That makes for some difficulties in the record books because the Michigan Atlantic record is 32 pounds, 10 ounces. It's classified as an Atlantic salmon, but there's no denying that it's a landlocked fish.

Salmon once were so thick in American rivers that indentured servants in colonial times had contracts that said they had to eat salmon only three times a week.

But man apparently just can't stand prosperity, and by about 1900 nearly all of the U.S. salmon runs had been wiped out by that infernal triumverate — dams, pollution and overfishing. That included the Lake Ontario Atlantics.

Salmon fishing in Europe had long been the province of the aristocracy, who owned the fishing rights on the salmon streams, or the rich, who could afford to rent those rights.

By the end of World War II, the same thing was true in North America because the only Atlantic salmon left were in places so remote that only the rich could afford to go there and fish for them.

A mystique soon grew around the Atlantic salmon, which were revered as the hardest-fighting fish in fresh water and the one that took the greatest skill to hook and land. I think steelhead fight just as hard and are just as acrobatic, although I will admit it's usually harder to get an Atlantic salmon to take a fly.

Some years ago I went to Nova Scotia to fish the Margaree, one of the world's most famed salmon streams. There, every fish caught is recorded, and the talk in the fishing hotels and restaurants every night is about which pool produced how many fish and on what flies.

I arrived to learn that because of a drought and commercial fishing boats offshore, no one had caught a fish for five days. I drove around that afternoon watching other anglers flogging the water with cast after cast as they put their flies through pools that probably didn't hold any salmon.

A strong believer in making my own odds, I said to heck with it and spent the next three days fishing for brook and brown trout and smallmouth bass in other streams and had a delightful time catching lots of fish that got little pressure.

When I checked in with the local fly shop at the end of that time, the owner was about as dour as the fish. He reported that he still had not heard of any salmon to record. So I made a great deal on a used Paul Young bamboo fly rod (which I still have) and headed home.

Today, most Michigan Atlantics are taken by trolling, and many probably are never recognized as Atlantic salmon. An Atlantic salmon looks very much like a shiny-bright, lake-run brown trout. The most obvious differences are the lack of spots on the salmon's adipose fin (the small second fin on its back) and the slightly deeper fork in its tail.

But an increasing number of anglers are fishing the Atlantics that return to the waters behind the Soo power plant and hang out for a few weeks each summer before making their fall spawning runs in the rapids.

Many fishermen have told me that these fish tend to be dour, the Scottish fisherman's term for salmon that are sullen and closemouthed, refusing fly after fly and plug after plug. But one angler reported a lot of success using tiny hair tube flies in sizes 12 through 16.

I have caught several Atlantics while fishing the rapids on the Canadian side of the St. Marys at the Soo, but they hit while I was casting flies to groups of chinooks. I have yet to figure out if the Atlantics mixed in among the chinooks are there to spawn, eat chinook eggs or merely rest while passing through.

Lake trout

As I said earlier, lake trout aren't salmon. Technically, they aren't even trout. They're char, a group that includes brook trout, Arctic char, dolly varden and bull trout.

But I think they should be included with salmon because they almost always are caught in lakes, at least in the United States, and because most are taken by trolling.

Lakers are the second-biggest members of the salmonid family. The world record is a 65-pound fish from Great Bear Lake in the Northwest Territories of Canada, but a 75-pounder was caught there that didn't qualify under sport-fishing rules, and a 102-pounder was netted from Lake Athabasca in Canada. The Michigan record is a 61-pound, eight-ounce fish caught in 1997 in Lake Superior's Huron Bay.

In the first half of the last century, lake trout almost disappeared from the Great Lakes, decimated by over-harvesting by commercial fishermen and the arrival of the predatory sea lamprey from the Atlantic Ocean.

Lamprey feed by hooking their mouths onto the body of a large fish like a lake trout, boring a hole into the fish's flesh with a tongue like a file and then sucking the fish's body juices.

While it might be hard for us to imagine today, lake trout were among the top four commercial species taken from Lake Erie through the late 1800s. (The others were whitefish, lake herring and sturgeon. Walleyes and perch were only a by-catch.)

But by the time World War II ended, sea lampreys had put such a dent in the lake trout population in the Great Lakes that natural reproduction had almost stopped and nearly all of the lakers left were reared in hatcheries.

Lake trout are fall spawners, laying their eggs on inshore reefs in less than 50 feet of water after the water starts to cool. That spawning habit was disastrous for lakers in the Great Lakes, where they arrived in the shallows just as thousands of sea lampreys arrived to stage offshore before running up rivers where the eels spawned.

Sea lampreys also will feed on salmon, whitefish and burbot, but these fish are harder to catch and latch on to. The slow-moving, bottom-hugging lake trout were much easier targets.

Lamprey-killing chemicals and electrical barriers in spawning streams greatly reduced the lamprey population in the 1980s, but at the same time streams were responding to efforts to clean up pollution, and that gave the environmentally sensitive lampreys more places to spawn.

The result was that by the mid-1990s, fisheries biologists estimated that no lake trout stocked in northern Lake Huron reached the spawning age of five. They were killed by the huge lamprey infestation that flowed from the eel's spawning grounds in the St. Marys River.

Today, new chemicals have been found that seem to be making a huge reduction in the lamprey population in the St. Marys, a river that produces more of the parasites than all of the other Great Lakes streams combined.

That offers hope that lake trout will achieve a self-sustaining population again and eventually end the need for humans to stock the lakes with a fish that evolved to live there.

The laker has spawned a lean trout/fat trout debate, which we should settle here. When white settlers first moved into places where lake trout lived, their descriptions showed there were several genetically and physiologically distinct forms of lake trout.

Two are left today. And while both are classified as Salvelinus namaycush, the lean trout lives in the four lower Great Lakes and in inland lakes throughout the northern states and Canada. The fat trout, or siscowet, lives only in Lake Superior.

The most obvious difference between the two is that the lean trout's body is more than four times longer than it is deep. A fat trout's body length is less than four times its depth.

Both forms have a lot of body fat, but in siscowets the fat content can be as much as 70 percent (it's 20 to 50 percent in lean lakers). Siscowet also prefer the icy cold water at depths of 300 feet or more, and the few I have seen look like lake trout that have swallowed a basketball.

Because they live at such great depths, siscowets are relatively rare catches for anglers. The handful I've seen were taken on Lake Superior in spring, when inshore water temperatures were in the 40s and siscowet came up above 200 feet following bait fish.

All real salmon, whether Pacific or Atlantic, have dark spots on a light background. Lake trout, like all chars, have light spots on a dark background.

In big lakes, lakers feed mostly on smelt, alewives, small ciscos, bloater chubs and even bottom huggers like sculpins. In places with a lot of prey fish, such as the Great Lakes and some of the big inland lakes in Canada, lakers can live more than 40 years and grow to enormous sizes. Fish bigger than 50 pounds might be 50 years old, and a 20-pounder probably has survived 20 seasons.

In smaller inland lakes, lake trout feed mostly on crayfish, insects and plankton. A 20-year-old fish in those lakes might be five pounds or less.

Lake trout feed deep, so most are caught by anglers trolling some distance offshore, and that requires larger boats. The vast majority of lakers are caught incidentally by people trolling for salmon and steelhead, but they often are targeted deliberately by skippers when salmon numbers are down.

Lake trout hit the same body baits and spoons as salmon and steelhead, and many anglers disparage lake trout as inferior fighters when compared to the other big salmonids. I think that's probably true of fish in the four lower Great Lakes, where lake trout are at the extreme southern end of their natural range.

There's also a problem of depth. Lakers often are taken from 100 feet down or more, and their swim bladder expands so much when they are pulled toward the surface that they are as effectively crippled as a diver with the bends.

But anyone who has ever taken a big lake trout on spinning tackle or fly in northern Ontario will attest that those fish fight just as hard as any salmon of the same size.

I have been fortunate to make three trips to lakes in northern Saskatchewan and Ontario in spring, when the water has just turned over and the temperature is the same from top to bottom.

The lake trout are cruising near the surface then, and I've caught them on streamer flies and even some dry flies (winged ants). They don't jump, but those two- to six-pound lake trout were every bit as strong and determined as a rainbow of the same size, slugging it out with long, slow runs and powerful head shakes.

An unusual Michigan fishing trip is to Stannard Rock, a submarine mountain that soars out of deep water, coming within about 120 feet of the surface 40 miles off the southern shore of Lake Superior.

Charter boats leave harbors around Marquette. It can be an uncomfortable trip on a windy day, but it's also a chance to deep-jig for 15- to 30-pound lakers that attack a lure savagely in broad daylight.

But then, you can do pretty much the same thing in the winter at Crystal Lake, a drowned river mouth inshore from Lake Michigan at Beulah, or at Higgins Lake. Anglers using big jigs and minnows catch 10- to 20-pound lakers through the ice, and anyone who has fought one of these fish in cold water will dispute any suggestions that the lake trout isn't a fine game fish.

Chapter 4

Trout

O NE OF MY FAVORITE TROUT FISHING STORIES, PURPORTEDLY true, was told by Ernest Schweibert, one of America's best-known fly anglers.

A man was fly-fishing on a stream with a drab brown wet fly called a cowdung, a tried-and-true pattern that had been developed a century earlier. The fly fisherman was doing well, getting a strike from a trout every few casts.

He was watched by two small boys who had ridden a horse out from town and were fishing with bait in a pool upstream and hadn't had a bite. Finally, one boy walked down the bank and called out to the wading angler, "Hey, mister! What are you using?"

"Cowdung," the fisherman said as he set the hook on yet another trout.

The kid walked back up the bank, conferred with his partner for a moment, then yelled again, "Hey, mister! Do you think horse shit would work?"

What really makes me laugh about that story is that many fishermen are so fanatical about catching trout that if a rumor went around that lion poop was a killer bait, zoos would have to establish security patrols to keep the lions safe.

We Michiganders live in the state that offers more public access to trout fishing than any other in the nation. It probably could offer the best trout fishing in the country, as well, if we concentrated on managing more streams as blue-ribbon fisheries, the way they do in Montana, Wyoming and other states that recognize the value of trophy trout waters.

I have a real problem with our trout regulations. When we increased the size limit for trout from 10 to 12 inches on a handful of streams in the Upper and Lower peninsulas, a lot of people had a fit, claiming they couldn't expect to take a legal limit of fish that size.

I admit some streams in the Upper Peninsula will never produce many brook trout longer than eight inches. The streams are just too small, too poor in nutrition and have too short a growing season. But a lot of other UP waters, and most in the northern Lower, should have plenty of brookies in the nine- to 12-inch range and browns and rainbows of 12 to 16 inches.

One reason they don't is that we let too many people kill too many fish before they have a chance to grow.

I was wading up a stream near Grayling recently, a small river that mostly produces small trout, when I encountered two bait fishermen wading downstream. One was towing a stringer on which were three brook trout, none of them within an inch of the legal minimum of 10 inches on that water. It was a practice I see on that river a lot.

When I pointed that out to the man and added that he would have a problem if he met a conservation officer at one of the access points, he tried to justify killing undersized trout by saying he had been fishing all day, and if he kept only legal-sized fish he would go home empty-handed.

I started to say that if he and people like him stopped killing all those small trout, maybe we could catch more keepers in a couple of years, but that would only have put us into a logic loop and I just continued upstream.

Don't assume that I'm one of the holier-than-thou types who preaches that every trout caught should be released. I've become convinced that a lot of people who preach the gospel of catch-and-release do so not because they care for the trout but because it lets them assume a trumped-up moral superiority.

We should have streams where no one can kill fish, and I would like to see the amount of no-kill water expanded. But the majority of our trout waters should be open to and managed for people who want to take a few trout home to eat.

It's easy for me to let trout go, or bass, for that matter, because I don't find them particularly tasty, at least not compared to bluegills, walleye and even saltwater species like cod. But my wife, Susan the trout cannibal, loves fresh trout, and I occasionally knock a couple over the head and bring them home as a treat. Even when I fish with the intention of bringing some home, though, I don't consider a day of fishing a waste if I don't fill a sack with a limit of keepers.

Now that I live in the one of the country's best fly-fishing states, it seems strange to think that when my great-grandfather was a boy, there were few trout in Michigan, and none in the Lower Peninsula streams that have become known worldwide.

Some brook trout were in the Upper Peninsula, but most anglers looking for big brookies went north of the Soo along the Lake Superior shoreline, as Robert Barnwell Roosevelt, Teddy Roosevelt's uncle, did in 1863. He wrote about that trip in "Superior Fishing," published in 1865. It's wonderful reading for anyone interested in the history of fishing in our state.

If you want to get technical about it, there were no trout in Michigan until about 120 years ago because brook trout aren't true trout but members of the closely related char family, which also includes lake trout.

Streams in the northern Lower Peninsula were jam-packed with grayling when Roosevelt passed the river mouths on Lake Huron. (He traveled through the area by ship, as did nearly everyone in those days.) But men attracted by a quick buck already had started the destruction of Michigan's forests, an environmental rape that, combined with overfishing, extirpated the grayling by the 20th Century.

There apparently were some rainbows that had been planted in the Great Lakes perhaps even before the Civil War. They entered a few streams to spawn, and once in a while someone caught one, but steelhead didn't become common until the Great Lakes states and Ontario started massive stockings 100 years later.

Brook trout from the UP apparently began to colonize streams in the northern Lower as the grayling disappeared, and early fisheries biologists also planted them in streams in the southwest Lower Peninsula.

Then Rube Babbitt, one of the best-known fishing guides on the Au Sable River in the grayling days, transplanted thousands of brook trout fry and a few rainbows in that river in 1877. Within a dozen years the fishing was so good it was drawing anglers from around the country, some of them the same people whose rapacious appetites had helped wipe out the grayling.

Six years after Babbitt brought trout to the Au Sable, a railroad train stopped along the headwaters of the Pere Marquette River and dumped the contents of a big pail normally used to haul milk. In that pail were the first brown trout imported from Germany by the U.S. Fish Commission, a predecessor of today's U.S. Fish and Wildlife Service.

Seth Green and Fred Mather were the great pioneers of fish culture — in those days devoted almost entirely to trout — and they worked tirelessly in the next few decades shipping fertile eggs and fingerlings from federal and New York state hatcheries to streams all over the country.

That was made possible by the completion of the first transcontinental railroad in 1869, but fertile fish eggs had been traveling by ship for decades. Michigan's first rainbows came from California the long way, around Cape Horn at the tip of South America and through the New York hatchery.

Green and Mather recognized the potential of the vacuum left by the disappearance of grayling from Michigan streams, but they weren't alone in their quest to put trout in every river that would support the fish. Thousands of enthusiastic amateur fish culturists hauled baby trout and eggs all over the country in everything from specially designed brood tanks to pails cooled by chunks of ice.

One of the most famous American fishing flies is the light Cahill, and the man who invented it, Dan Cahill, was a brakeman on the Erie & Lackawanna railroad. Cahill and his friends often loaded pails of trout eggs or fingerlings on their trains and dumped them in any track-side stream that looked feasible.

Tom Awrey was an old man when I met him 30 years ago, well into his 80s, and he told me that when he was a boy in Chicago, his father and some of his father's friends would order trout fingerlings that arrived by train in large pails from eastern hatcheries.

Awrey remembered accompanying the men at age 10 as they carefully shepherded the pails of trout on trains to northern Michigan, where the fish were dumped in streams the men loved to fish.

Nearly all of the fish were rainbows. Awrey said that was because most anglers disliked brown trout, which they thought were far too hard to catch and preyed heavily on other trout.

But Americans eventually came to admire and even revere the brown trout, and I'm glad they did. These fish have provided me with a lifetime of pleasure, entertainment and study, and while I'm better now at catching them than I was as a child more than 50 years ago, I never take momentary success for granted.

It has always struck me that the trout I remember best usually aren't those I caught but those I didn't. When I'm having trouble sleeping and wile away some time by thinking about fishing, it's most often about the ones that got away, and the woulda-shoulda-coulda that might have made a difference.

Like the fish that was rising ever so quietly for midges on the surface of a tiny tributary to the Manistee River. I had caught a couple of dozen six- to 12-inchers that evening, and when I dropped a No. 16 mosquito pattern above it, I figured this fish was something similar.

I had stepped into a loop on the fly line, so I cast the fly and started to clear the line from my wader boot just as the fish sipped down the mosquito. When I raised the three-weight rod, it felt as if I were trying to raise an anvil. The fish tore by me, and I could see it was a brown trout of at least 22 inches.

But when it came up tight, the mess around my boot prevented the fish from pulling line from the reel, and the four-pound leader tippet snapped like a cobweb.

I'll never forget an afternoon in Wyoming when I cast to a big cutthroat trout, one of a half-dozen I could see in a pool on the Yellowstone River. I saw the fish take the fly, and I struck. There was a satisfying weight on the line and some strong head shakes for a few seconds, then nothing.

It wasn't the first fish I had seen kick off, so I cast to another fish a little upstream. The same thing happened. It was only after I had rolled over a third big fish before losing it that I took a second to check the fly.

The point of the hook was gone, undoubtedly broken off when I had let it touch a rock on a careless back-cast.

And when I think about trout I have caught, it's usually not the biggest fish but the ones that were the most satisfying to catch.

Like the 15-inch brown in the Au Sable that was rising in a foot-wide pocket against the bank surrounded on all sides by logs. I knew I would get only one cast at it, and it had to be perfect. It was, and I slid him out over the woodwork and into the open river before he knew what hit him.

Or the 12-inch brookie surface-feeding on something I couldn't see in the Union River in Porcupine Mountains Wilderness State Park in the UP. That fish refused six fly patterns before it took a No. 16 floating nymph. I put 50 casts over that brookie in a half-hour and never spooked the fish.

Or the two-pound brown lying motionless at the tail end of a foot-deep flat in the upper Manistee on a bright day when the water was so clear you could count the fish's spots 50 feet away. When I made the cast with a No. 18 dry fly, the two-pound test tippet cast a shadow on the bottom that looked as thick as a ship's hawser. It took me nearly 20 minutes to wade into a position where I could cast without putting the line over the fish, and I broke into a sweat every time my foot made the tiniest ripple, but when I finally got into position, the trout took the fly on the first cast.

More books about fly-fishing for trout cross my desk than about any other form of angling. I don't know what it is about this facet of our sport that makes participants think they must wax rhapsodic to prove their commitment.

Among the recent offerings was one by a guy who took an extended summer trip with his daughter in an effort to understand the deeper meanings of life through fly-fishing. What it really came down to was, he had screwed up his life, gotten divorced, wasn't feeling very good about himself and needed some time to get his head straight.

Another book purported to be about fly-fishing for dummies. That writer obviously was dumb enough that he didn't realize that fly-fishing is so learning-intensive that dummies shouldn't attempt it. This is not to say you need a PhD to fly-fish for trout. I've known wonderful fly anglers who never graduated from high school. But that doesn't mean they were stupid. They simply didn't get the educational opportunities some other people did, and their knowledge of the sport was encyclopedic.

It also fascinates me that fly anglers command so much literary attention, even though they make up about five percent of the national angling fraternity. Even in places like Michigan, where there are fly-fishing opportunities galore, I figure maybe 10 percent of anglers regularly fish with a fly rod.

The one time you can make a clear exception to that rule is during the hatch of the giant Hexagenia mayflies in late June and early July. Just as everyone is Irish on St. Patrick's Day, it seems that everyone is a fly fisherman when the hexes start to pop.

The Hexagenia hatch is on as I write this. And even though my desk is less than five miles from the Au Sable and the Manistee rivers, and friends are calling about all the giant brown trout they are catching, I've only been able to get out on four nights.

This year the hex hatch coincided with a busy travel schedule, and the few nights I was home, the bugs often didn't hatch where I decided to fish. I still caught several 18- to 21-inch browns on hex spinners, but the wild feeding binges that a thick hex hatch can produce never materialized, and I didn't get any of the 22- to 25-inch monsters I've caught a handful of times in previous years.

But that's the way the cookie crumbles during the hex hatch. I've seen nights where I stood for hours at a spot that should be perfect Hexagenia hatch water and never saw anything bigger than a mosquito. But on the same night friends on the same stream a couple of miles away had a blizzard hatch and caught several trout longer than 18 inches.

Of course, a few times I've been the one who had the hexes and the fish when my friends were blanked, so I guess it all works out in the long run.

The hex hatch is something special. First, it happens after dark. Once an angler has experienced the sensations of standing on a night-shrouded stream, listening to whippoorwills and the million other little noises that fill the night, he usually looks forward to doing it again.

Second, it brings out huge numbers of big trout, fish 18 inches and larger, which normally would never dream of wasting their time picking a mayfly off the surface in broad daylight. These big fish are cannibals, living on other fish, mice and frogs, and they spend the daylight hours loafing under stream banks and downed logs while they wait for hunting hours.

The hex hatch deserves a book all to itself. In fact, it has one, "In the Thrill of the Night," by Detroit-area angler Dan Catau. This book should answer nearly all questions about catching trout when the big flies are out, from where to go to what flies to use to the tactics in using them.

The hex hatch is one of the rare times a fly angler can expect to do as well or better than a bait fisherman. The water is often covered with millions of juicy mayflies, either hatching or returning to lay their eggs, and they offer such a tremendous amount of protein that even the biggest trout gains far more energy from the flies than it uses to eat them.

Sometimes, when a hex hatch starts while there is still enough twilight to see, I've watched big trout come to the surface and suck in a half-dozen or more flies at each rise, and the fish would rise non-stop every few seconds for 30 minutes or more.

Big trout are so keyed on the big mayflies that many anglers pull out a fly rod for the first and only time that year. The hex hatch is when I see people heading for the streams with 30-year-old white Shakespeare Wonderods and yellow Eagle Claws in their hands. These old rods work about as well as anything because most casts during the hex hatch are less than 30 feet.

If you wonder how you see a rising trout at night, the answer is that most of the time you don't, or at least not clearly. On nights with a bright moon, it's amazing how well you can see what's going on around you, especially after your eyes have had a couple of hours to get accustomed to the dim light. But most years the hatch doesn't coincide with bright moonlight, or there's cloud cover. I've also noticed that on nights when humans can see well, so can the trout, and they are tougher to approach and cast to.

Most experienced hex anglers pick a spot they know well. The ideal spot would be near an area with a silty bottom, where the flies live as nymphs for three years before hatching for a two-day adult life span. The place should be wadeable (deep holes can be a problem in the dark) and offer good trout cover.

I like to get to the spot an hour or two before dark to stake my claim and work the water over with a brown drake or a hex spinner. (Some trout like early-bird specials.)

When darkness falls, I wait for the hatch or spinner fall. Sometimes they happen, sometimes they don't. Most often, the hatch starts at 11 p.m. or later, and the spinner fall comes anywhere from 30 minutes to three hours after that.

Through the years, I've become pretty good at estimating the distance from me to a slurping sound that marks a rising fish. Because I arrive early enough to acquaint myself with the waters in daylight, I have a decent idea of where that slurp arose in relation to me and the surrounding trout cover.

Usually, I do the same thing I would do in daylight, cast to an area I think is 10 feet or so above the fish and try for a drag-free float (although that is less important in night fishing). Sometimes I hear the rise, then strike and find myself attached to a fish. More often, the rod jerks in my hand, I jerk back reflexively and I'm into a trout.

I rarely fish in Michigan with a fly rod heavier than a five-weight, but the hex hatch is an exception. Then, I usually pull out a seven-weight, and my leader tippet is eight-pound fluorocarbon rather than the two to four pounds I use in daylight. The fish can't see the leader as well, and the chances of hooking a real leader-buster longer than 20 inches is better than at any other time of the year.

Fly fishermen learned a long time ago that the key to catching trout is a natural presentation of the lure. And in recent years American bait fishermen have learned what Europeans did centuries ago — that if they switch to longer rods, nine to 12 feet, they can present a bait that looks a lot more natural and is more likely to draw a strike.

Everyone who has fished with a worm for trout knows that the best presentation is to let the worm drift downstream on a slack line from a position directly upstream from the fish. (This assumes that you got into position without kicking up too much of the stream bottom.) Not only does the worm reach the fish before it sees the line, there is less drag on the bait and the line, and the worm rolls and tumbles pretty much like a worm that isn't attached to a hook.

Drifting a worm straight downstream is a great way to get to fish hiding under a log or undercut bank, but if you use a long rod, it's an even better way to present a worm in a natural manner.

A longer rod also works well with spinners. It allows the angler to control the speed with which the spinner moves through the water and to control its drift over underwater structures and through pools by varying the amount of line in the water.

I have a 10-foot Stimula rod made by Shimano that I use for nearly all of my bait-fishing for trout. I bought it in Chicago, and when I called Shimano to find out where I could buy some more, I was told, "Gee, that's a rod we make for the European market. We don't sell them here. I don't know how that one ended up in a tackle shop in Chicago."

This rod works beautifully with two- to four-pound test line, but the tip is a lot stiffer than American noodle rods of the same length, which means I also can use it to cast for bluegills or perch.

For trout fishing, I rig the bait under a float about three inches long and the thickness of a pencil. The line is attached to the float by slipping the monofilament through small neoprene rings, one at either end of the float. This lets me vary the depth of the bait by sliding the float up and down the line to suit the depth of the water.

I add split shots, usually BB size, to the line under the float until only about a half-inch of the tiny red tip sticks above water when a night crawler is attached to the hook.

Now I have a rig I can flip underhanded 15 to 20 feet upstream and let drift down the current toward me while the rod keeps all or nearly all of the line off the surface of the water.

The float is so close to neutral buoyancy that it goes under if a fish so much as breathes on it. And when a fish grabs the bait and runs with it, it feels almost no resistance from the bobber.

Letting the bait drift with no line touching the water not only helps fool fish, it reduces the chances of snagging. (Although I've always said that if you don't lose a half-dozen hooks on a bait-fishing excursion, you're not doing it right.)

Most bait anglers use worms for trout. They work, but I know a few anglers in Grayling who specialize in catching large trout on bait, and they rarely use anything but minnows.

Smaller fish make up 90 percent of the diet of a big brown trout, a fish longer than 16 inches. That makes sense for a fish that spends nearly all of its time preserving energy. If you have to leave slack water and use calories swimming against a current, it's more energy-efficient to make one dash after something the size of a minnow than 50 attacks on something the size of a mayfly.

Brook trout

Some writers have described the brook trout as the "Aphrodite of the hemlocks." That's a slur against the fish. Aphrodite might have been the epitome of beauty in Greece a few thousand years ago, but if you go by most of those Aphrodite statues in European museums, she would have been hard-pressed to squeeze into a size-16 dress.

A male brookie in his fall spawning coat is one of the most beautiful creatures in the world. His back is shaded from a deep, blackish-green on the back to pale olive on the sides. His back and sides are covered with paler, worm-like tracks and spots, and mixed among the light areas are brilliant red spots with lavender margins.

His belly is the color of a Lake Superior sunset, sometimes with black stripes outlining the red, and his fins fade from a flaming reddish-orange at the rear to black, with a defined white stripe along the leading edge.

I've always been puzzled by comments by angling writers in the 19th and early 20th centuries that brook trout were easy to catch because they came back and slashed at a fly time after time. Maybe there has been a change in brook trout genetics since those words were written, but my experience has been that while it's easier to get a brookie to rise to a fly the first time, it's less likely to strike again if you miss.

I often can get a brown or a rainbow to hit a fly again if it didn't feel the sting of a hook the first time. But once a brookie has been spooked by a bungled strike, that's usually the last rise you get from that fish for an hour or so.

If you wonder why brook trout in Michigan average about half the size of those farther north in Ontario, it's for the same reason that Scandinavians are taller on average than Italians — they have different gene pools.

Michigan brookies are part of a southern population that mostly lives in smaller rivers and lakes. These fish grow slowly and don't live as long, usually less than seven years.

Canadian brook trout live much longer, up to 15 years, and grow much faster. In this aspect brookies resemble northern pike and lake trout, whose biggest specimens also come from the extreme northern end of their range.

But the same is true for mammals like bears, big cats and even elephants. Scientists have explained this phenomenon through Bergman's rule.

Bergman's rule says that bigger-bodied animals are more energy-efficient, and members of the species tend to get bigger the farther they are from the Equator. It's less clear why this should work for cold-blooded critters like fish.

In the past decade it has become obvious to fisheries biologists that there are two strains of brook trout, perhaps even two subspecies. (And some would argue that coaster and salter brookies are a third subspecies.) One strain is the fish that live in streams in Michigan, Wisconsin and Minnesota, and even survive in relic populations down to the Georgia Appalachian highlands (where they moved in during the last of the ice ages).

These fish grow to 14 to 16 inches, maybe 18, tops, and they don't live long. Careful management can increase the average size well above the six inches we see today, but a fish bigger than two pounds will always be exceptional.

Then there are the brook trout that inhabit the lakes of Ontario's Laurentian Shield, a landscape carved out of some of the world's most ancient rocks, and sub-Arctic rivers like the Sutton and Albany. This strain averages two to three pounds (18 to 22 inches), and five-pounders are not uncommon. Fishing contests in places like Thunder Bay, Ontario, are usually won by brook trout that top eight pounds. The world-record brook trout — 14 pounds, eight ounces — came from Ontario's Nipigon River, which cuts through the shield.

A few months ago, I went ice fishing at Thunder Bay in northern Lake Superior, and the first brook trout that came up through the hole was a big-bellied 19-incher that went at least three pounds. But the truly remarkable thing was that the local anglers I was fishing with hardly remarked on it other than to say, "Nice fish."

This is the kind of brook trout Robert Barnwell Roosevelt wrote about in "Superior Fishing," when he described a fishing trip along about 100 miles of Lake Superior shoreline north of Sault Ste. Marie.

From his description of fishing at the mouths of rivers and along some of the steep bluffs that fall into the big lake, he probably was fishing for coasters, a strain or perhaps subspecies of brook trout that spawns in a river yet spends two or three years of its adult life feeding in big, open water, a life cycle much like that of steelhead or salmon.

Numerous stories in magazines and books from the 1800s detail the spawning runs of these fish, and the brook trout found in a handful of Michigan streams at the northern tip of the Lower Peninsula when white settlers arrived probably were coasters.

That kind of lifestyle for some brook trout makes sense, especially when you look at the salter brookies that migrate along the New England coastline to spawn in freshwater streams after spending their growing years in the Atlantic Ocean.

I've seen some salters, and they have a smoky-gray color that looks a lot like the coloration of sea-run Arctic char. And the brook trout I have seen that people told me were coasters also are more silvery and much less colorful than fish from inland streams.

I could take one of the brook trout from a stream I fish near Grayling, put it in a 1,000-gallon tank by itself and feed it crayfish stuffed with mayfly larvae for five years, and it probably would never exceed two pounds.

And that makes sense, too. Why would nature evolve fish that can reach their reproductive potential in streams that don't supply enough nutrition?

Brook trout like cold water, preferably below 55 degrees, and they are less tolerant of pollutants than most other trout. They are fall spawners, making their redds in streams in late September and October in most of Michigan. But they also spawn in lakes if the water stays highly oxygenated through the winter.

Brookies will eat almost anything. Fish in small streams seem to feed more heavily on insects, but all brook trout are aggressive predators on smaller fish and are enthusiastic cannibals.

The South Branch of the Au Sable River in the northern Lower Peninsula and the Indian River in the Upper Peninsula are two of the best streams to catch bigger brookies (12 to 16 inches). But I have caught a lot of keeper-sized fish in small streams all across the western UP. In one river in Porcupine Mountains Wilderness State Park, you can catch brookies from bathtub-sized pools in the granite of what was a pretty good-sized waterfall earlier in the year. When the water level falls, these pools still get a trickle through them, but the fish are trapped.

The Michigan record brook trout is nine pounds, eight ounces, caught in Clear Lake in 1996.

Brown trout

I once came across a well-known, elderly angler who was spearing salmon in the Pere Marquette River and tossing their carcasses on the riverbank. When I told him this was not only stupid but illegal, he said he didn't care, he was going to kill as many salmon as possible because they were competing for spawning grounds with "the native brown trout."

I found myself at a loss for words. Salmon hadn't affected the trout population, and trying to wipe out salmon by spearing a few was like trying to empty the river with a teacup.

But the most ridiculous part was that brown trout are not native to Michigan. In fact, they were introduced to the Pere Marquette not long before that old fisherman was born.

In the 1880s, the old United States Fish Commission decided to bring in some European game fish to replace native species, mostly brook trout, which had been decimated by overfishing, dam building and pollution.

They brought in two species, carp and brown trout, and many of today's anglers might be surprised to learn that the brown trout was despised at first as an oversized, skulking, fish-eating trash species.

Today, the brown trout is at the apex of the trout angler's pantheon because of the same attributes that originally earned it such scorn — it's wary and hard to catch, it grows bigger than native brook trout, and it fights like a bulldog.

Brown trout have become favorite targets of Great Lakes anglers, who nearly always troll for them. These fish are stay-at-homes, usually hanging off river mouths and along shorelines, and in April and May they often are found just outside the surf line on the beaches.

My buddy Mike Gnatkowski, a charter skipper out of Ludington, fishes for steelhead in the Pere Marquette River all winter and on his bigger boat for salmon miles offshore on Lake Michigan all summer.

But early spring finds him trolling body baits just off the beaches, sometimes in water as shallow as eight feet, looking for browns that average about five pounds but sometimes surpass 15.

These Great Lakes fish look like footballs, with fat, round bellies and small heads, and small-boat anglers can catch them all summer within a mile or two of shore.

Brown trout originally had a natural range that spread from western India to Scotland. But unlike the closely related Atlantic salmon, which crossed the ocean to North America, brown trout never ventured far from the shoreline.

Brown trout have been the target of anglers for millennia. An early geographer wrote nearly 2,000 years ago that the Macedonians caught "the fish with speckled skins," and apparently used artificial flies to do so. And Dame Juliana Berners nearly 600 years ago described dressings for flies used to catch brown trout in England.

The Brits expanded the evolutionary horizons of the brown trout, loading tanks of brown trout eggs on ships bound to British colonies and trading ports around the world. Because of the British love of trout fishing, browns now can be found near the snow-clad peaks of the Hindu Kush in the Himalayas and off Tierra del Fuego at the tip of South America.

I've driven through a searing desert near Perth in Western Australia to fish for browns that officials from an English penal colony released in mountain streams. I've caught them in Chile, where they were imported by homesick Limey cattle ranchers. And I've caught them 5,000 feet up in the Drakensberg Mountains in South Africa.

But browns didn't reach the United States until near the end of the 19th Century, largely because there were tremendous numbers of native trout and other game fish, and the Americans tossed the Brits out before they developed the technology needed to transport live fish eggs across oceans.

When brown trout finally were brought to this country, they often multiplied quickly in streams where native trout and smallmouth bass had been decimated. But unlike brook trout, which usually would take just about any reasonable-looking fly, browns proved much harder to fool.

Sometimes, they would take only an artificial fly almost identical in size and color to the naturals hatching on the stream, a concept alien to American anglers. Until then anglers hadn't paid a lot of attention to matching the hatch, which the English had been doing for a century.

Then American trout anglers like Theodore Gordon, Edward Ringwood Hewitt and George LaBranche in the late 19th and early 20th centuries worked out patterns that imitated American aquatic insects. And just as important, they developed techniques for fishing with these flies on American waters, which tend to be much rougher and faster than British streams.

One of the most effective ways to fly-fish for big browns is with streamers, overgrown flies that look more like a hardware fisherman's crank bait and which imitate bait fish and crayfish rather than insects.

Streamers used to be lumped generically under the name "bucktail" because most had a wing made from that material. The original streamers apparently were copied from flies Canadian Indians made from the hair on a deer's tail or from polar bear fur.

Fly tiers like Roy Steenrod, Carrie Stevens and Don Gapen refined the crude originals into classic minnow imitations like the bumblepuppy, gray ghost and muddler minnow, and superb anglers and writers like Ray Bergman, Joe Bates and Joe Brooks showed the world how to catch big browns on them.

I love catching fish on dry flies, but early in the season and on rainy days I'll open up the meat-fishing box and pull out a streamer that looks like something a big brown would consider worth chasing and eating.

The first brown trout brought to this country came from Germany, which is why many old-timers referred to them as German trout or Von Behr trout. They soon were followed by browns from Loch Leven in Scotland. The Loch Leven fish had thick, black spots but no red spots, and the German variety had red spots scattered among the black. Most brown trout caught in Michigan have the red spots, but interbreeding in hatcheries for more than a century has so mixed up the gene pool that differences among the strains have long been moot.

While I deliberately live a few miles from the headwaters of the Au Sable and Manistee rivers, both famed brown trout streams, I think the best brown trout fishing in Michigan rivers in recent years has been in the Pere Marquette. That river gets better plants of trout than the other two, and while purists might rant about their love of wild browns, I think that's a large pile of crap.

I don't know how many times I have gone to a meeting where people have fulminated about the need for more spawning waters for natural brown trout, then we've settled back to see slides or a video of Bill or Charlie's trip to

Montana or Colorado, where they caught a batch of big browns — all of which were planted by the state.

Don't get me wrong. I would like to see many more miles of Michigan rivers managed for natural reproduction. But I also see nothing wrong with a put-andtake fishery in other streams, especially since I defy anyone to tell the difference between the way planted and stream-born fish fight after they have been in the river three or four years.

The place where no one seems to have a problem with planting trout is in the Great Lakes, and I would like to see more effort go to planting browns and less to planting salmon. The Great Lakes brown trout, mostly of the Seeforellen and Wild Rose hatchery strains, grow quickly and to large sizes. Fish exceeding 20 pounds are caught routinely, and 10 pounds has become the norm out of many Lake Michigan and Lake Huron ports.

I like these fish for a couple of reasons. First, they tend to stay near shore, in 60 feet of water or less, so they are easily accessible to small-boat anglers.

They also like to hang out at river mouths and the drowned river-mouth lakes inside the Great Lakes proper, like Lake Manistee and Pere Marquette Lake. That makes them accessible for a fair amount of the year to shore fishermen casting from piers.

Second, I like a mixed-bag fishery more than another that is comprised of a single species. A lot of people seem to long for a return to the days when they would catch nothing but coho or chinook salmon. Not me. I love picking up a rod when a fish strikes and not knowing if it will be a salmon, lake trout, steelhead or brown (or an Atlantic, if you're fishing in Lake Huron).

Brown trout do well in Michigan partly because they tolerate warmer water than most other trout. They can easily handle 80-degree water temperatures that would kill or incapacitate a brook trout, although browns prefer water in the low to mid-60s.

But I've also become convinced that their preference for warmer water is one reason we see enormous variation in the brown trout population and growth rates in streams in northern Michigan.

If you look at the brown trout's original homelands, you'll be struck that few of these places get anywhere near as cold as does northern Michigan.

Glasgow, Scotland, where I was born, is at 56 degrees north latitude, nearly 1,000 miles north of my home in Grayling and 1,200 miles north of Detroit, and yet Glasgow and the rest of Scotland get little snow.

The same is true right across the brown trout's ancestral homeland. Macedonia, Turkey, Spain, France, you name a place where brown trout evolved naturally, and it will have a milder winter and cooler summer than we see in Cadillac or Grayling or Marquette.

If you fish for brown trout in Wyoming or Montana or Colorado, you'll find the best fishing isn't in the mountains but on the fringes, places where the winter is tempered by sunny days in which temperatures rise into the 50s in January and February. The fish also inhabit rivers that are mostly bigger and warmer than ours.

I moved to Grayling in 1990, and since then we've seen a steady improvement in brown trout fishing in the Au Sable, Manistee and other well-known streams. Part of that improvement is better stream management by the state Department of Natural Resources, but I'm convinced it's no accident that in those 12 years we've had some of the warmest winters ever recorded in

Michigan (and the United States, for that matter).

Brown trout have the biggest natural size variation of any freshwater fish in Michigan, with the possible exception of the channel catfish. The state-record brown trout, taken from Lake Michigan in 2000, is a whopping 34 pounds, 10 ounces. But any brown bigger than five pounds taken from an inland stream is a rare trophy, and the average brown caught in a Michigan trout stream is probably less than 12 inches.

With all the genetic mixing and matching of the past century, many of our brown trout probably have the sea-trout gene that causes them to spawn in a river and spend the rest of the year feeding in big water, like their first-cousin, the Atlantic salmon.

That's probably the genesis of the 28-pound, four-ounce brown that St. Joseph charter skipper Ken Neidlinger landed aboard his boat in the St. Joseph River in 2001. Most sea-run (or lake-run) browns look so much like an Atlantic salmon that most people can't tell them apart, but this fish looked like a scaled-up version of the 12-inchers people catch on dry flies in rivers all over the state.

Instead of being silvery, it had an overall brown and yellow coloration and lots of black and red spots. And while brown trout that return to a river tend to regain some of their juvenile colors, this one was so typical of a stream fish that it might have spent much of its life in the St. Joseph, living in a deep pool and dining on salmon and trout fingerlings that came down a tributary creek.

I've snorkled under a lot of the trout structures built in our streams during the Civilian Conservation Corps days, and I'm always amazed at the number of 16- to 24-inch browns I see loafing under there.

But big browns like this don't make their living coming out in midday to eat a half-inch fly. They mostly eat smaller fish, including other trout, although they will happily dine on crayfish, mice or anything else that looks like it would make a suitable meal. And they hunt at night, when most trout anglers are in bed.

I suspect that the heavy angling pressure on most of our trout streams has had an effect on the fishery. When you have someone wading down a river every 30 minutes (or sometimes three minutes) from May until September, it only makes sense that the fish will adjust their lifestyles to compensate for the disturbance.

Rainbow trout

I once read that rainbow trout (undoubtedly steelhead) were introduced to the Great Lakes as early as 1858. Another account places their introduction in 1876 (the same year George Armstrong Custer earned everlasting fame by screwing up at the Little Bighorn in Montana).

Whenever they arrived, rainbow trout quickly became a favored game fish. They were much easier to catch than the newly arrived brown trout, and they were spectacular jumpers.

Today, rainbow trout are in the minority in most Michigan streams, with the exception of the migratory steelhead that were discussed in the chapter on salmon.

Rainbows like colder water than browns, from about 55 to 60 degrees, but they can live in water up to 75 degrees if it is well-oxygenated. They also do well in lakes.

For reasons I've never understood, rainbow trout, a fish that obviously evolved in the Pacific Coast drainage, used to be listed in the genus Salmo along with Atlantic salmon and brown trout.

Now they have been reassigned to the genus Oncorhynchus, which includes other Pacific salmonid species such as coho and chinook salmon, and that seems to make more sense.

Most fish books list three rainbow subspecies — the migratory steelhead, the stream-resident rainbow and the Kamloops trout, a steelhead originally found in British Columbia that never left fresh water but spent its non-spawning time in big Kamloops Lake.

Today, rainbow genetics have been so intermixed that it's doubtful there are any strains of pure stream rainbows left (with the possible exception of some fish transplanted to southern Argentina a century ago). One biologist told me the problem with planting rainbows in a stream is that "half of them turn out to have steelhead genes, and they head down for the big lake as soon as they are old enough. And the other half are so dumb and easy to catch that they get cleaned out in a couple of years, and so it's tough to get a naturally reproducing population going."

I like rainbows because they are usually willing to take a dry fly, thanks to their predilection for insect prey over bait fish. It's one reason I often fish the Manistee above Cameron Road Bridge, because few things are more fun than playing a cart-wheeling, one- to two-pound rainbow that grabbed a No. 14 Adams fly cast on a three-weight rod.

But rainbows are also an excellent species for spin fishermen. They usually like small, flashy spinners, the kind with blades less than an inch long. That's also true for big steelhead.

Other good streams for resident rainbows are the Pine River in Lake County and the Pere Marquette, which is primarily a brown trout stream. And I've caught some nice rainbows in Paint Creek in Rochester.

Rainbows caught on quickly in Michigan in the last decades of the 19th Century and first decades of the 20th. Relatively easy to raise and hardy enough to transport well, they were popular species in the Au Sable, Manistee, Pere Marquette, Sturgeon and Muskegon, but the most famous rainbow fishery in the Eastern United States developed in the rapids of the St. Marys River at Sault Ste. Marie.

The fish apparently were planted there before 1900, and by 1920 Ernest Hemingway wrote about the Soo's fabulous rainbow fishing for the Toronto Star. Ray Bergman, one of America's finest fishing writers of his generation, extolled the wonderful and wild Soo rapids fishery in his marvelous book "Trout," which went through several printings in the 1930s and spurred thousands of anglers to try their hand there.

Stream rainbows grow very slowly. It normally takes about four years for a resident stream rainbow to reach 13 inches and one pound. A steelhead feeding in a big lake usually grows bigger than 10 pounds by that time.

But even big rainbows show an amazing preference for tiny insects as food. Some studies have shown that mayfly and caddis fly larvae, beetles, ants and the nymphal forms of other aquatic insects make up 70 percent or more of a rainbow's diet.

Stream rainbows are spring spawners, with the females making nests when the water reaches about 50 degrees. Rainbows that live in lakes without suitable tributary spawning streams often will spawn in the shallows where little creeks enter or leave the lake.

There is no state record for a stream-resident rainbow, mostly because there's no real way to separate those fish from the migratory steelhead. As you might expect, the state-record steelie, 26 pounds, eight ounces, was caught by a trolling angler in Lake Michigan.

But if you're fishing most Michigan streams in summer and catch a rainbow bigger than three pounds, you've got yourself a trophy.

Splake

A couple of winters ago, I found myself staring through an underwater television camera at some big walleyes slowly milling around my jigging spoon 20 feet under the ice.

The walleyes were interested in the spoon but were ultra-cautious. Then a big shape materialized from the gloom. It was a splake, a solid eight-pounder, and it flashed through the walleyes like a torpedo, driving them away.

It disappeared for a few seconds, then came slicing back across the screen and dashed out of sight. The rod in my left hand began jerking violently, line started peeling off the reel, and I realized the fish had grabbed the baited spoon.

I tried to put some brakes on the fish, and it went nuts. We could see it flashing back and forth on the monitor, and within 30 seconds it had wrapped the line around three other lines and the TV camera cable.

I managed to crank everything up until we could see the fish through the ice, about two feet below us and three feet from the hole. At that point, what with the television camera, the fish and the other lures, I had so much weight on the line I didn't dare apply any more pressure, and I broke the line as I tried to reach the fish with a hand gaff.

If you think steelhead are good fighters, wait until you tangle with a splake. This fish is a hatchery cross between a male brook trout and a female lake trout, but I always think of it as a steelhead on speed.

Unlike many hybrids, splake are often fertile. But there are few naturally reproduced splake, largely because they can breed back with the parent stocks. The name is derived from "speckled," the common Canadian term for brook trout, and "lake."

Splake can be hard to identify. Most look more like a brook trout than a lake trout, but splake from the Great Lakes can be almost as silver as a salmon. A good rule of thumb is that any fish from the Great Lakes or an inland lake that looks a lot like a brook trout but is bigger than four pounds is probably a splake.

Most big splake are caught in the Great Lakes by trollers (the Michigan record is 17 pounds, seven ounces, from Big Bay de Noc), and I suspect most are written off as an oddly colored laker.

Splake feed aggressively on almost anything they can catch, with a decided preference for smaller fish.

Chapter 5

Perch

THERE IS LITTLE MORE ENJOYABLE ON A WINTER'S DAY THAN sitting in an ice-fishing shanty with a big school of eagerly biting perch below. It was on a day like that on Little Bay de Noc, an arm of Lake Michigan on the southern shore of the Upper Peninsula, that I hooked what I thought must be a good walleye from the way it bent the three-foot ice rod.

As I got the fish near the hole, I was delighted to see it was a huge perch, and a few minutes later a ruler confirmed it was the biggest of my life, a 15-incher that weighed two pounds. For a few minutes I just sat and admired its beautiful contours and colors. The sides were as brassy as a carnival watch, the dark bars stood out like a convict's stripes, and the fins were a brilliant red-orange.

I finally came to my senses and realized that I hadn't done the most important thing with this fish — take it to the other shanty where I could show it off to my fishing buddies and gloat. I barely had gotten outside when the door of the other shanty opened and Kim Papineau, a professional walleye tournament angler from Escanaba, held out a fish and said, "Look at this!"

It was a 16-inch perch that weighed nearly three pounds and made mine look commonplace. I hid my fish behind my back, made the appropriate congratulatory noises and retreated to my hut.

After the various species of sunfish, yellow perch are the most commonly caught freshwater fish in Michigan and one of the most common in the country.

Giants like those caught in Little Bay de Noc, lakes Erie and St. Clair in southeast Michigan and Lake Simcoe in Canada — about 70 miles north of Toronto — are the exception. Most perch are school fish, five to nine inches long. They will happily take everything from minnows to worms and like shallow water, so they easily can be caught from shore by kids and casual anglers.

Yellow perch once were a staple for party-boat skippers out of Great Lakes ports like St. Joseph and Grand Haven on Lake Michigan and Port Austin on Lake Huron. But perch numbers have fallen dramatically in the Great Lakes. An invasion of fish-eating birds called cormorants might be part of the problem in the Les Cheneaux Islands in northern Lake Huron, but scientists think the root cause is competition between newly arrived zebra mussels and a native freshwater shrimp called gammarus, a remnant of the ice ages that lives in deep, cold waters.

Zebra mussels came from the Baltic Sea and have exploded in the Great Lakes in numbers as much as 1,000 times higher than in their homeland. (No predators or diseases here keep them in check.)

Interestingly, two areas where perch continue to thrive are Lake St. Clair and Lake Erie. These are shallower and warmer than the rest of the Great Lakes, places where the gramerus does not do well. It's replaced by another species of freshwater shrimp that not only competes with zebra mussels but eats zebra mussel feces, which is too big for gramerus to consume.

Species

The yellow perch, Perca flavescens, is the only perch species in North America. It is a member of a family of fish that also includes walleyes, saugers and darters.

The average size of yellow perch is about nine inches and a half-pound. The European perch, Perca fluviatilis, shares the same convict stripes and orangy fins, but it has a more silvery body and can reach a weight of more than 15 pounds. The yellow perch world record is four pounds and three ounces, a New Jersey fish from 1865 that is by far the oldest record in the International Game Fish Association book.

Yellow perch reach six inches long in about three years and 10 inches in about six, and the great majority of fish we put in our buckets in Michigan are in that age range. A 12-inch jumbo is about 10 years old, and the rare 15-incher is more than 15.

Perch feed heavily on minnows, including baby perch, but they also eat large numbers of aquatic insects, fish eggs (which they usually pick off vegetation), small crayfish and snails.

HABITAT PREFERENCE

Perch inhabit lakes, ponds and rivers across the entire northern half of the United States and southern Canada, from the Maritime provinces to the Rockies.

They like bodies of water deeper than 20 feet, giving them a winter refuge, something important to fish that feed actively all winter. Perch tend to school in open water and around weed beds, and they are cool-water fish with a preference for temperatures about 60 to 70 degrees.

Perch also can overpopulate an area, especially in small lakes and ponds, and produce a population of stunted adult fish. But in big waters, like the Great Lakes and Lake St. Clair, there is so much food and habitat that it is common in spring and late fall to fill buckets with fish averaging 10 inches.

SPAWNING

Perch spawn early in the spring when the water reaches about 45 degrees, depositing their gelatinous strings of eggs on weed beds and brush piles in water less than 10 feet deep.

Adults abandon the eggs after spawning, and more than 99 percent of the fry don't make it to a length of three inches at the end of their first year. They are prey for all kinds of other fish, including their bigger cousins, the walleye.

TOP WATERS

You couldn't do better than Lake St. Clair and western Lake Erie for perch fishing in Michigan, especially in May and October. These big waters produce lots of little perch and have tons of food, which means more of the little ones grow to be 10- to 14-inch jumbos.

Houghton and Higgins lakes in the northern Lower Peninsula also are noted perch hot spots, along with Saginaw Bay. Little Bay de Noc and lakes Gogebic and Michigamme are good Upper Peninsula perch waters.

TECHNIQUES

Most perch probably are caught on worms by casual anglers who toss out bait in hopes of hooking sunfish, perch, bass or anything else that comes along.

But if you are deliberately targeting perch, nothing beats small minnows (one to three inches long) fished under a bobber in summer or on a small jig through the ice.

Perch can be amazingly fussy biters, something I began to understand after I started using a Vista-Cam underwater camera a couple of years ago. We dropped the camera in clear water in several lakes and were amazed to see that our baits sometimes were surrounded by dozens and perhaps hundreds of perch that looked at them curiously, then ignored them.

We tried jigging the baits quickly, then slowly, then letting them sit still. We lifted them toward the surface and let them fall to the bottom. We switched jigs and baits, going from minnows to wax worms to night crawlers, again usually with little or no effect.

Then something we didn't understand would tell the fish it was time to eat, and we watched perch after perch rush over and seize bait that had been ignored minutes earlier.

The underwater camera confirmed what most anglers know from experience — perch congregate by size, and if you catch one six-incher, then the rest of the fish you catch will be in the same size range. If you want bigger fish, wait for the first school to move on or start casting 100 feet out around the edges of the school, where you'll find the bigger, more solitary fish that are the survivors of millions hatched in that year-class 10 years before.

Another thing the camera showed was the fascinating perch-walleye relationship. Walleyes eat perch, but I have watched as six-inch perch showed no concern when a 20-inch walleye showed up to see what was going on.

But the perch disappeared as it started to get dark, mostly settling on the bottom, while the walleyes continued to feed.

For the past couple of years, I've been going to a small lake near my home, where I row a cataraft and troll for perch with tiny crank baits one to two inches long made by Yo-Zuri and Rapala. I've tried some realistic imitations of baby trout and baby bass, but the colors that work best are chartreuse and bright orange in the Yo-Zuri snap beans and fire tiger combinations with the midget Rapalas.

FOOD VALUE

Perch fillets often sell for $12 to $15 a pound, considerably higher than anything else in the fish store. What more do you need to say? Many people think perch is the finest fish in fresh water, even better than its big cousin, the walleye.

Perch are delicious, but people who have had heart problems, like me, rarely get to eat them because they have to be fried to taste right. And because it takes about 40 average perch to make a meal for four people, a lot of anglers have bought perch-scaling devices that fit on an electric drill to speed up the process.

Limited commercial perch fisheries continue on some of the Great Lakes, but not in Michigan waters. Most fresh perch you see for sale in our stores come from the Ontario side of Lake Erie.

White perch

Imagine a white bass without stripes and shrunk to about half its normal size. That's a white perch, a member of the same family as white and striped bass and an exotic invader that reached the Great Lakes above Niagara Falls about 50 years ago. (It reached Lake Ontario 100 years before, probably through the Erie Canal.)

White perch live a long time, but those in the Great Lakes are showing evidence of a common problem: stunting because of overpopulation. A five-year-old white perch should be about nine inches long, but those in the Great Lakes are usually half that size.

It's a shame because they are fun to catch with ultralight tackle and very good to eat. You also can teach kids to catch them in large numbers on worms, tiny jigs and spinners.

White perch include small fish in their diet but eat more invertebrates, especially insect larvae. In summer, white perch often can be seen picking hatching insects off the surface, and that's a good time to fish for them with a dry fly. (I've had a lot of success with No. 8 brown drakes and Adams.)

White perch are extremely wary, and a school will run off if a boat comes too close. If you hook one and want to catch more, anchor the boat, or drift through the places where you caught the fish and then motor slowly around the area in a big circle until you are back upwind or up-current.

Chapter 6

Northern pike

THE NORTHERN PIKE HAS THE MOST WIDESPREAD NATURAL distribution of any freshwater fish. It circles the northern hemisphere in a relatively narrow band that originally extended from about 40 degrees north latitude all the way to the Arctic Circle.

The only other fish to approach this distribution is the salmon. But salmon include more than a dozen species, with six to 10 salmon species in North America, depending on which taxonomic system you accept.

But whether you catch it in Ireland, Russia or Michigan, a northern pike is a northern pike.

"The pike is a hard beast to manage," said Todd Grischke, a state Department of Natural Resources fisheries biologist. "Bass are almost entirely sport fish, and bass anglers hardly ever kill one. Walleyes are food fish to almost everyone, even to the tournament walleye anglers.

"But pike are a sport fish for half of the people, and a food fish for the other half, so it's hard to come up with a management policy that makes a majority of the anglers happy."

Grischke was commenting on the Michigan DNR's decision to lower the daily pike bag limit from five fish to two in 2002. Previously, the rule was five bass, pike or walleye in any combination. That could be a mixed bag of five, or five of any one species.

Predictably, when the word got out, my e-mail and voice mail began drawing heated complaints from some anglers, who said things like: "It's hardly worth going fishing for two pike." Others praised the move, saying: "This change is long overdue. If we want to develop some trophy pike fishing in Michigan, we have to give more pike a chance to grow."

I can understand why some people would be upset with the changes imposed by the DNR, especially ice fishermen who are pike specialists. They spend a lot of winter weekends traveling to lakes in northern Michigan that produce a lot of these toothy water wolves.

But my support goes to the DNR and the anglers who want to see our pike grow bigger. They are remarkably long-lived fish, and the only way to let a few reach their potential maximum size is to give them more time to grow.

If the decision had been mine, not only would I have reduced the bag limit, I would have increased the minimum size of 24 inches for keepers to at least 30 inches. The reason is that while northern pike are among the biggest of freshwater fish, they are also among the slowest-growing, at least in their native northern waters.

I occasionally get questions from anglers who wonder why Michigan doesn't produce many trophy northerns like those taken from fly-in lakes in northern Canada.

The answer is complex, and part of it has to do with the size, geology and age of our lakes. (We don't have enough really big inland lakes with lots of shallows.) But our biggest problem is that so many people fish for and keep pike, the fish don't live long enough to reach trophy sizes, even in the biggest lakes.

Pike can live 25 years or more (the medieval stories about 100-year-old pike are myths), and any pike bigger than about seven pounds is certainly a female. I have fished a lot of those fly-in lakes in places like northern Saskatchewan, the Northwest Territories and Alaska, and we caught huge numbers of pike bigger than 20 pounds and a few nudging 30.

But we also released them to live to fight another day. The same is true in Ireland, where many people think the next world-record pike will be produced.

Water bailiffs kill every pike they see on most trout waters in Ireland and Great Britain, but the Irish have established trophy fishing in several streams and lakes, and the result has been a phenomenal northern fishery that draws anglers from around the world.

Compare those waters to the lake on which I live in Grayling, Lake Margrethe. It has an excellent pike population that is exploited mostly in the winter by ice fishermen.

I often wander onto the lake on a nice winter day and schmooze with friends who have ice shacks or move around and fish from snowmobiles. It's also common for me to see three to six barely legal pike on the ice at each stop.

What surprises me is how the lake continues to produce such good numbers of pike year after year. But it doesn't surprise me that most caught weigh less than five pounds, and a fish bigger than 10 pounds is rare.

Things are a bit different at Wakeley Lake, a federally managed site about 10 miles east of Grayling. The rules at Wakeley allow artificial baits only, and all species of fish must be released. The lake is open only from mid-June through August.

Many people don't fish Wakeley because they want to bring something home. Besides that, no motors are allowed, not even electrics, and it's a half-mile walk from the parking lot. (Many locals have come up with various push carts to get canoes and rowboats to the lake.)

So not only do most Wakeley fish live to fight and spawn again, there is considerably less fishing pressure than on many other lakes. And it's not a coincidence that Wakeley Lake consistently produces some of the biggest pike I see or hear about in Michigan.

But big pike can come out of surprisingly small waters. A couple of summers ago I was fly-fishing for bluegills on a lake barely a half-mile across, a place where I had caught a few 12-inch hammer-handle pike but nothing bigger.

I was using a tiny popper and had just hooked another bluegill when the water boiled behind it and the three-weight rod developed a serious bend. Since I had never seen a bluegill take off 30 yards of line, I figured a pike or big bass had eaten the fish I was playing.

It took 15 minutes to learn that my first guess was right. It was a pike of about 15 pounds (38 inches long). Though it had almost instantly bitten through the three-pound test tippet, its attack on the bluegill was so violent that it got the thick part of the leader wrapped around its head and gills.

After I got the pike untangled, I looked down its throat and saw the hapless bluegill, bloodied but alive. Reaching in gingerly with my pliers, I got the gill out, released the pike, removed my popper from the bluegill's mouth and let it go, too.

I was delighted with catching the pike and getting my popper back, and I suppose the fish were as happy as could be expected under the circumstances.

Let's give the new pike regulations a chance. If you don't think it's worth going fishing for two fish, maybe you need to think a bit about why you fish. If you think it's primarily about putting food on the table, I suggest you check out the seafood section in your local supermarket. You can buy a huge variety of fish for far less than it costs to go fishing, after you figure in the cost of tackle and trips.

Female pike reach sexual maturity at about four years old in the southern Lower Peninsula and as late as six in the colder lakes of the northern Lower and Upper Peninsula. Pike that have reached the legal minimum size of 24 inches are nearly all older than 10 — but most pike don't live 10 years.

Nearly every pike angler has watched videos of monster fish in the 36- to 48-inch range from northern Canadian waters like God's Lake in Manitoba, Great Bear Lake in the Northwest Territories and the Vermillion Lake system in Ontario.

All of those fish are at least 20 years old, and the biggest are probably older than 40. The American-record pike is a 46-pound, two-ounce fish caught in northern New York state in 1940. The International Game Fish Association recognizes as the world record a 55-pound, one-ounce pike caught in Germany in 1986. The Fresh Water Fishing Hall of Fame lists a 55-pound, 15-ounce fish caught in Czechoslovakia in 1969. But those giants are like pip-squeaks compared to several fish bigger than 70 pounds caught before official world records were begun, including a fairly reliable report of a 90-pound pike caught in Ireland in 1862. Of the nine pike listed as International Game Fish Association line-class world records, four came from Alaska and four from Sweden. An examination of these records shows that three things are needed to produce world-class pike — an abundant food supply, cold water and the opportunity to live for 20-plus years. Michigan has many places that offer the rich food source and cool conditions, but it's tough for a pike to survive more than 10 years in a place that sells more than a million fishing licenses every year.

Pike in the South often reach 28 to 30 inches and five to six pounds in six years, about twice as fast as northern pike. But few Southern pike live longer than six years and rarely reach trophy size. Smaller pike, fish less than 10 pounds, prefer water temperatures of 60 to 70 degrees. But giant pike are like trout or whitefish in seeking water 55 degrees or colder.

Most places that produce trophy pike are at latitudes ranging from the Upper Peninsula north. It is almost impossible to reach those pike lakes in Canada without the services of a fly-in lodge or bush pilot. And nearly all of them impose a strict no-kill, catch-and-release policy, though some allow fishermen to keep a barely legal fish to eat.

Pike are early spawners, laying eggs in shallow streams, shoreline marshes and weedy bays where the water is shallower than four feet deep. It's common for them to spawn in areas that are dry only a couple of weeks after the pike eggs hatch. Pike spawn as soon as the ice melts — some while the lake is still covered with ice if the water temperature reaches 40 degrees.

This early spawning is why few lakes hold large populations of both pike and muskies. Muskellunge spawn about a month after northerns, when the water is 10 to 20 degrees warmer, and the newly hatched muskie fry make perfect food for ravenous fingerling pike.

The easiest way to tell northern pike from muskies is the same method used to differentiate members of the char family (like brook trout and lake trout) from true trout (like browns and rainbows). Northern pike have light spots on a dark background. Muskies have dark spots or bars on a light background (just as chars have light marks on a dark background, and trout have dark spots on a light background).

But how do you tell a silver pike, which has unmarked, silvery sides and yellow fins, from a clear muskie, which has unmarked greenish sides and orangish fins? While silver pike are no longer considered a subspecies of northerns but a genetic mutation, it's still easy to differentiate them from muskellunge.

Muskies have scales only on the upper half of their cheeks and gill covers. Pike cheeks are fully scaled, although only the top of the gill covers have scales.

Redfin and grass pickerel are much smaller members of the pike family, averaging less than a foot long and one pound, and rarely exceeding five pounds. They inhabit some southern Michigan waters, but their splotched sides usually make them easy to identify. If all else fails, the angler can check if the cheeks and gill covers are fully scaled (a sure sign of a pickerel). The slightly larger chain pickerel has been introduced in Lake Erie but rarely exceeds two pounds.

If you still can't tell if the fish is a pike or muskie, roll it over and look at the madrepores, small openings that run along the bottom sides of the jaw. Pike have 10 or fewer madrepores (usually five on each side); muskies have 12 or more (usually six on each side).

Pike will feed on any fish up to about half of their own size, including other pike. One of the biggest northerns I ever caught, a 43-inch fish that weighed about 20 pounds, hit a 13-inch pike that had grabbed a six-inch black-and-white Rapala crank bait. The big pike hit the smaller one just behind the gills, and the rear treble hooks on the Rapala sank into the 20-pounder's jaw.

Pike longer than two feet seem to prefer bait fish in the six- to 12-inch range and eagerly eat yellow perch, small walleyes, whitefish, bass, suckers and other pike. Suckers are perhaps the best live bait for pike, and a 10-inch sucker suspended four feet under a big float has probably accounted for more large pike than any other method in Michigan.

Pike also eat frogs, crayfish, mud puppies and other small creatures, and they are willing to sample anything smaller than a beagle they spot swimming on the surface.

Ten years ago I was fishing on Houghton Lake early on a June morning when I saw a small wake moving toward a mother mallard and her mostly grown ducklings. It took a second to realize that the wake was produced by a large fish swimming just beneath the surface, an assumption confirmed a few seconds later when the water exploded under one of the ducklings.

I got a glimpse of a greenish body about three feet long, then all was still except for the rest of the quacking ducks, who paddled frantically across the water.

Nothing remained of the duck that was attacked but a few feathers floating on the surface. I'm convinced it had been eaten by a large pike, because there's not much else in Houghton Lake that looks like that predator and is big enough to eat a two-pound bird. (I've heard stories about muskellunge in Houghton Lake, but I've never met anyone who caught one there.)

Where and when to fish

The decision to drop the daily pike limit to two drew some of its strongest opposition from the people around Houghton Lake. It's such a good pike lake that many anglers from southern Michigan go there to target that species, especially during the winter. But I'm convinced that in the long run, the change will be good for Houghton Lake, because it also has enormous potential to become a trophy pike lake and produce a lot of 20-pounders.

Other top pike waters in Michigan include Fletcher Pond in Alpena and Montmorency counties, which consistently produces pike well above the state average. That's mainly because the power company that regulates a dam on the impoundment is required to maintain water levels that enhance pike spawning.

Lake Mitchell near Cadillac offers good pike fishing, as do Hardy Pond on the Muskegon River, Munuscong Bay on the St. Marys and Manistique Lake in the Upper Peninsula.

Pike feed actively through the winter, allowing ice anglers to take them with tip-ups, jigging spoons and spears. Pike also feed voraciously after spawning in early spring. Many northerns are caught in the hottest months of the summer, but that's probably because more anglers fish for them in July and August than at any other time.

Most pike specialists say the best time to catch the biggest northerns is the fall, when they, like many other predators, go on a feeding binge in preparation for winter. Big pike have had all summer to recover from the rigors of spawning and put on the weight they lost.

Michigan can grow big pike. Northerns must be at least 40 inches long for catch-and-release fish and 18 pounds for catch-and-keep, and the state record is 39 pounds. But an 18-pounder is still an exceptional fish, and the great majority of Michigan pike are less than 34 inches and seven pounds.

The statewide minimum for keeping northerns is 24 inches, at which point a pike weighs three to four pounds. (There is no minimum size in the Michigan-Wisconsin boundary waters.)

Some medieval authors credit pike with living 100 years and weighing more than 100 pounds. Though these writers greatly exaggerated the pike's longevity, they probably weren't that far off on its size. There are several fairly well-documented cases of pike in the 75- to 90-pound range taken in Europe in the 1700s and 1800s, although most were not caught by angling.

Northern pike grow fairly slowly in Michigan, taking four to five years to reach 12 inches. By contrast, pike in Tennessee and Alabama can reach 12 inches in one to two years. But Yankee pike live a lot longer than their Southern cohorts, and Michigan produces fair numbers of pike in the 15- to 20-pound range.

Techniques

A few years ago I inherited a tackle box belonging to my wife's grandfather, who spent his summer vacations trolling for pike in northern Ontario. Although he had a few large bucktails in the box, most of his pike tackle consisted of rigs designed to hook or clamp a large dead minnow.

Pike can be caught by trolling plugs and spoons, casting plugs, spoons and spinner baits, and still-fishing or trolling with live or dead bait. Northerns are voracious, and small pike often will attack lures half their size.

A good standard for pike lures is to choose models six inches or longer. Jointed lures with an enticing wriggle are still among the most popular plugs for pike.

While they often are referred to as water wolves, pike are more like the lions or tigers of fresh water — ambush-feeders that lurk in heavy cover and dart out at prey fish that make the mistake of passing within their four- to eight-foot striking range.

A good technique is to troll shallow-running lures or baits parallel to weed beds, especially along the outside edges in three to five feet of water in spring and six to 10 feet later in the summer. Another productive method is to let the boat drift or move under the trolling motor 30 to 40 feet off the weed beds while the angler casts a floating lure toward the weeds, allowing the bait to sit for a few seconds before starting an angled retrieve toward the boat.

My favorite time to catch pike is early spring, just after ice-out, when fish are hanging out in water so shallow you can often see them 50 feet away. Casting surface plugs or big, floating or shallow-running streamer flies along the edges of the weeds sometimes results in three or four wakes racing toward the fly at the same time.

Pike hit like a ton of bricks and fight powerfully for a few minutes, but they usually tire quickly (although they tend to fight longer than muskies). For trolling or plug-casting, a seven-foot bait-casting outfit rigged with 16- to 20-pound line will handle a northern of just about any size. Some anglers use wire leaders, but I've been using 20-pound mono for years and rarely lose a fish because of a cut-off, especially when fishing with plugs.

Some friends and I recently made a fly-in trip to the Boundary Waters Canoe Area Wilderness on the Minnesota-Ontario border, a wonderful network of lakes and rivers with numerous northern pike.

We were mostly fishing for walleyes and smallmouth bass, so we used reels loaded with four- to eight-pound monofilament. A lot of pike still struck our plugs and jigs, and only about 10 percent of those hits resulted in cut-offs, even with line that light. But a 10-percent cut-off rate can be expensive when you catch 100 pike a week on lures that cost $5 each.

In early spring, just after the ice melts, pike usually can be found in four to 10 feet of water in bays, regaining their strength and basking in the waters that warm the fastest.

My standard fly for this fishing is a five-inch-long red-and-white bucktail or Lefty's Deceiver (a saltwater pattern), which I tie to imitate a red-and-white Daredevle spoon, one of the oldest and most effective pike lures ever.

I used to fish these streamers on a 12-weight tarpon rod simply because they were so air-resistant that it was hard to cast them on anything lighter (and Sharp's Law holds that 90 percent of casts with big streamers must be made into the teeth of a 15-knot wind). But the development of new fly-tying materials has allowed for long streamer flies — lighter and less bulky than the old models — offering bigger and flashier silhouettes in the water.

Another good early-season tactic is to cast weedless lures into marshes in bays or any area where grasses poke above the surface, again in water four feet or less. Pike that have spawned recently often choose such places to recover, and they watch the surface in shallow water as carefully as they watch the openings in the weeds. A good outfit for this kind of fishing is a seven-foot spinning rod with 12- to 14-pound line. These rigs cast well and allow an angler to cover a lot of water.

Pike don't seem to be fussy about the condition of their food, and bait fishermen often catch them by letting a dead minnow lie on the bottom near a likely pike haunt. A better option for the bait fisherman is a large float, not a round plastic bobber, but one of the streamlined models developed in Europe. These will float a big bait as well as a round bobber, but their slick shape allows them to be pulled underwater without the pike's being aware of any resistance.

As the water warms in summer, pike leave the shallows for cooler pastures. This is especially true for fish bigger than about 15 pounds, which don't like water warmer than 55 degrees. But unlike bass and walleyes, which often go deeper than 20 feet, pike prefer to stay in the upper reaches and usually can be found in less than 20 feet of water near or in a weed bed.

In summer, fish the shallows around weed beds with artificials in the morning, before the water has a chance to warm up. I like to fish jigs in the early hours, when the fish are relatively lethargic, then switch to a spinner bait or crank bait as the water warms.

In the afternoon, with the shallows heating up and the sunlight making maximum penetration, I often switch to a heavier spoon or in-line spinner bait to fish the cooler, dimmer waters along drop-offs at the mouths of bays.

Later in the day is also a good time to try natural baits in deeper water. The angler still should stay near weed beds or other structure that offer ambush cover, such as a downed log or boulder. Big pike tend to prefer big baits, and some of the most successful pike anglers I know often use 10- to 13-inch suckers under a big float. What is really surprising is the number of times the angler hooks and lands a fish, only to discover that a two-foot pike had attacked a bait fish half its own length (which shouldn't be surprising, because the major predator on hammer-handle pike is bigger pike).

Fall is the time to fish grass flats up to 15 feet deep with big plugs that run about three feet deep. Many anglers are convinced that big baits are the secret to catching big pike, and they use lures designed for muskies after learning that even small pike won't hesitate to grab a foot-long chunk of muskie lumber.

Chapter 7

Sunfish

FOUR HUNDRED YEARS AGO, ENGLISH PLAYWRIGHT BEN Jonson said of the strawberry, "Doubtless God could have made a better berry, but doubtless God never did."

If we replace berry with bluegill, Ol' Ben would have left us a pretty fair description of the most available, amazingly tasty and, ounce for ounce, scrappy fish in Michigan or any other waters.

I always have thought that if bluegills grew to the same size as their bigger cousins, the black bass, no one would dare step into fresh water. A couple of years ago I was taking underwater pictures in a lake near Grayling when I felt something hitting my right ankle. I looked back and saw I had strayed too close to the nest of a six-inch male bluegill, who expressed his objections to my presence by biting the hairs on my leg.

When I swung around and got nose to nose with him, the little bugger didn't swim off, but flared his gills and attacked the diving mask of a creature hundreds of times his size.

I also might point out that if bluegills grew to the size of bass, we would need to use tarpon tackle to fish for them, because once a six-ounce bluegill manages to turn his slab body sideways, it feels as if the angler is trying to land a fish 10 times as big.

Bluegills originally lived in the eastern half of North America but have been transplanted to every state. They like clear, warm-water lakes and ponds that lack current, and they mostly are found hanging out in and around underwater weed beds.

Like other sunfish, they spawn for the first time when the water reaches 60 to 70 degrees — late May in southern Michigan to late June in the Upper Peninsula. And while bluegills sometimes can be seen guarding nests in water so shallow the fish's dorsal fin almost breaks the surface, those are usually the smallest and weakest fish in the population. The biggest bluegills typically spawn in deeper water a little farther from shore.

Bluegills often spawn a second time in the dog days of summer. In the South, some bluegills can be found on beds all year, although most spawn in March. Each male guards one nest, which usually is visited by several females who deposit eggs in it. Bluegills are such prolific breeders they often overpopulate smaller lakes, resulting in a mass of stunted fish that rarely exceed six inches.

A spawning male bluegill is one of the most resplendent sights in fishdom and a true challenger to the brook trout for the title of underwater dandy. The males develop thick, puffed-up chests of a coppery-orange that almost glow. Their backs grow darker — almost black in some — their sides show metallic shades of yellow and bronze, and the stripes that run from their backs to their bellies darken, too.

The tip of a bluegill's gill cover is black to navy blue, but it gets its name from the curved, powder-blue border that runs along the bottom of the head from the back of the mouth to the rear of the gill plate.

Though people often talk about places they can catch 12-inch bluegills, a fish that size is a giant that will weigh nearly one pound. The world-record bluegill, caught in Alabama more than 50 years ago, weighed four pounds, 12 ounces and looked like an Olympic weight-lifter on steroids. Most fish that go into the bucket in Michigan are about eight inches, and a stringer of 10-inchers is something to brag about.

Bluegills are mostly insect eaters, but they also prey on snails and the eggs and fry of other fish (including other bluegills). If you sit in a canoe that lies motionless over a shallow, weedy flat on a windless day, or wade into such a place and stand still for five minutes, you soon will see bluegills coming out of the weeds and going about their business.

Those that guard nests never stray far from them, but others will have small territories of a few square feet they patrol like a guard on his rounds, and they are constantly pecking at things growing on or clinging to the stalks of underwater plants.

Other sunfish species

There are 32 sunfish species in the United States. Excluding the two biggest, largemouth and smallmouth bass, which are discussed in another chapter, Michigan is home to seven other species.

ROCK BASS

They like clear, cold, rocky lakes and cool, slow streams with lots of vegetation and rocks for cover. Shaped much like the bigger bass and equipped with red eyes, rock bass can grow to a foot or so but more often are seven to 10 inches. (The world record is a three-pound fish from Ontario.)

They feed mostly on aquatic insects and crayfish, but they apparently will eat about anything. The biggest one I caught, an 11-incher in Ontario, hit a piece of plastic bag I put on a hook after running out of worms. Rock bass often hit a lure so hard that for a few seconds the angler thinks he has hooked a smallmouth, but they give up quickly.

WARMOUTH

This is the most heat-tolerant of the sunfish, seeking water warmer than 80 degrees and living happily in water temperatures warmer than 90. That's how they have adapted to shallow lakes and slow rivers with solar-collecting mud bottoms, and why they are largely absent from the Upper Peninsula.

Warmouths also are called stumpknocker because of their habit of rapping their noses against downed timber as they pick off snails and aquatic insects. A giant is 10 inches and a pound, but most never exceed six inches.

They fight well for their size and often can be picked out of heavy weeds by lowering the bait into an opening in the greenery.

GREEN SUNFISH

The smallest of the clan found in Michigan, most green sunfish caught here are in the four- to six-inch range. They prefer clear water but can tolerate a lot of silt.

They mate with most of the other sunfish species and form hybrids, so it's often hard for an angler to tell exactly what he has caught. But a good indication of a purebred is the distinct blue-green lateral line on the sides and a yellow-green margin behind the black spot on the gill cover.

This sunfish likes thick weeds and heavy cover, handling warm water about as well as the warmouth.

PUMPKINSEED

If you see a lot of small sunfish in the shallow, weedy waters along the edges of a lake, they're probably pumpkinseeds, another miniature fish that can reach 10 inches but rarely exceeds six.

Pumpkinseeds, named for their oval shape, are among the most brilliantly colored sunfish, with orange bellies the color of a midsummer sunrise. They are easily identified by the tiny red spot at the back end of the gill cover. They live as far north as Hudson Bay in Canada. They also are among the easiest fish for kids to catch, because they will eat just about anything they can get into their mouths.

REDEAR

This species averages a little larger than bluegills in size, with 10- to 12-inchers fairly common in bigger lakes. They like quiet water and weeds, and they can be maddeningly difficult to fool into taking bait.

Redears are called shellcrackers in the South because they eat so many snails, but they also will eat aquatic insects. They can be identified by the thin red margin that circles the entire rear portion of the gill cover. Excellent fighters, they rarely take artificial lures and are often caught by bait fishermen who were targeting bluegills. They are uncommon in the Upper Peninsula.

LONGEAR

The longear is another midget fish that likes slow, clear water with some weeds. It is probably misidentified most of the time because it can look much like a bluegill, especially in spawning colors, or a pumpkinseed, especially when it has a small red spot on the gill cover.

The giveaway on close examination is the dark gill cover, which has a light rear margin, is about twice as long as it is deep and points up slightly.

Longears average four to six inches and are decent fighters for their size. They are found mostly in the southern half of the Lower Peninsula.

BLACK AND WHITE CRAPPIES

These are closely related sunfish with deep, thin bodies, and they are prized more for their taste than their fighting qualities.

Black crappies, sometimes called calico bass for their darkly speckled sides, are more common in Michigan, where a 12-inch fish is big. They prefer clear, deep lakes with good weed growth. White crappies, which have blurred vertical lines on their sides, like slightly warmer and murkier water, and they tend to grow an inch or so larger.

While both species are voracious minnow eaters, they also feed on plankton, especially when algae blooms. That's why they often are found suspended at various depths and might reject minnows, spinners and small jigs they hit eagerly the day before.

Both species are schooling fish, so when anglers catch one, they continue to work the immediate area with the same baits and techniques hoping for more. Black crappies are more likely found deeper and near weed beds. White crappies often are suspended along the edges of drop-offs and around dense underwater structure, which is why many Southern anglers sink piles of cut brush into lakes.

Many anglers say the best technique for crappies is at night, using a bright lantern suspended above the water to attract bait fish. The crappies are drawn by the natural bait and lurk in the watery shadows just beyond the reach of the light.

TACKLE AND TECHNIQUES

I suspect most American adults have cherished pictures of themselves as four-year-olds, exhibiting a gap-toothed grin as they hold up the sunfish that was their first catch.

Sunfish are the perfect fish for kids because they are found everywhere, there are lots of them, they are easy to catch most of the time, and they can be caught from shore.

Even two- or three-year-olds can learn to catch sunfish with a cane pole, a piece of fishing line, a hook, a piece of worm and a bobber. The kids need only lay the bobber on the water, wait until they see it go under and then lift the fish out of the water and swing or drag it to shore.

Sunfish get their name from the brilliant gold and yellows that mark spawning males, but they could just as easily be named for their preference for daylight. While the biggest bluegills and redears are usually caught just after dawn and just before dusk, sunfish activity comes to an abrupt halt after sunset. That's because sunfish usually share the water with largemouth bass, which are active night feeders and have sunfish ranked high on their gustatorial hit parade.

For older anglers, a worm-and-bobber rig works just as well with a light spinning rod. I like to use two- to four-pound line, and I also like rods nine feet or longer because they let me reach out and lay the bait carefully into an opening in the aquatic vegetation that would be hard to reach by casting.

For the past couple of years I've also been fishing for bluegills with inch-long crank baits called Snap Beans from Yo-Zuri. I have an ultralight rod that will let me cast the tiny lures 40 to 50 feet, and the sunfish smack them like a five-pound bass taking a No. 9 Rapala. If the fish are deeper, I sometimes add a split shot or two ahead of the little lures to get them down four to five feet.

The best all-around bait for sunfish, especially bluegills, is a two-inch piece of juicy night crawler. Using a whole worm is a waste that offends my Scottish soul, and it's not as effective, because sunnies are masters at grabbing a free end of the bait and pulling it off the hook.

Sunfish can be fussy, so serious angling requires an assortment of natural and artificial baits that might need to be switched throughout the day.

For sunfish in deeper water, six feet or more, I've found that crickets and grasshoppers seem to work better than worms. The best way to tempt these fish is to hang the bait under a slip bobber and let the canoe or boat drift with the wind, because deep sunnies are usually suspended sunnies.

If you don't have an electronic fish finder to locate the fish, vary the depth of the bait from just above the bottom to mid-water to just under the surface on different drifts.

Sunfish have superb sight, at least at close range. Many is the time I've seen a nice bluegill or redear swim up to my bait, eye it for long seconds from an inch away, then swim off without tasting it. They also will take the bait in their mouths, decide it's not what they want and spit it out without the angler's knowing the fish was there.

I've also seen sunfish ignore the bait but peck hard at a split shot a foot up the line. The split shot is no bigger than the letter "o" on this page, but the fish apparently think the tiny black ball is a snail or egg. I suspect that's what happens on days when bobbers jiggle on the surface a lot but are rarely pulled under.

Sunfish also can be line shy. On many occasions I started fishing with 10-pound line because that was what was on the reel and I was too lazy to change it. I watched fish after fish swim up to the bait and turn away without even making a close inspection. Usually, I could start catching fish by switching reels or reel spools for two- to four-pound line.

I saw a perfect example of bluegill wariness a couple of summers ago when I was wade-fishing in a small, clear pond with a 10-foot lightweight rod, a streamlined float an inch long and worms for bait. The fish were extremely finicky, so the tiny float helped me cast to them without spooking them. In a couple of hours I caught and released maybe 60 bluegills. As I got out of the water, a man fishing with a couple of small children walked up and asked what bait I was using.

He and his sons also were using worms, but they hadn't caught a fish, even though they had had a few bites. When I looked at their tackle, the problem was obvious. They were fishing a gin-clear pond with 15-pound line, red-and-white plastic bobbers as big as an orange, and huge hooks better suited for pike. We took a few minutes to rig their rods with six-foot leaders of four-pound fluoro-carbon line, small floats and No. 10 hooks, and on their first casts all three hooked fish.

Sunfish are the perfect species to teach kids to fly-fish. They usually hit poppers, rubber spiders and bulky dry flies like Royal Wulffs and humpies. But don't overlook hatch-matchers like brown drakes, Hexagenias and stone flies in lakes where those insects hatch commonly, or ant and beetle patterns for days when those insects are shaken out of water-side trees by the wind.

When a sunny hits a dry fly or popper, it usually sucks it under (often with an audible "shlooop"), then turns sideways and heads down. Young anglers usually can hook them simply by raising the rod and tightening the line.

If the fish show no interest in dry flies, try a sinking fly like bead-head hair's ears, small woolly worms, stone-fly nymphs and even traditional wet flies like the Greenwell's glory and coachman. The best retrieve is usually done by fig-ure-eighting the line around the fingers, which keeps it fairly tight so the angler can feel the pull of a take.

I like to wade in lakes and ponds for sunfish. Many of the waters are clear, and the fish can be spooky, so I use the same long leaders I use for trout in low, clear water, 10 feet at a minimum and more often 12 to 14 feet, and light tippets in the two- to four-pound range (5X-6X.)

Just about any fly rod will work well for sunfish, but lighter line weights, three to five, are better suited to the small fish. And because they are often waist deep in water, many anglers prefer the added leverage advantage they get from a 10-foot rod.

My favorite sunfish fly rod is actually a short one, a six-foot, two-weight model from Temple Fork that sells for about $70. It is perfectly matched to the size of the fish and will cast a No. 10 grasshopper 40 to 50 feet, as long as it isn't straight upwind.

That's enough writing about bluegills. It's a sunny spring day outside my office window, and the big bluegills should have moved onto the sand flat in front of our boathouse. I'm grabbing that two-weight and taking a break.

FOOD VALUE

A plate of fried bluegills with a green salad and a glass of New Zealand sauvignon blanc is one of the few meals that will get me to defy my cardiolo-gist. Some people think perch is the tastiest fish in fresh water, but I will argue for bluegills every time. The meat is white and flaky, and don't forget to use a sharp knife to scoop out the bluegill cheeks.

Pumpkinseeds taste as good as bluegills, but you often spend an inordinate amount of time cleaning fish for a relatively small amount of meat.

At least the equal of the bluegill in quality and size, redears aren't seen on the table as much simply because they are less common and harder to catch. I wish more longears lived in the lakes around our home in Grayling, because they are superb eating, even if they do run small. But I do know a couple of lakes in the southern part of the state where I can catch a stringer-full two or three times a summer.

Another bluegill taste-clone, green sunfish, would be marvelous table fare if they grew about twice as big.

Crappies are so tasty that many people spend the whole summer fishing for them. I find the meat a little soft, but it hardens a bit if baked.

Warmouths are mediocre table fare, and they are so small that most people can't be bothered cleaning them.

Rock bass taste good, but a lot of the ones I catch have parasites in the flesh that, while harmless, aren't very appealing.

Chapter 8
═══

Muskies

A MYSTIQUE SURROUNDS THE MUSKELLUNGE BECAUSE IT looks dangerous. We humans fear and are fascinated by big, toothy predators, whether they're fish like muskies, fowl like eagles or overgrown cats like lions.

The truth is that muskies aren't dangerous — unless you're a bass, carp, perch or other fish less than 18 inches long (including other muskellunge), or unless you're handling one as you remove a lure from its mouth.

I've heard the stories about people who had toes bitten off as they dangled their feet from a dock, but I haven't documented a single instance when a muskellunge bit anyone who wasn't molesting it in some way.

Proof of their relative innocuousness is found in Lake St. Clair, which might have the world's biggest concentration of these overgrown pike. Estimates are that upward of 50,000 or more muskies live in the lake, many bigger than 20 pounds, which makes them as big or bigger than the average barracuda in tropical waters.

Lake St. Clair has no shortage of people, either, many of whom swim from boats anchored in ideal muskie habitat. But while you can document the rare barracuda attack on a human in salt water, I've never heard of anyone injured by a muskie in Lake St. Clair. And if you have, I wish you would tell me, because it would make a heck of a story.

Muskies have fascinated people for a long time. We know the Ojibwa peoples who lived in Michigan before whites arrived called them something like "mask-inonge," which probably meant "ugly fish" but could have been "big pike" or "deformed pike."

Before we proceed, let's try to settle the question of how large muskies grow. There are numerous accounts by early fur traders and settlers of muskies that were up to six feet long and went 80 to 100 pounds. One angler on the St. Lawrence River played and lost a muskie that left some huge scales on the hook, and a biologist estimated the fish weighed about 100 pounds. The annual rings on fish scales can be used to estimate size and age.

But the generally recognized world-record fish is 69 pounds, 11 ounces, caught by Louis Spray at the Chippewa Flowage in Wisconsin. No fish bigger than 70 pounds has been recorded since that one was caught in 1949, and fish bigger than 40 pounds are extremely rare. The official record books list only about a dozen fish bigger than 50 pounds that have been entered since Spray landed his monster.

If 80- to 100-pounders were out there, you would think someone would have caught at least one, especially in the past 20 years, when specialty anglers have been flying all over the place in attempts to set world records.

The Michigan record for a purebred muskie is a 49-pound, 12-ounce fish taken from Thornapple Lake in 2000 (though the state Department of Natural Resources' fishing guide still lists a 48-pounder). And while tiger muskies usually are smaller than purebreds, the Michigan and world-record tiger is a 51-pound, three-ounce fish caught in Lac Vieux Desert on the Wisconsin border in the western Upper Peninsula in 1919. It's one of the oldest records in the books.

A 20-pound muskellunge of any kind will earn you a master angler patch in Michigan.

Here's something else to consider: The biggest northern pike grow at the northern end of that species' range, which includes a lot of trophy pike lakes in northern Ontario, the Northwest Territories, Saskatchewan and Quebec. These areas never were affected by settlement and never were fished much until outfitters began flying people in 20 years ago.

But muskies like warmer water (Michigan is near the northern end of their range) and live in places where people settled and farmed. That means they have been far more accessible, and under far greater fishing pressure, both commercial and sport, for a couple of centuries.

My best guess is that some of the old reports were true and that a few 80- to 100-pound muskies were taken (probably by netters) from prime muskellunge waters like the St. Lawrence River, Lake Erie and Wisconsin's Chippewa Flowage.

But those would have been extremely old fish, probably older than 30. The chance that a muskie would live that long today, when most states and provinces have a minimum limit of about 36 inches, is slim, indeed.

The muskie's original range was limited to eastern and central North America, from about 35 degrees to 50 degrees north. (It probably evolved from the northern pike in warmer times.)

Pike and muskellunge are so closely related that they sometimes produce a hybrid called a tiger muskellunge. It also is produced by hatcheries for stocking. Pike and muskellunge parted ways recently in geological terms, but it was so long enough ago that they have many genetic differences, and the hybrid tiger is sterile.

Muskellunge normally spawn in May or June, when the water reaches about 50 degrees. They grow quickly, reaching 10 to 12 inches in their first year and the Michigan keeper limit of 42 inches in about 10 years. Muskies transplanted to southern states grow a bit faster than northern fish, but because they rarely live longer than 12 years, they rarely exceed 25 pounds. A Lake St. Clair trophy fish of 50 inches and 30 pounds is at least 15 years old, and a 35-pounder is probably about 20.

Lake St. Clair is unusual in having large populations of muskies and northern pike. Pike spawn about a month before muskies. When baby muskies hatch a week or two after they are spawned, they are the perfect-sized meal for juvenile pike, which are then three to four inches long.

But Lake St. Clair is so big that it offers niches for both species, so a lot of muskies are hatched where there aren't many pike. The major predator on 12- to 18-inch muskies is a bigger muskie. The population balance seems to be healthy, though, and Lake St. Clair anglers routinely catch and release four to six muskellunge in the three- to 10-pound range for every 20-pounder.

Adult muskies and pike usually don't compete for food. Big pike, larger than six or seven pounds, like water temperatures of 50 to 55 degrees and depths less than 10 feet. Big muskies, larger than 15 pounds, prefer water around 70 and deeper than eight feet. Muskies and pike usually occupy such different habitats that it is relatively rare for trolling muskie anglers on Lake St. Clair to hook a northern.

Fisheries biologists once listed three types of muskies: northern, Great Lakes and clear. But there was disagreement over whether they were true subspecies or merely local color variations. Subsequent transplants of fish around the country have so mixed up the gene pool that the question is now meaningless and all three variations can often be found in the same lake.

On a trolling trip with Mike Pittiglio, a charter captain who runs the boat Muskie Mania, we caught a 24-pounder and a 25-pounder on Lake St. Clair, and their coloration defined why biologists used to list three subspecies.

The 24-pounder was quite pale, its back shaded a lavender gray and the spots on its sides well-defined and irregular. The 25-pounder, caught a quarter-mile away, had an olive back, and the spots on its sides were oblong and arranged in vertical rows. We also caught one smaller fish that had clear sides, and another with wavy bars instead of spots (but it had the pointed tail fins of a true muskie, and not the rounded fins of a tiger).

Most anglers have heard the muskie described as "the fish of 1,000 casts" or even "the fish of 10,000 casts." That brings amused looks to Lake St. Clair trollers, who usually catch and release six to 10 fish a day and often double those numbers.

But power trolling works only in places where you have large numbers of fish and limited underwater vegetation. In many lakes, casting is still the only practical way to catch muskies, and it's such a low-percentage activity that most muskellunge caught by casting are probably caught by people who were trying to catch other species.

I saw a fascinating example of that during a Professional Walleye Trail event on Lake St. Clair. After I watched the fleet head out in the morning, I went muskie fishing with Mark Orlowski on his boat named Fishin' Pole. It was a great morning, and I landed and released what is still my personal-best muskellunge, a 51-inch fish that weighed 28 pounds. Most 50-inchers are 30 pounds or better, but this one's hollow flanks showed that it hadn't eaten for a while. Had I caught it a couple of days later, it might have had a five-pound bass in its belly.

When we got back to the dock, I returned to the tournament weigh-in site and interviewed the anglers as they came off the stage. Six of the walleye pros told me they had caught and released 48- to 52-inch muskies that bit on drifted crawler harnesses. And several other pros told me they had big muskies that broke off, mostly because the walleye anglers use line that tests 10 pounds or less.

What makes that experience so amazing is that most muskie lakes don't give up one 48-inch fish all year (a 48-incher is about 25 pounds). And yet Lake St. Clair will produce multiple fish that size and bigger in one day for people who aren't trying to catch them.

You will hear the same thing if you talk to the bass professionals who fish in tournaments on Lake St. Clair. They routinely hook up with big muskies that grab tube baits, crank baits and spinner baits, especially in mid-lake and along the Canadian shore.

If they hook a small muskie, less than 15 pounds, the bass pros tend to break it off quickly. Time is money for these guys, and the next cast could produce a fish that makes the difference between going home empty-handed and cashing a $50,000 check. But when they hook a big muskie, 20 pounds or better, most of the pros say they can't help playing and landing it just for the novelty of catching a fish that big on light tackle.

Lake St. Clair gets the bulk of the muskie hype for two reasons. The first is that it has a heck of a lot of muskies and big ones, which no one can deny. But the second is that it is only a few minutes' drive from Detroit and within a few hours of the great majority of the state's anglers.

Many other places on the Great Lakes and some inland lakes also have excellent muskie populations and don't get much pressure. I suspect the reason muskellunge aren't caught on many more Michigan waters is that we don't fish for them. Go to any inland lake and count the number of people you see trolling an array of 10-inch plugs or casting eight-inch bucktail spinner baits. It's doubtful you'll have to use more than the fingers on one hand all season.

One overlooked muskellunge fishery is the St. Marys River in the Upper Peninsula, especially around Raber Bay. A motel owner there has told me about a Wisconsin muskie specialist who shows up every summer with a 20-foot boat rigged for trolling.

This man spends two weeks catching and releasing big muskies every day, then disappears for 50 weeks. He doesn't bring a fishing buddy, and he never mentions what he is doing. The motel owner found out one day when he was fishing for walleyes about a half-mile away, saw his guest's boat and looked through binoculars to see the Wisconsin fisherman slide a four-foot muskie back into the water.

Lake Skegemog near Kalkaska has Great Lakes and tiger muskies, and Thornapple Lake, which produced the state and world-record tiger, is still a good place to hunt big fish, both the tiger and purebred varieties.

Tiger muskies have been introduced in many waters. I was fly-fishing for bass at Lake Ovid in Sleepy Hollow State Park a few years ago when a fish inhaled the popper. I thought it must be a state-record largemouth bass. When the fish jumped 20 feet from me, I thought it was a big northern pike, and it wasn't until I got it in my hand that I saw it was a 30-inch tiger muskellunge.

This is probably a good place to talk about the muskellunge's fighting ability. Many fishing books talk about the power of the muskellunge and the way it often leaps like a salmon. I'll agree that a muskellunge is one of the strongest fish in fresh water — for a relatively brief period. In fact, I would argue that you can make the same comparison between the fighting abilities of muskellunge and northern pike that you can between largemouth and smallmouth bass.

Like the largemouth, the muskellunge's most intriguing quality is its size. Grass pickerel look like midget muskellunge, right down to the bars on their sides, and they fight hard for their size. But you don't hear people brag about or mount the 14-inch grass pickerel they caught, although that would be a monster for the species.

The biggest muskie I've seen was in the St. Lawrence River in upstate New York. I was snorkeling along the edge of a weed bed where it fell off into deep water, and saw a big shadow move into the weeds at the edge of vision as I approached.

I used a spearfishing technique, and instead of approaching the spot head on, I backed off and circled around behind. Moving in slowly, I parted the weeds and saw the fish ahead of me, staring balefully to the open water of the river. It was big, and allowing for the effects of underwater vision (which tends to magnify things), I would guess it went at least 40 pounds.

I lay still and watched it, but after about 30 seconds I must have done something to alert the fish, because it turned sideways, looked at me briefly, then slid slowly into deep water. When I told the owner of the motel where I was staying about that fish, he told me several anglers had hooked it, and some had even got it close enough to see it, but it had always gotten off.

Like largemouth bass, muskellunge tend to fight hard for a few minutes, then quit and sulk. By contrast, smallmouth bass and northern pike tend to fight all the way to the boat. The muskie probably has the same physiological problem as the largemouth, with lactic acid building up in its muscles so quickly that it simply can't fight long.

I've caught muskellunge on casting spoons, spinner baits and buzz baits in Canada. The biggest I've caught with that technique, a 21-pound fish, came from Rice Lake east of Toronto and followed the lure to the boat three times before it struck, something muskies do with infuriating regularity. I finally got it to hit by swirling the big bucktail buzz bait back and forth in front of its nose in a figure-eight pattern with the rod tip a foot underwater.

I made three complete revolutions, with the muskie hanging motionless in the water about two feet away before it darted forward and nearly pulled my arm out of its socket on the strike.

I have fished Lake St. Clair several times for muskies using casting techniques and have never done better than getting a fish to follow. Some muskie specialists there swear by large brass spoons with red-jeweled eyes, but most also tell me that a good day is catching one fish, and two is a bonanza.

That's why most of my Lake St. Clair muskellunge fishing has been done by trolling, using 10- to 12-inch plugs like Believers, Wileys, Lokis and Swim Whizzes in perch, frog, carp, pike and smallmouth bass colors that mimic the muskie's prey.

Trolling for muskies requires a lot of specialized tackle, so it's primarily the province of a relative handful of muskie nuts. Many have 200 or more giant lures that cost $10 to $25 each. In addition, the muskie catch rate increases in direct ratio to the number of lures in the water. So if you're fishing the Canadian side of Lake St. Clair, where you are limited to one rod per angler, you will be considerably more successful in a boat that can hold six anglers than one that can hold two.

Trolling works well on Lake St. Clair because of the enormous population of muskies. This is a species usually described as moody, sulky and reclusive, which should make an angler think in terms of quality rather than quantity.

I imagine the muskie is considered the fish of 1,000 or 10,000 casts because most are just not hungry enough to eat, or the angler's lure doesn't look enough like what they've been eating to trigger a feeding response.

So if you're casting a spoon on an inland lake with a population of 500 muskies, and you put the lure in front of 50 a day (even if you can't see them), your odds aren't very good. But if you're trolling in a place that has 50,000 muskies, and you can put six to 12 lures in front of a few thousand by trolling for five hours at three to four miles per hour, your success ratio will increase dramatically.

A recent trip with Pittiglio aboard the 31-foot Muskie Mania was an object lesson in why big boats work best for Lake St. Clair muskies, and how to fish them.

There have been some interesting changes in recent years. In the 1950s, the late Homer LeBlanc, Lake St. Clair's legendary muskellunge guide and one of its most fascinating characters, devised the power-trolling system that revolutionized muskie fishing not just on that lake but anywhere it can be done.

LeBlanc developed a technique of trolling lures at different depths close to the boat, often with the rod tips in the water. The greatest distance he would troll behind the boat was usually about 40 feet, and he preferred half that distance. He almost always set one lure in the propeller wash five to 10 feet behind the boat.

But that was before the introduction of planer boards, which gave anglers a method of getting trolling lures 100 feet out from the sides of the boat, where fish were less likely to be upset by the boat's passage. The planer board system also had the advantage of bringing the lures along just in time to intercept fish that were moving out to the side to get away from the commotion of the approaching craft.

Today, anglers like Pittiglio use a combination of the LeBlanc method and planer boards. They fish several lures close to the hull (with one- to two-pound weights clipped to the lines to get the lures down to various depths), and several more well out to the sides on planer boards.

"I think a lot of time muskies hit the lure because they want to kill it, not because they're hungry," Pittiglio said. "It's like they're saying, 'Who do you think you are?' It doesn't hurt to tick them off."

It also doesn't hurt to have a nice wind chop to break up the light coming through the surface and make it tougher for the muskie to distinguish the bait from a real fish, Pittiglio said.

On this day we were on a busman's holiday. Even when he doesn't have a charter, Pittiglio is such a muskellunge fanatic that he still goes fishing, usually with the pals who often mate for him. They include his younger brother Adam; Bryan Bombalski and Tony Radaj, friends he has known since Sterling Heights High School, and fishing buddy Mike Zainea.

Pittiglio believes strongly in the value of solunar tables, which use moon phases and time of year to predict the best fishing times each day and the best days each month. On this day we had an hour-long minor period starting at

2:30 p.m. and a major period (theoretically the best fishing) starting at 9:05.

"I really see the effects of those minor and major periods," he said. "We went 10-for-12 (fish) yesterday, but we didn't get them until late, during a minor period."

Pittiglio hopped out of his seat and rang a small ship's bell mounted in the cockpit.

"I almost forgot to ring the dinner bell and tell them the minor period has started," he said.

Ten minutes later, a reel sang out and Adam Pittiglio landed a beautifully marked 24-pounder.

"He knows he better not lose it," Mike Pittiglio said as the pungent odor of muskellunge slime filled the cockpit. "When we're fishing for fun, if you lose a fish, you have to go into the penalty box and sit in the cabin until it's your turn to play a fish again."

Minutes later, another fish struck. I was up and played it for a few minutes, and I could see when it surfaced a couple of times that it was bigger than the 24-pounder we just landed. But when the fish was 30 feet behind the boat, I had to stop reeling while we cleared the line, and the muskie kicked off. I managed to talk my way out of the penalty box by pointing out that if I were stuck down there, I couldn't take pictures or notes.

Fishing muskies on Lake St. Clair will spoil you. Most muskellunge lakes don't give up one 30-pounder a year, but on Lake St. Clair it's typical for a half-dozen or more to be entered in a weekend tournament. Pittiglio's biggest fish on Muskie Mania went 36 pounds, one ounce, and one day in 2001, "we released a 31-pounder and had a 33-pounder hit 30 seconds later," he said. "We're crying if we don't get 10 fish a day."

Lake St. Clair is also unusual in that it's the only place I've heard people complain about too many muskies.

"There are a ton out here, but the problem is that there's a whole bunch of little ones that grab the lure before a big one can get to it," Pittiglio said. "That's why in July and August, when the water warms up, I like to fish mid-lake.

"You don't get as many out there, but they're nearly all big, 45 inches or more. I caught 16 muskies over 30 pounds last season, and I bet 12 of them came from mid-lake."

In the past 10 years, exotic zebra mussels from Eurasia have made a dramatic difference in the water clarity in Lake St. Clair. In 1990, about four feet was the average depth at which you could see a white plastic Secchi disk (used to test water clarity). Today, it's more than 10 feet. While that has decreased the population of walleyes, which prefer murkier water, it has been a boon for sight-feeders like muskellunge and smallmouth bass. Their populations probably are at record levels. It's not unusual for an angler to catch 50 or more smallmouths a day.

The increased clarity can make fishing tougher on calm days. But Pittiglio said the best thing that has happened is that "the fish are getting bigger. Ten, 12 years ago, a 30-pounder was something. Then they raised the minimum size to 42 inches, and 30-pounders became pretty common. I'd like to see the limit moved to 46 to 50 inches. You'd see 40-pounders then. Raising the limit wouldn't make much difference to muskie fishermen, because they hardly ever kill a fish."

Reports from the Michigan-Ontario Muskie Club, which has been keeping records and running tournaments on Lake St. Clair since 1946, support that argument. The record book shows that in 1960-87, no more than three 30-pounders were entered in any one year. Only four years had three fish that size, 13 years had one, five years had two, and seven years had no 30-pounders entered.

But in 1992-2000, after the 42-inch limit had time to take effect, the number of 30-pound-and-larger muskies landed each year increased to 13, 13, 20, 12, 15, 11, 13, 28 and 20.

The club records don't include every big muskellunge caught on Lake St. Clair, but they do track trends, and for the past decade the average size of the fish caught has definitely increased.

There are so many big muskies in Lake St. Clair today that the annual fluctuations might be more reflective of weather conditions and fishing effort than the number of fish available.

"The best time to catch big muskies is October, November and December," Pittiglio said. "That's when they're feeding like crazy, fattening up for the winter. Some years, you can get out during those months. Other years, the weather is just so bad nobody is fishing."

At 26, Pittiglio is one of the youngest charter captains on the Great Lakes. He quit a job as a tool designer and went into debt to buy a 31-foot Sea Ray with a 12-foot beam and twin 454 big-block engines.

"Muskies are all I fish for," he said. "I used to mate for Steve Jones (one of St. Clair's legendary muskie captains), and he taught me a lot.

"I don't know how true it is, but a lot of guys think the sound of the big-block 454s attracts muskies when you're trolling. Some of the guys with smaller engines put on mufflers that are tuned to sound like a big block."

That belief in the right sound is shared by skippers around the world, who tune their exhausts to produce a sound they think will draw fish, whether it be muskies or marlin.

Though the most effective technique for catching muskies on Lake St. Clair is trolling, it involves a lot more than simply motoring along for hours and washing the paint off big plugs. Pittiglio and his crew change lures constantly, sometimes looking to see if a different color will draw fish, sometimes making changes because light levels have changed. Pittiglio said duller colors work best on cloudy days and at dawn and dusk.

"First, you have to find the fish," he said. "Then you have to find how deep they are. Then you have to see if there's a color they like better than others. When it comes to muskies, the harder you work, the more you catch."

As each fish is caught, or even hits a bait and gets off, three crew members keep track of the color and swimming motion.

"Today we're getting the most hits on solid-body lures with yellow bellies," Pittiglio said. "Yesterday, we got all of our fish on jointed lures with white bellies. What I can never get over is how it changes from day to day. You can come out here one day and get a dozen fish on a perch Loki. Then you can come out the next day, at the same time, in exactly the same conditions, and nothing will hit that lure. The minute you think you've figured them out, they make you look stupid."

Despite their size and predatory nature, muskies can be tentative about striking a bait. At 7 p.m., the drag on a starboard side rod screeched for a half-second, then went quiet. At 7:11, another starboard rod did the same.

At 7:15, a port-side rod went "click . . . click, click . . . click . . . click, click," and Bombalski picked it up. "It feels like a small muskie," he said, but after a few seconds it kicked off. Bombalski reeled in the lure to check it, and tooth marks on the fresh paint proved he was right.

"Three rips and three zips," he said. "It just baffles me how a muskie can hit a lure with three big treble hooks on it and not get hooked. If I just handle a lure, I get the hooks in my fingers."

Pittiglio said: "I just realized I forgot to pay the fish. These are Canadian fish, but I've got some Canadian quarters." He pitched coins into the wake. Thirty seconds later, a reel screamed, Bombalski grabbed it and landed a seven-pound muskie, and we all threw every coin in our pockets into the water.

At 8:30 p.m., we got another rip-and-zip on a starboard-side rod, but Pittiglio wasn't concerned: "We still have a little while to go. The major solunar period doesn't start until 9:05."

After 35 minutes, Radaj said, "OK, the major period started. Where are the fish?"

Pittiglio said: "How do you know if the muskie's watch is set the same as yours?" He barely got the words out of his mouth before a port-side rod started bucking and screaming as a big fish made a serious attack.

Pittiglio yelled: "WHADIDITELLYA!" as I grabbed the rod and felt a heavy weight and some powerful head shakes. The fish made a couple of runs, but as I said earlier, muskies fight hard, they don't fight long. We soon had it in the boat, where we weighed it at 25 pounds and put it back over the side.

The day ended with five muskies caught and released and seven more missed. Three were four to seven pounds and the others 24 and 25, beautiful fish that in other parts of the country would be the catch of a lifetime. We also caught a 14-inch smallmouth bass that must have had sex on its mind, because it wasn't much bigger than the jointed plug it attacked.

"I just love muskie fishing," Pittiglio said as he steered Muskie Mania home across the night-shrouded lake. "I wish I could do it every day."

Asked what he planned to do in the winter, he didn't hesitate before answering: "Get depressed."

Chapter 9

Sturgeon

A COUPLE OF YEARS AGO, A LAKE STURGEON WEIGHING 320 POUNDS washed ashore dead at Buffalo, N.Y., on the eastern end of Lake Erie. It was the biggest of its species ever recorded, or at least verified by a certified scale.

And it raised again the controversial question of just how big these prehistoric fish can get and how long they can live.

A 208-pound sturgeon netted in 1952 in Lake of the Woods, Ontario, was aged at 152 years by using a microscope to count the rings in its scales, which are laid down annually like growth rings in a tree trunk.

Fish continue growing until they die, and biologists realized that if the scalering count were correct, 300-pound-plus fish reported from the 18th and 19th centuries had to be more than 200 years old.

For a while, the scientific pendulum swung against the long-lived theory, with some biologists arguing that the scale-ring count must not work for sturgeon the way it does for other species. But it has swung to the other side now, and many biologists today think sturgeon can live to incredibly old ages if we give them the opportunity.

It won't happen in my lifetime, but I like to think my six-year-old granddaughter Alexis, my fishing buddy since she was three, will someday fish in Michigan with a realistic expectation of landing a trophy that weighs more than 200 pounds.

That can happen if the Great Lakes sturgeon recovery program bears fruit, but it's a tenuous proposition from biological and political standpoints.

The fisheries biologists who document the success of the program sometime around 2050 would be the grandchildren of those who started the sturgeon research in the 1990s. Based on the uneven history of the state's environmental movements, and our wildlife bureaucrats' crisis-oriented approach to management, many people doubt that any research program could last that long.

There are many historical reports about sturgeon taken from the Great Lakes that weighed 300 to 400 pounds, but most of those weights were estimates and should be taken with a grain of salt. To gauge the relative value of estimating fish weight, watch one of the Saturday morning fishing shows in which the host holds up a three-pound bass and says, "This is a nice five-pounder, maybe six."

But that 320-pound sturgeon found near Buffalo adds validity to reports of a 310-pounder caught and weighed by commercial fishermen in Lake Superior in 1922, numerous 200- to 300-pound fish weighed by commercial and sports fishermen in the Great Lakes in the 20th Century, and a 193-pounder caught in Mullet Lake in 1974 that was weighed publicly.

Sturgeon have been around about 250-million years, and with the related paddlefish, have the most ancient lineage among freshwater fishes. They are listed among the modern bony fishes, like bass and trout, but their skeletons are mostly made of cartilage, like sharks and rays. When we look at a sturgeon, we're probably looking at something that is very much like the first fish to develop hard skeletal parts.

But man has not been kind to them, and of the roughly 25 worldwide species, only the lake sturgeon and white sturgeon of the American West are not considered endangered.

Sturgeon look prehistoric, with a shark-like shape, long, flat noses and bodies covered with armored plates. When the fish are young, the armor sports a ridge of sharp spikes along the back, but the spikes smooth out when the fish reach about 50 pounds, at which point they're no longer in much danger of being attacked and eaten.

Colossal as they seem to freshwater anglers, lake sturgeon are nowhere near the biggest members of the family. That honor goes to the beluga sturgeon of Europe and Asia, which can top 3,000 pounds. The white sturgeon of North America can flirt with the one-ton mark.

The smallest member of the family is the European sterlet, which tops out at about 20 pounds and was almost exterminated to obtain the golden caviar that was a favorite of Russian czars and the socialist autocrats who succeeded them.

Beluga sturgeon were almost fished out of existence for their eggs, which produce the famed beluga caviar that sells for more than $100 an ounce. But the beluga, the lake sturgeon and every other member of the family have been hurt far worse by dams and pollution, which drastically reduced the available spawning areas.

No one has completed an extensive study of the sturgeon population in Michigan, although one is under way. But the educated guess by biologists studying the species is that when white settlers arrived, Lake Michigan had a population of 11-million sturgeon, and that figure is about 11,000 today.

Sturgeon apparently move up big rivers like the Detroit, St. Clair and Manistee in late winter and early spring, then spawn on gravel bars and other places where structure breaks up a flow of fast water.

Sturgeon once spawned by the millions in a rapids in the Detroit River that has long since been dredged away. The fish were so thick that people said they could almost walk across the river on their backs. People speared and shot the spawning sturgeon, stacked their oily carcasses on the bank like cordwood and used them to fire the boilers of lake steamers.

Lake sturgeon are vulnerable to overfishing because of their reproductive strategy. Fish like walleyes spawn their fourth year and school by the tens of thousands every year, but sturgeon usually don't reach sexual maturity until about age 15 and 42 inches for males, and 25 years and 56 inches for females.

And while a female sturgeon can produce hundreds of thousands of eggs (about 5,000 for each pound of body weight), she spawns only every four to nine years, and males every two to six. In any given season, only 10 to 20 percent of the fish make a spawning run. Until recently, no one realized that under the old size limits, with fish legal at 36 inches, most sturgeon caught by anglers were taken out of the population before they had a chance to breed once.

Sturgeon were hated at first by commercial fishermen. The big fish destroyed nets they blundered into, and many commercial fishermen and anglers carried pistols in their boats to shoot any sturgeon they caught.

But by the late 18th Century, commercial fishermen realized there was a market for the caviar roe and the delicious meat. (Some think it tastes like veal.) In addition to meat and caviar, sturgeon were in demand for isinglass, a clear, gelatinous material found in their huge swim bladders that was used to clarify jellies and beer.

After the commercial market developed, sturgeon were targeted mercilessly until they were nearly wiped out. In 1885, the U.S. Fish Commission tallied 8.6-million pounds of sturgeon from the Great Lakes, 5.2 million from Lake Erie alone. Thirty-five years later, that figure was down to 25,000 pounds. Lake Michigan's sturgeon production went from a peak of 3.8-million pounds in 1889 to 2,000 pounds in 1929, a reduction of 99.5 percent.

Bob Haas, who heads the state Department of Natural Resources research laboratory on Lake St. Clair, estimates the lake holds about 30,000 to 50,000 of the ancient fish.

The average sturgeon that biologists catch in their trawls or long lines in Lake St. Clair is about four feet long and 50 pounds, with the odd six-footer that weighs about 100.

"We get bigger ones on the line occasionally, but they get away," Haas said. "Our gear isn't made to catch them."

Biologists have had 150- to 200-pound fish up to the side of the research boat in their nets but had to release them, he said.

In Lake St. Clair and the St. Clair River, anglers are allowed to keep one sturgeon from 42 to 50 inches per season. Otsego Lake near Gaylord is open for sturgeon fishing all year, with the same bag limit, a 42-inch minimum and no maximum size. Anglers aren't allowed to keep sturgeon in other Michigan waters except for Black Lake in Cheboygan County, where a limited spearing season is permitted.

Most sturgeon caught today are taken accidentally while anglers fish for other species, and the catch surprises the angler as much as the fish. But anglers can target the fish with fairly high expectations in places on the St. Clair River and Lake St. Clair.

Most sturgeon fishing is done at night, and it's not unusual for an angler who knows what he's doing to catch and release four to eight per trip. A few might weigh up to 100 pounds, although 10 to 30 is more common. In most of the state, sturgeon fishing is limited to catch-and-release, and in the few places where there's a season, the bag limit is one per year.

A couple of years ago I joined some biologists who were catching and tagging sturgeon in the Detroit River. On earlier trips I had seen 50- to 100-pound fish caught, equipped with a radio transmitter and a micro-tag, then released. But on this trip I was surprised to see the fish that got the biologists most excited was a tiny fish less than a foot long.

"That's the most valuable sturgeon we've ever seen," said Nathan Caswell, one of the biologists. He explained that not only is it rare to catch a sturgeon that small, it would remain in the study longer than older fish and perhaps provide valuable data about what pre-pubescent sturgeon do in the years before they mature.

Fighting a big sturgeon is a lot like fighting a shark of the same size. I once hooked a 62-pound lake sturgeon that gobbled a carp bait on a bottom rig in the Detroit River.

The Detroit River reminds me of the St. Lawrence, one of the best carp grounds in the country in terms of big fish. I was convinced that if I groundbaited a section of the Detroit River for a couple of days I could attract and catch a trophy carp.

Because I was hoping to catch a fish of 30 pounds of more, I was using a medium-heavy spinning outfit with 14-pound line and a 14-pound fluorocarbon leader. The rod was laid across an English electronic bite alarm that gives an audible signal of a take.

The bite alarm sounded while I was standing about 50 feet away talking to another angler (one of the beauties of using an alarm for bottom fishing), and when I reached the rod, line was spooling off at a right smart clip. The reel was made for this kind of fishing and had two drags. I had set the rear drag so I could put the rod and reel down with the bail closed, but the fish still could take line easily. I lifted the rod, turned the handle and engaged the front drag, which was set for the pressure I wanted to play the fish.

I had the drag set fairly tight, about the same pressure I would use for a 20-pound carp, but it hardly slowed down the speed at which I was losing line. I slowly turned the drag tighter, and the fish still moved away steadily.

It wasn't a real run, at least not in salmon or steelhead terms. It was more of a walk, but that didn't prevent the fish from stripping more than 100 yards of monofilament off the reel before it stopped.

As I played the fish for 15 to 20 minutes, I thought I was tied into Moby Carp. I was entertaining Walter Mitty dreams of sending its picture to my English friends for their edification and envy when I got my first look at it deep in the water. I didn't know what it was, but it sure as heck wasn't a carp.

This fish didn't jump. But I have seen huge sturgeon on the Columbia River system in Washington, fish that probably were 10 feet long and weighed more than 400 pounds, clear the surface by the height of a man.

When I finally saw the fish was a sturgeon, I wanted to land it and get some measurements. We brought it alongside the boat, and it lay docilely while we took its length and girth with a tape measure. It made no effort to escape and seemed unconcerned about being handled.

A few years later, I saw the same docility exhibited by a 95-pound sturgeon a couple of research scientists netted in the lower Manistee River. They tied a rope around its body just ahead of the tail and tied it to a dock while they prepared to surgically implant a transmitter.

The fish swam about quietly on its leash in a couple of feet of water, and when it came time for the operation, my wife, Susan, took the rope in her hand and led the fish to the waiting scientists as easily as she would have led a puppy.

The way most people fish for sturgeon is with cut bait or a ball of night crawlers, which the fish senses with the barbells (whiskers) under its nose and picks up with a tube-shaped mouth it can project downward several inches.

Scientists who caught sturgeon in the St. Clair River on trotlines (sunken lines about 200 feet long with a hook every 10 feet) deliberately put different baits on the hooks and kept track of the results to see if the sturgeon showed any preference. The fish preferred round gobies about three-to-one over other baits.

I've heard a number of anglers complain about the strict new limits on sturgeon and say they'll no longer fish for them. But I'm all for the limits and think the state should go even further and eliminate catch-and-keep sturgeon fishing.

If you cut back to a single fish a year, why do you need to keep any? As I said earlier, I won't see the day when 200-pound sturgeon are no longer rare in our lakes, but if giving up killing sturgeon now means 200-pounders for future generations, that's not a hardship for me, but a privilege.

Chapter 10

Catfish

I HAVE FIRSTHAND EVIDENCE THAT HUGE CATFISH LIVE IN Michigan. A big flathead once tried to eat me.

I was diving with a friend, Dick Burke, in Lake Erie, looking for a shipwreck site in about 40 feet of water. This was a few years ago when the algae blooms were often so thick you couldn't see your hand in front of your diving mask, but on this day the bloom was down and we could see a good 10 feet.

Burke was using a handheld metal detector and had picked up a reading that indicated a substantial hunk of metal lay under the sand. I knelt on the bottom and started to push a long, steel probe into the sand to try to locate the thing when my left leg jerked violently and I was spun around onto my back.

I looked down the length of my body and was stunned to see that a huge catfish had most of my left flipper in its mouth and was shaking me like a dog shaking a rag. When it was biting my flipper, the thing looked to be about eight feet long, and the head seemed about the size of a nail keg. But looking back later, after I had stopped shaking, I would say it was realistically four to five feet.

I thrust out with the steel rod I was using to probe the sand and gave the fish a couple of hard raps across the noggin. At the second bang, it let go and flashed off into the gloom.

Burke saw it before it let go, and when I looked at him after it swam off, his eyes looked like saucers behind his face plate. I was breathing so hard I was exhaling clouds of bubbles the size of a compact car, and once I made sure my foot was still there, we ascended slowly and climbed into the boat.

I can't honestly say I saw it well enough to be absolutely sure of the species.

The whole incident, from the time it grabbed me until its tail disappeared, lasted less than 10 seconds, and as you might imagine, I kicked up a pretty good cloud of silt in the scuffle.

But based on the size, shape and color, I think it was a big flathead, probably about 60 pounds. There are no blue catfish in the Great Lakes system, it was too big for a channel cat (the color was a greenish-brown), and I don't remember whether the tail was forked.

The catfish probably was going about its business of vacuuming any unfortunate prey it could find near the bottom when it saw this black thing that wiggled and looked edible. The fish must have been as surprised as I was when it latched on to something even bigger than itself.

Michigan is home to five species of catfish (or five of interest to anglers). They are the flathead, which is the biggest; the channel catfish; and three bullhead species — black, brown and yellow.

Channel cats and flatheads are among America's biggest freshwater fish. The world records stand at 58 pounds for the channel catfish and 123 pounds for the flathead. (The state records are 40 pounds for the channel cat and 47 pounds, eight ounces for the flathead.)

But the flathead is not even close to being the world's biggest catfish. The Eurasian wels can exceed 600 pounds (the rod-and-reel record is 212 pounds, 12 ounces), and several South American, Asian and African catfish exceed 300 pounds.

All catfish have sharp, strong, barbed spines in their dorsal and pectoral fins. If you have the misfortune to get stabbed by one, it hurts. (You are listening to the voice of experience.) And the cut often becomes infected because catfish slime gets driven into the wound, along with any other bacteria or contaminants that were on your skin.

In addition, small catfish, called madtoms, which are too small to be of interest to anglers, have a fairly potent venom in their spines. It produces a level of pain similar to a hornet sting. (Again, you are listening to the voice of experience.)

Even a dead catfish can be hazardous. I once stepped barefoot on a bullhead skeleton that some idiot had thrown onto a lawn after cleaning the fish. The spine penetrated deep into the bottom of my foot, and the next day the foot was swollen to twice its normal size. It returned to normal the next day, but I was hobbling for most of a week.

Channel catfish and flatheads are amazingly strong. I usually fish for them with a specialized carp-and-catfish rod I bought at Cabela's, an 11-footer called the Predator. Not only will it cast two ounces of lure and sinker more than 100 yards (I fish for catfish mostly from shore), it has enough backbone that I can crank down the drag on a big Penn spinning reel and beat the fish fairly quickly on 12- or 14-pound line.

Flatheads are found only in the southernmost parts of the state. They prefer water in the 75- to 80-degree range, and there are reports of flatheads that reached 20 pounds in 10 years (they probably lived more than 20 years).

The biggest flathead ever recorded was a 139-pound fish netted by a commercial fisherman. That's probably near the maximum size for the species, although 90- to 100-pounders are hooked or netted fairly often.

Flatheads like big, slow rivers and big lakes and reservoirs. They also like sunken timber and driftwood, where they often will spend the day hanging out and not doing much of anything before hunting at night.

Some catfish are notorious for eating stink baits, god-awful mixtures of rotting fish, chicken, meat scraps and flour that are stuck in a big ball around a hook.

But flatheads don't show the same taste for dead baits and scraps as channel cats and bullheads (and blues in the South), preferring live fish or fresh cut baits. I don't have much experience with flatheads, but those I have caught were taken on a live six-inch sucker or three or four recently deceased minnows on the same hook.

I've caught a couple of flatheads using floats, but I've had more success with the bottom-fishing system the English call a running ledger. The fishing line is passed through the hole in an egg sinker big enough to take the bait to the bottom (usually one to two ounces, depending on the speed of the current and how far you have to cast).

A good quality barrel swivel is attached to the main line, and a two-foot fluorocarbon leader (the same test as the main line or slightly less) is tied to the lower end of the swivel. Tie the hook to the leader, add the bait and you're good to go.

The advantage of this rig is that the angler can leave the bail of the spinning reel open, and when the fish picks up the bait, the line will slip through the sinker with almost no resistance.

You can turn this into a bolt rig by crimping a split shot on the line about three feet above the sinker. If a fish grabs the bait and runs off quickly, the split shot will stop the line from running freely when it hits the egg sinker, and that abrupt stop usually is enough to drive the hook home.

I've caught flatheads up to 20 pounds in the Kalamazoo and St. Joseph rivers, and I once hooked a big catfish in the Huron River near Flat Rock that looked like a flathead and had to weigh at least 40 pounds. (We saw it briefly a couple of times.) Unfortunately, the fish was hooked on eight-pound line, and when it decided to swim around a snag in mid-stream, there was no way I could stop it.

Flatheads are the kinds of critters that put the "ug" in ugly. They have a laterally compressed body, with a huge mouth that's wider than most of the head, and the lower jaw protrudes slightly.

They have eight tactile whiskers that can taste things as well as our tongues do, with the added advantage that the fish can do so without bringing potential food objects into their mouths. There's one whisker on either side of the mouth, four under the chin and two more protruding from the top of the head near the nostril openings.

These fish usually are a yellowish-brown on top of the body, fading to a mottled, dingy yellow on the sides. The tail is almost square on the end, and they usually have a bulging belly and small, beady eyes.

Flatheads are extremely strong. When hooked, they fight to stay near the bottom, and you usually know you have hooked a big flathead long before you see it by the angry head shakes that are felt through your forearms as well as the rod butt.

Some day I would like to spend a week on the Kalamazoo or another good flathead stream and do nothing but concentrate on catching a really big specimen. I suspect that with some advice from local experts, and a three-pound carp or sucker for bait, I might land a couple as big as the one that got away in the Huron.

The Detroit River always has looked to me like a place that should produce a state-record channel catfish. Contrary to what most people think, this is a cool-water species that likes big water and a bit of current.

People who don't know much about fishing will tell you that channel catfish are pure scavengers that feed only on the bottom. Anyone who has trolled lures for walleyes on Saginaw Bay or cast plugs for bass in the Grand River knows that is a pile of doo-doo.

If you look at a channel cat, you'll see that its mouth is located pretty much in the same place as a pike or walleye's mouth, right on the front of its face.

Those whiskers help it locate live prey like small fish, crayfish and insect larvae that live on the bottom and make up the bulk of a catfish's diet. But these powerful, brainy fish also will slam a plug or crawler harness in mid-water or a jig bounced along the bottom.

Channel catfish are one of the most underappreciated game fish in Michigan. They are ubiquitous, found in waters from the Indiana border to the south shore of Lake Superior, and they are also among the biggest and strongest fish in fresh water.

On top of all that, channel cats are absolutely delicious, assuming you take them from waters where toxic pollutants haven't reached levels that make the fish dangerous to eat.

Channel catfish are beautiful, at least in my eyes. Their bodies are sleek and powerful and remind me of a salmon or steelhead. They are usually dark blue on the back, and the sides are a silvery blue, sometimes with a faint olive overlay.

Two of the easiest ways to identify a channel cat are the deeply forked tail and the dark spots scattered over the body. Fish bigger than 20 pounds sometimes don't have spots, but the forked tail is still the giveaway in Michigan, because our state doesn't have the blue catfish (which also has a forked tail and unspotted sides).

I've caught a lot of channel cats in Michigan. Some were taken on dead baits when I was bottom-fishing in lakes for carp, but many were caught on jigs and small crank baits when I was fishing for smallmouths in rivers, and some were taken on night crawlers and spinner rigs when we were trolling for walleyes. I've caught channel cats on spoons when we were trolling for salmon and steelhead in Lake Michigan, and I've even caught them on streamers when I was fly-fishing for bass.

Channel catfish are river creatures that prefer a moderate current, but they are very much at home in lakes. They like sand or gravel bottoms, and while they prefer water warmer than 70 degrees, they still feed actively when the temperature is in the 50s. (But I've never caught one through the ice, not even in lakes where I catch them routinely in the summer.)

These catfish respond well to the ghastly stink baits, even though they are aggressive predators that feed primarily on small fish, crayfish and snails. Many people think of them as bottom-feeders. They will eat bottom-dwelling fish like darters and stonerollers (another species of tiny catfish), but they also pursue active swimmers like sunfish, shad and spot-tail minnows.

If you fish for channel catfish from shore, the bolt rig described above works well with commercially prepared stink baits and homemade dough baits. Most channel cats caught in Michigan weigh less than five pounds, so a lighter rod rigged with 10-pound test line is not only strong enough, it makes for a much better fight.

Channel cats grow more slowly than most other catfish, and in Michigan it usually takes about five years for them to reach 12 inches and three-quarters of a pound. A five-pounder is at least 10 years old, and fish bigger than 20 pounds undoubtedly are older than 20.

But I'm still convinced that the Detroit River has to hold huge channel cats, and one of these days I'm going to find out by dropping a perforated bucket of frozen, rotted fish parts to the bottom on a line.

I'll let that percolate in the river for three or four hours and then come back and lower an underwater TV camera next to it. I'll be surprised if a number of big channel cats haven't been attracted to the bait.

And if they have, the next thing that's going down is a dead gizzard shad on a 1/0 hook.

The catfish family also includes three Michigan species that would win any contest for the toughest fish to kill — the yellow, brown and black bullheads.

Bullheads can survive in water that is nearly devoid of oxygen by coming to the surface to gulp air. They can take water temperatures in excess of 90 degrees for weeks at a time. And they can overcrowd a lake like no other species, sometimes exceeding 1,000 pounds of bullheads per acre. The result of that overcrowding is fish with tiny bodies and grotesquely oversized heads.

I came to the United States from Scotland as a kid and was already a fanatical angler by the time I arrived. My butt still tingles when I think of the consequences of the time I got a gang of kids to help me dam a stream behind my great-grandmother's home in the old Kingdom of Fife, creating a short-lived trout pond where I caught some lovely six-inch brown trout on a fly I tied myself.

Unfortunately, that lovely little burn was also the water supply for some farmers downstream, who showed up en masse at my great-grandmother's door to ask why their cattle were suddenly without water.

One of the first fish I met after arriving in the United States was the black bullhead, which came inshore in spring in huge numbers, gobbled worms like they were going out of style and fought wonderfully on the new, ultralight spinning systems to which I had just been introduced.

Nearly 50 years later, I still look forward to May, when the bullheads gather in the shallows of Lake Margrethe near my home in Grayling and take worms as if they were going out of style.

All three bullhead species average about a pound in Michigan, with three-pound fish being something to brag about. The world record for the black bullhead is eight pounds, 15 ounces; the state record is three pounds, seven ounces. For the brown, the world record is six pounds, two ounces and the state record three pounds, 10 ounces. For the yellow, four pounds, eight ounces is the world record, and three pounds, seven ounces the state record.

Black bullheads are easy to identify because of their color, but I sometimes have a hard time differentiating between the brown and yellow species. Brown bullhead in the South usually have mottled sides, but our northern brown bullheads often lack the mottling and aren't much darker than the yellows.

I usually make the determination by looking at the whiskers, which are light yellow or gray on the yellow bullhead and dark brown to black on the brown bullhead. The tail is more rounded in the yellow bullhead and square in the brown.

Yellow bullheads like clearer water with a lot of weeds, which harbor the snails, scuds and insect larvae that make up most of their diet. They live less than 10 years, but it takes five or six years for them to reach a weight of one pound at 12 to 13 inches.

They like cooler water than the other two bullhead species, 75 to 80 degrees, and their preferred habitat is small lakes and slow-moving streams.

Black bullheads can live longer than 10 years, and they like turbid water, soft bottoms and water temperatures above 80 degrees.

It takes seven to eight years for a black bullhead to reach a pound, and a fish that weighs three pounds is a true graybeard that was fortunate enough to be spawned in water rich in clams, snails, fish eggs and insect larvae.

Brown bullheads prefer waters warmer than 80 degrees and tend to live in deeper waters than their bullhead cousins (which explains why they are more common in bigger lakes). They also can live longer than 10 years. Our northern fish reach the one-pound mark in about six years; southern fish reach that weight in three years.

Bullhead fishing is almost always done on the bottom, although some anglers combine a bottom rig with a float. Bullheads also are most active at night, so another popular rig uses small bells on the rod tip to announce a bite.

Worms are the standard bait for all three species, but I've caught a lot of bullhead on dough balls flavored with chopped-up sardines (the canned variety), ground-up night crawlers and canned cat food.

For tackle, I like a six-foot spinning rod designed to handle four- to six-pound line. The bottom rigs usually have a quarter-ounce to a half-ounce of weight, so heavier line isn't necessary. The fish have big mouths for their size, so a No. 2 or even 1/0 hook isn't too large, especially if you can hide the hook completely inside the bait.

For children, a closed-face spinning reel with eight-pound line is a good choice. It's rarely necessary to make long casts, and snags are rarely a problem because bullheads don't run. Bait the hook with a night crawler.

While bullheads aren't the world's best fighters, they are fun on light tackle and have the added advantage of being delicious. The brown and yellow species fight better than the black, which usually gives up a few seconds after being hooked and simply spins around and around in the water as it is reeled in.

The proper method of cleaning bullheads is to skin them. Hold the head of the fish — being careful to avoid the spines — and make a shallow cut all the way around the body behind the head.

Grab the skin behind the head on one side with a pair of pliers and pull it all the way back to the tail. Now do the same with the skin on the other side.

Next, bend the head back until the backbone breaks, or cut through the backbone with a knife. Hold the fish's tail with the pliers and pull on the head. The entrails will follow the head in one piece.

Cut off the tail and rinse out the body cavity. The best way to cook bullhead or any small catfish is to batter and deep-fry them, making it simple to remove the backbone and rib bones with a fork once the fish are on a plate.

Chapter 11

Suckers

I
N THE LAST WEEK OF MARCH, THE RIFLE RIVER AT OMER IS USUALLY high and muddy, swollen by spring rains and the tail end of the snowmelt. Below the U.S.-23 bridge, where the river is about 100 feet wide, the banks are almost sure to be lined with anglers casting into the small, white-water wavelets.

The season is not-quite-still-winter and not-quite-yet-spring, and the fishermen will wear everything from down coats to T-shirts, depending on their tolerance for cold or, in some cases, capacity for alcohol.

At night, bonfires blaze near the water, and people fish into the small hours with rods and reels and big nets, the latter usually hanging from the end of a 20-foot pole and winched out of the river with a hand-cranked rig scavenged from an old boat trailer.

What draws all these people is the annual sucker run. Some come because they can catch and release 50 fish in a few hours, but most are there to fill car trunks and truck beds with immense loads of white suckers that will be smoked, canned or ground up to make suckerburgers.

You don't have to spend much time on the banks of the Rifle to figure out that this isn't the fly-fishing set.

One hint is an overstuffed sofa that sits in the mud, with one charred cushion and the other still smoking from a blaze started by sparks from a bonfire. There's also the bumper sticker on a nearby truck: "My child was inmate of the month at County Jail."

Millions of suckers run in many Michigan rivers each spring, and showing up to catch them has become as much an annual ritual for some as deer camp.

Some groups set up their sucker camps for a week or more.

They come to Omer in pickup trucks hauling trailers behind them, and with as many as 20 people to a camp one day in 2002, the parking area soon looked like a frontier town in one of those Clint Eastwood spaghetti westerns. People sat playing euchre and pinochle at long tables, where groups of women soon would be cleaning and canning the fish in huge, steaming kettles. The men brought loads of fresh suckers up from the waters and kids got underfoot, chased each other around and fell into the river.

"This is the best time of the year," said Faron Smith of Harrison. "It even beats deer camp, because nobody cares if you're loud here."

Smith had just shinnied out on a long pine pole hanging 10 feet above the river and attached an American flag to the end. The pole is used by members of his camp to winch suckers out of the water with a large umbrella net.

The camps sometimes get raucous, especially on weekends when the alcohol consumption rate increases dramatically. On one Friday night, a man was standing knee deep in the 40-degree water, grabbing two- to four-pound fish out of a net and tossing them toward big wooden boxes half-sunk in the water. The fish are kept alive there until they are processed.

But the man was so drunk that two fish fell into the river next to the boxes and escaped. A couple of his friends clambered down the bank, grabbed the drunk by the arms and led him away, explaining, "Every year it's the same. He's fine until he opens that second bottle of peppermint schnapps."

There are about 60 species of suckers in North America. They are closely related to Asian loaches, some of which are popular aquarium fish. The five sucker species that live in Michigan lakes and streams are the river redhorse, golden redhorse, northern hogsucker, creek chubsucker and the white sucker.

To be technical, three more suckers are found in Michigan — largemouth and smallmouth buffalofish, which can exceed 70 pounds but are more common in the 10- to 20-pound range, and the quillback, which can reach 12 pounds and averages five. These fish are found mostly in the southern parts of the Great Lakes drainage, but few anglers lump these fish with smaller suckers, just as few think of largemouth and smallmouth bass as the overgrown sunfish they really are.

The species that draws the most attention is the white sucker, which makes a spring spawning run up rivers in numbers so thick that it's common for experienced anglers to catch 100 in a day. White suckers live 10 to 15 years and reach sexual maturity at three to five. They can reach a maximum weight of more than eight pounds, but the majority run one to two pounds for males, two to four pounds for females.

Like other suckers, the white has an array of sensory pores on the thick lips of its underslung mouth, and it uses these pores to locate food as it runs its mouth over the bottom.

The sucker's diet is composed almost entirely of things that are small and harmless — midge, mayfly and caddis larvae, bits of algae and well-rotted leaf detritus. It sucks the food and mud into its mouth, then separates the wheat from the chaff with its gill strainers.

Suckers can spawn in streams or lakes. Those that run the rivers can negotiate stiff rapids, and after running the fast water they spawn over well-washed and well-aerated gravel bottoms. The fish that spawn in lakes usually choose shallow, rocky places.

Unlike salmon, which run from the Great Lakes, suckers might run upstream from a lake or from a lower section of a river. The timing of the spring run depends on warming water and rains that raise the water level and signal fish waiting downstream that plenty of water will be on the spawning beds. The run usually begins in late March and ends by mid-April.

The initial stages of the run draws anglers, who fish with rods and reels, but starting April 1, things get serious when the netters are allowed to start fishing from small barges anchored in the river and with big, hanging nets lowered to the riverbed at night. The netters often bring up 100 pounds of fish at a dip.

My favorite sucker rig is the same 10-foot spinning rod I use for salmon and steelhead, and the fishing technique is similar, too. The rod isn't a noodle rod. It has a much stiffer tip and easily will cast a quarter-ounce lure or weight 50 yards with six-pound monofilament line. Several manufacturers offer similar nine- to 10-footers, rods designed to let the angler feel the bait or lure move along the bottom, react quickly to strikes, then play a fish in heavy current.

In slow current, a one- to two-inch piece of night crawler works well for suckers, but if the water is moving fast, as it usually does in the Rifle, nothing beats a No. 8 treble hook tipped with a piece of green or red sponge foam.

I like to fish with a one-eighth-ounce jig head and a two- to three-inch curly tailed plastic jig, adding small split shots about a foot above the jig to get it to the bottom. But on one recent day I caught only two fish on jigs while people using foam caught 20. When I switched to a single No. 6 hook with a couple of half-inch pieces of green sponge, I hooked fish on three of the next five casts.

Whether using jigs or foam, the number and size of the split shots depends on the current speed. The trick is to add just enough so you feel a tick, tick, tick as the jig skips along the bottom. Too little weight, and the lure won't get down where the fish are; too much, and it will hang up on the bottom too often.

The best jig and foam colors usually are chartreuse, red or yellow, but when the fish are plentiful, color doesn't make much difference. A major problem when fishing for suckers in streams is that the bottom usually is matted with old line wrapped around rocks and other natural obstacles, adding to the chance you will get snagged, so bring lots of jig heads and treble hooks.

And bring a good measure of patience, not because of the need to wait for fish, but because you will spend a fair amount of time trying to free snagged hooks from the bottom or untangling lines from up to a dozen others.

Chapter 12

Carp

A BOUT A DOZEN YEARS AGO A MAN NAMED GEORGE VON
Schrader called and asked if I wanted to fly-fish for carp in northern
Lake Michigan. It sounded like a good weirdo story, so I met him a few
days later at Garden on the southern shore of the Upper Peninsula.

George is dead now, felled far too soon by a heart attack, yet I never think of
him without a big smile of gratitude for introducing me to one of the most fascinating and rewarding forms of fishing I know.

Every now and then I see his goofy grin and oversized ears on television,
when they rerun the "In-Fisherman" show. He introduced thousands of TV
anglers to Lake Michigan carp fishing, and I have to admit I still choke up a little.

A few weeks ago I went to the Bahamas to catch bonefish. Playing a nice six-
pounder, I enjoyed the initial run as the fish ripped away with the fly line and
50 yards of backing, but I couldn't help thinking, "It's fast, but it's not as strong
as a carp."

My biggest carp on a fly (a No. 6 olive woolly bugger) is a 28-pound fish
George netted after I fought it for 45 minutes on a six-pound tippet. And the
day I finally land a 30-pounder, I'll hold it up to the heavens for him to admire.

Carp are the most underappreciated and reviled fish in the United States.
Europeans have long known that they are a superb game species (although
hard to catch), and they are a good food fish when caught from unpolluted
waters. In the decade before World War I, commercial fishermen on Lake Erie
sent as much as nine-million pounds of carp a year to markets in New York and
Chicago, most of it processed into gefilte fish.

Carp can be caught by several methods. My favorite is with a fly rod, but they also will take small rubber jigs cast on a spinning rod and a variety of baits ranging from worms to dough balls to that worldwide favorite, corn.

Best of all, there are thousands of lakes and rivers in Michigan where you can catch carp, and the Great Lakes offer some of the best carp fishing in the world.

It surprises me that some canny Michigan fishing guide hasn't done what my expatriate English friend Bernie Haines has done on the St. Lawrence River in New York state — set up a carp fishing operation where Europeans and Japanese will come to fish and pay $1,000 a week for the privilege.

Bernie has an established camp where anglers fish with European techniques — 12-foot spinning rods, electronic bite indicators and catapults to throw out ground bait. A Michigan guide could offer sight-fishing from a flats boat with fly and spinning gear in water so clear you could see the fish coming 100 yards away.

There are dozens of Carp rivers in the United States that were named long before carp were introduced to this country in the 1880s, contemporaneously with the then-exotic brown trout. I suspect fur traders and other European explorers saw suckers, buffalofish, quillbacks and other species that bore a passing resemblance to carp in the new rivers they came across.

Remember, this was a time before television, or libraries for that matter, when most people had only the vaguest idea of the world 20 miles beyond their homes.

The carp initially was hailed as a great food and game fish by American fishermen, who disparaged the brown trout as a skulking cannibal that was much harder to catch than the brook trout it largely replaced.

But by 1900, the brown trout had gained reverence as the second-most desirable fish in North America (after the Atlantic salmon). The carp, which had spread to nearly every body of water east of the Mississippi, was considered an alien monster that displaced native species and turned once-clear lakes and ponds into mud pits.

My English friends look at our disdain for carp as further proof that George III really screwed up by letting the colonists win. A couple of years ago we took a couple of them into a big discount store to buy fishing licenses. (They had flown to the United States specifically to fish for big carp.)

As we stood in line at the sporting goods counter, their attention went to an overhead TV screen where an outdoors video was playing. I'll never forget their looks of horror as they realized that it was a carp shoot, and that these low-rent Yankee bow hunters actually thought it good sport to slaughter thousands of carp in a weekend just for the hell of it.

I love to fish for carp because they are among the strongest and biggest fish in fresh water. I am convinced that if you tied a 20-pound carp and a 20-pound salmon tail to tail, the result would be a draw.

I also can catch them by sight-fishing with a fly or spinning rod in the clear waters of the northern Great Lakes, wading in rivers like the Grand and Huron or still-fishing more turbid waters like Kent Lake, Saginaw Bay and the Kalamazoo River.

Carp are cyprinoids, oversized members of the minnow family, and in their native lands east of the Danube River in Europe, their numbers were controlled by predators and diseases. Even when introduced to places like England

and France during the late Middle Ages and the Renaissance, carp were largely in balance with the rest of the ecosystem, although even then they had a reputation for being hard to catch (more true 500 years later).

A 17th Century rhyme held that "hops and turkeys, carps and beer, came
into England all in a year." That wasn't true, but it was historically pretty close.

Carp in western Europe probably were first stocked in monastery fish
ponds. (The monks usually had a royally granted monopoly on selling fish to
the locals.) And many streams were stocked with carp fingerlings that escaped
when ponds overflowed during floods.

There are three basic forms of the common carp: commons, which are fully
covered with scales; mirrors, which have a handful of oversized scales; and
leathers, which are essentially scale-less. Mirrors make up about two or three
percent of any carp population, and the rare leathers less than one percent.

Izaak Walton, the unrepentant bait-flinger whose "Compleat Angler" is still
recognized as a literary masterpiece and a great how-to book, wrote in 1653: "If
you will fish for a carp, you must put on a very large measure of patience, especially for a river carp. I have known a very good fisher (to) angle diligently four
to six hours in a day, for three or four days together for a river carp, and not
have a bite."

Nearly 350 years later, his advice still holds true, and the carp angler is at
the apex of the fishing hierarchy in most parts of Europe. Ironically, coarse fish
like carp, roach and rudd are rarely killed there, but game species like trout
and salmon almost always are.

The reason English carp are so hard to catch is that they are naturally
among the smartest of fish, and they are the product of 500 years of unnatur-
al selection by anglers, who caught and removed the easy carp from the population, leaving the wary.

English carp were the province of a handful of die-hard, secretive specialists
and didn't become a popular sport fish there until about 1990, when an angler
invented something called the hair rig. The bait doesn't go on a hook but on a
three-inch length of fine line whipped to the hook shank near the eye.

English carp were notorious for mouthing a bait and spitting it out if they
encountered anything that felt like a hook. But with a hair rig, the carp can feel
only the bait, and when it sucks it in, the fish pulls the hook with it.

Not that the hair rig made English carp fishing all that easier. This is a country where anglers boil field corn with carefully selected amino acids in hopes
of enticing a bite. One English carp angler I encountered on the St. Lawrence
River said he made an annual trip to North America because he could catch as
many carp in a day as he could in several years at home, and more 20-pounders
in a week than an English angler would take in a lifetime.

Fortunately for us Yanks, the carp here are still relatively fat, dumb and
happy, although they are far smarter and warier than most of our native fish.
Many of our waters teem with huge numbers of carp, big and small, which have
never been targeted by anglers. Only a few have felt a hook, and most were
caught by people fishing for something else.

Carp are among the biggest fish in American waters, but they also are
among the shiest. The national hook-and-line record is a 57-pound, 13-ounce
fish caught in the Potomac River near Washington, D.C., and the Michigan
record is a 61-pound, eight-ounce carp taken with a bow and arrow. While
many people talk about taking 30-pound carp routinely on dough balls, the

truth is that if those fish were put on a scale, few would exceed 20 pounds. And few of those anglers could consistently catch carp bigger than 20 pounds if they had $100 riding on it.

FOOD PREFERENCES

Many anglers think carp largely eat aquatic vegetation, but the carp's primary foods are insect larvae, scuds (freshwater shrimp), small crayfish and the occasional hapless minnow.

Carp are accused of turning clear lakes into muddy ones, but that's because the fish were thrown into bodies of water where they had few natural enemies and could compete better than most native species. That resulted in an overpopulation of carp, and once their preferred foods were in short supply, they turned to vegetation to survive while many native species disappeared.

Anyone who doubts the carp's preference for insects and crayfish need only stand on a bluff above a rocky bay anywhere on the Great Lakes and watch the big, dark shadows cruising the shallows.

One of my favorite spots to watch is a scenic parking area on U.S.-2 along the southern shore of the Upper Peninsula a few miles west of the Mackinac Bridge. From there, when the sun penetrates the crystal-clear waters of Lake Michigan at the right angle, you can spot cruising carp swimming parallel to the shoreline from 100 yards away.

These fish are hard to catch because they are on a mission. Occasionally I climb down the dunes to the beach, wade 20 yards offshore and toss black stone-fly nymphs, woolly buggers and other proven patterns as schools of carp swim past a few yards away. I've caught a couple of fish there, but 99 percent ignore my offerings, I suspect mostly because the sandy bottom is not the kind of place they are accustomed to feeding.

To catch carp consistently, look for a clear, shallow bay, with waters four feet deep or less, where the bottom is covered with stones ranging in size from a golf ball to your head. Huge numbers of aquatic insects and crustaceans make their homes in these areas, and this is where carp feed.

Sometimes I take a break from fishing to watch the carp, especially if there's a nearby elevation (and I've already caught a couple of fish).

Unlike those sand-flats cruisers that pass with purposeful tail strokes, carp in the feeding zones tend to meander along, zigzagging left and right as they pick off a morsel here and a tidbit there. If the water is shallow enough, usually less than a foot, the carp's tails and dorsal fins stick up through the water and flash wetly in the sun as the fish go down to root a bug or crayfish out of the rocks. They look exactly like tailing bonefish and redfish in southern waters, and like their southern cousins, tailing carp are usually suckers for a fly or lure dropped gently five feet ahead and three feet beyond and then twitched carefully past their noses.

People who have mostly encountered carp in warm, muddy lakes don't know that this is the last habitat carp prefer. They like clear water, and they also prefer cool water. (The latitude of their ancestral home in Asia is about the same as Michigan.)

When carp were dumped into American lakes and rivers by the federal government 125 years ago, no thought was given to the possibility that without natural predators and with the ability to eat everything from fish to clams to algae, carp would create an environment in which they dominated.

But that happened quickly. And when carp were dumped into clear lakes with a limited supply of crayfish, minnows and aquatic insects, they didn't die off, as the native fish did. They switched their diet to plant life and soon turned the lake into a muddy weed factory.

Bernie Haines, who operates the Golden Salmon Ranch carp camp in Massena, N.Y., says carp need two other factors to grow to trophy size (bigger than 30 pounds). The first is big water, which offers a greater supply of food. The second is big predators, which remove the sick, weak and dumb fish and keep the population at a level the food supply will sustain.

That explains why the Great Lakes system (of which the St. Lawrence River is part) produces so many huge carp. The water temperature is ideal, the food supply is enormous, and big predators ranging from muskellunge to salmon help keep carp numbers balanced.

Haines' arguments were reinforced some years ago when I fished at a private lake in France owned by another Englishman who micro-managed the lake so it had a population of about 150 carp that weighed 20 to 30 pounds, 50 that went 30 to 40 pounds, and maybe 20 that exceeded 40 pounds (including a couple of 50-pounders). Just the possibility of catching a 40-pounder drew scores of Englishmen each summer to fish this lake for $900 a week.

When I was there, the host was awaiting the arrival of a truck from Yugoslavia with more brood stock, 50 carp in the 20-pound range that he was introducing to the lake to expand the gene pool. But also in that truck were a dozen wels, huge Eurasian catfish with mouths like a dredge bucket that can exceed 10 feet in length and 600 pounds. (The fish he was expecting were about 75 to 120 pounds.)

When I asked the lake owner if the wels were there to offer further enticement to anglers, he said, "Oh, no. Their job is to eat the 10- to 15-pound carp and keep the lake in balance."

One thing I still haven't figured out about the Great Lakes: Where are the little carp? In smaller lakes and rivers, I sometimes catch carp smaller than five pounds, but carp that size are so rare in the Great Lakes that if I catch one I'm usually on the telephone to tell my carp-fishing friends. Yet there have to be large numbers of small carp in these waters because there are large numbers of big ones.

Not only are small carp rarely caught in the Great Lakes, they are rarely seen, even in northern waters so clear the fish are easy to spot. My guess is that the little guys in the big lakes live in deeper water and don't enter the shallows to feed until they are big enough that few predators will bother them. But that's only a guess.

TACKLE

Lots of people catch lots of carp on a $10, six-foot spinning rod rigged with a $10 spin-cast reel. Their strike indicators are small bells attached to the rod tip, and the bait is usually a dough ball or a couple of pieces of corn.

But when you talk to people who use such rigs, they probably will tell you about a lot of big fish that got away, carp they could have landed if they had better rods and reels with drags that give an angler a better chance against powerful fish.

Most carp angling is done from shore, so 10- to 12-foot rods designed for six-to 14-pound line are a great choice. These are not like the American noodle rods designed for steelhead fishing. The carp (and catfish) rods have a lot more backbone, stiffer tips and easily will cast a two-ounce weight 75 to 100 yards and a three-ouncer 100 to 150 yards. They allow the bank angler to reach a lot more water than someone who uses a shorter rod designed for fishing from a boat.

Several American companies offer good, 10- to 12-foot carp and catfish rods for about $60. And in the day of the Internet, anglers can order excellent European rods online from firms like England's Fox Tackle for $100 on up. Top European carp rods exceed $500, like the best American fly and spinning rods.

Carp aren't top-level predators that will attack a lure, so the key to success with bait is to bring the carp to you. This normally entails a good bit of waiting.

Because the rod is usually placed in a rod holder while the angler awaits a strike, the best reels are bait-feeder spinning reels, which have two drags. These reels initially were developed for ocean pier fishermen, who also spend a lot of time waiting for strikes. The first drag is at the top of the spool, and the angler usually sets that for the pressure he wants while fighting the fish.

The second drag is at the rear of the reel, and this is set loosely. When the second drag is set, the primary drag is disengaged, so if a fish picks up the bait, it can move off with it and feel almost no pressure from the line. When the angler sees he has a fish running with the line, he picks up the rod and turns the reel handle or throws a lever to engage the front drag. That lets him set the hook, and the fight is on.

Shimano, the big Japanese tackle company, holds a patent on the system, which allows the angler to engage the front drag by turning the reel handle. So most bait-feeder reels from other manufacturers require the angler to throw a lever to engage the front drag. The Shimano system is the most convenient, but I also have a couple of Silstar and Penn bait feeders I like about the same.

Carp also can be caught on bait-casting tackle, and reels like the Ambassadeur 6500, Shakespeare Medalist and Pflueger Trion work well. I also like long rods, and 10- to 12-foot bait-casting rods that handle six- to 14-pound line are hard to find and expensive, although a friend who is a dedicated carp angler and resident of North Carolina swears by light surf-casting rigs.

If I'm fishing in relatively open water without a lot of snags, I use eight-pound test monofilament on my carp reels. If the water is clear, I might go to six-pound mono. I carry spare spools for each reel, which allows me to change in a minute. I also tie on a four-foot piece of fluorocarbon line — the same breaking strain as the main line — as a leader. Fluorocarbon is virtually invisible underwater, and I've gotten into the habit of using fluorocarbon leaders for virtually all my fishing, even tying three-foot section as leaders on the braided super-lines.

If the water is snaggy, weedy or muddy, with visibility less than two feet, I prefer 12-pound monofilament. Hooked carp often head for the nearest underwater obstacle, and the 12-pound line offers a good balance between abrasion resistance and visibility to the fish.

BAIT

The thing to remember when selecting carp baits is that these fish are basically overgrown minnows, and they act more like prey fish than the predators you would expect from something this size.

The standard carp bait in the United States and Europe is corn. Most Americans tend to use canned sweet corn, but Europeans and top American carp anglers use field corn, which has bigger kernels and stays on the hook better.

Europeans also flavor their corn with an assortment of fruit essences and other secret ingredients. (One of my favorites is strawberry Kool-Aid powder.)

Relatively few Brits use the dough balls that many people consider the standard American carp bait. But I've found that dough balls work well if you flavor them, and another good bait is a thick paste made by crushing Frosted Flakes and oatmeal together in a bowl.

You can fish these mixtures by squeezing them around the hook to form a ball, but a better method is to use a swim feeder. Take a 35-millimeter film canister and poke a couple of dozen holes in the side. Put a snap swivel through a hole at one end.

Tie a three-way swivel into the line just above your leader and snap the film canister onto the open ring of the three-way.

Stuff the film canister with your crushed cereal mix (you also can mix in a few grains of corn). Put some corn kernels on the hook or hair rig and cast out the whole thing. The mixture in the canister will slowly seep into the water, drawing fish to the area. Eventually, one of the fish will find your corn bait.

If you plan to become a serious carp fisherman, think about buying an 11- to 13-foot rod, a bait-feeder reel and even an electronic bite indicator (which you can buy on the Internet). This last device is a black box about the size of a cigarette pack that screws into the top of a bank stick (a pole shoved into the mud to support a rod).

After the bait is cast out, the rod is laid on top of the bite indicator with the line running through a groove in the top of the box. The bail is left open or the back drag of the bait-feeder reel is set to allow line to run freely.

When a fish takes, the bite indicator lets out an electronic tone to indicate a run. If you use more than one indicator, the tones can be set at different pitches so you know which rod has the fish, and most have small lights that blink rapidly to indicate a strike at night.

WATERS

It's getting harder to catch carp as more people take up the pursuit, and in a perverse way that's making more people interested in catching carp. I'm of two minds about that. I love fishing for these superb fighters, but I also like going to wonderful carp waters and knowing I'll probably be the only one fishing them.

At least for a little while.

In Michigan, Saginaw Bay has probably the richest carp grounds, evidenced by the huge numbers of carp killed during bow hunting contests in the spring breeding season. The fish thrash and roll in the shallows by the thousands. But Saginaw Bay is also very turbid, compared to the rest of the Great Lakes, which makes it fine for fishing with bait but impractical for sight-fishing.

Sight-fishing for carp is like sight-fishing for bonefish, except the quarry is much larger. The truth is, it's almost exactly like sight-fishing for redfish (channel bass) in Florida. The fish have the same shape, same feeding habits and are nearly the same color.

Some superb sight-fishing areas are the Garden Peninsula along the southern shore of the Upper Peninsula, and just about any clear, rocky bay from Epoufette on Lake Michigan to De Tour on Lake Huron. The key is to wear polarized sunglasses (which let anglers see into the water much better), and to fish prime hours, 10 a.m. to 3 p.m., when the sun's angle is best for seeing fish.

To me, the most fun way to fish for carp is to wade for them, casting flies or small jigs ahead of and beyond the fish. Some anglers fish from a boat, but they have to pole the boat along because running a motor warns the carp that something is wrong. And a carp that has been warned will ignore every lure you put in front of it.

Goldfish

For a long time we have treated the Great Lakes as if they were some kind of giant aquarium, and sometimes we get results that fit that assumption.

Nearly 25 years ago I was walking the southern shoreline of Pelee Island in western Lake Erie, casting out among the rocks for smallmouth bass and rock bass, when I spotted an orange glow in the water.

You have to realize that unlike the clear, green Lake Erie of today, where underwater visibility routinely exceeds 20 feet, the Lake Erie of the late 1970s looked more like pea soup, especially during summer algae blooms.

I was fishing a worm/small spinner combination, so I cast it just ahead of the thing that was barely visible in two feet of water but seemed to be moving slowly across the bottom. I began a slow retrieve, set the hook when the spinner suddenly got heavy and was surprised when the thing shot off down the steep bank and peeled line off my ultralight spinning rod.

Five minutes later I was utterly gob-smacked, as my New Zealand friends say, when I landed a goldfish. As brilliant as a newly picked orange, it went at least three pounds, and there was no question that it was a goldfish. This thing looked just like the critters we used to buy at the dime store — if you had put those little tank polluters on steroids for a couple of years.

Today, I can catch goldfish anytime I want by going to the Little River in Windsor, just across the Canadian border from Detroit. Not only does it have a good population of midsize common carp, fish that average six to 10 pounds, it has a lot of goldfish that have gone back to the wild state.

The last time I fished there I was using corn, my favorite carp bait. This variety was a canned Pescaviva brand, especially made in Italy for carp anglers and cherry-flavored, I think. I was still-fishing on the bottom when I saw a pale shape moving through the water on the far side.

I reeled in one rod, cast the corn across and a few minutes later was rewarded with a take as line peeled off the reel. I set the hook, played the fish and soon had a two-pound goldfish in the net, but few people would have recognized it.

This wasn't like the brassy fish I had seen in Lake Erie. It was a fish with a charcoal-gray back and off-white sides and underbelly. It had reverted to the original colors of Carassius auratus, the hues it bore before Chinese aquaculturists began selecting 4,000 years ago for the brilliant fish we keep in our homes.

Wild goldfish have become common in the Great Lakes drainage, mostly in slow-moving streams, and most were released by people who got tired of keeping them in fish tanks. They also are common in Europe. The American-record fish is two pounds, 13 ounces, taken from Lake Michigan.

I have caught them in a host of color patterns, including some wild mixtures of red, white and brown like the koi carp so popular in Japan.

Goldfish are related to carp and can create hybrids with them, but the offspring seem to inherit the smaller stature of the Carassius genus. They take the same baits carp do (corn and dough mixtures). While the common goldfish seem to fight about as well as most two- to three-pound fish, a friend tells me he knows of a lake in Oakland County filled with fancy fantail goldfish "that can't fight their way out of a paper bag."

FOOD VALUE

For the heck of it, I brought a two-pound goldfish home one day, baked it and ate it. It was good, with slightly oily flesh the color of a salmon or steelhead. (It apparently had been feeding heavily on crustaceans.)

The problem with carp (and goldfish) is that they eat so many insects, crayfish and other critters from the bottom of the food chain, they amass toxic chemicals even faster than most predatory fish. Carp from Great Lakes waters and most of our major rivers are unsafe to eat. That's a real shame, because if they were edible, we could ship tens of millions of pounds a year to Asia and Europe.

But if you get a chance to try a nice five- to eight-pound carp from an inland lake where they are safe to eat, go ahead. The state Department of Natural Resources has a booklet that shows toxicity levels for fish everywhere in Michigan.

You probably will be surprised to learn how tasty carp are. Another option is to visit Cicero, Ill., near Chicago. The U.S. Carp Fishing Championships are held in the Chicago River every fall, and we love to take our British visitors to a street in Cicero where all the bars serve carp sandwiches from farmed fish.

You can imagine the reaction of the Englishmen, who would never dream of killing a carp and hold them in such high esteem that some put anti-bacterial ointment on the hook scar before releasing a fish.

It's the only way we can get back at the Limey buggers for hammering us in our own contests year after year.

The fish of Michigan

TROUT AND BASS

SMALLMOUTH BASS

(Micropterus dolomieui)

Michigan average: 2-4 pounds.

Michigan record: 9 pounds, 4 ounces.

RAINBOW TROUT

(Oncorhynchus mykiss)

Michigan average: 10-14 inches.

Michigan record: 26 pounds, 8 ounces (steelhead form).

LARGEMOUTH BASS

(Micropterus salmoides)

Michigan average: 2-4 pounds.

Michigan record: 11 pounds, 15 ounces.

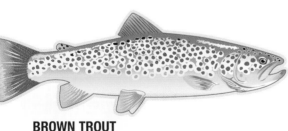

BROOK TROUT

(Salvelinus fontinalis)

Michigan average: 8-10 inches.

Michigan record: 9 pounds, 8 ounces.

BROWN TROUT

(Salmo trutta)

Michigan average: 12-16 inches.

Michigan record: 34 pounds, 10 ounces (Great Lakes fish).

MUSKIE AND PERCH

STURGEON

(Acipenser fulvescens)
Michigan average: 8-30 pounds.
Michigan record: 193 pounds.

MUSKELLUNGE

(Esox masquinongy)
Michigan average: 10-15 pounds.
Michigan record: 48 pounds for Great Lakes variety; 45 pounds for inland variety.

NORTHERN PIKE

(Esox lucius)
Michigan average: 2-4 pounds.
Michigan record: 39 pounds.

WALLEYE

(Stizostedion vitreum)
Michigan average: 1½-3 pounds inland; 2-6 pounds in Great Lakes.
Michigan record: 17 pounds, 3 ounces.

YELLOW PERCH

(Perca flavascens)
Michigan average: 6-10 inches.
Michigan record: 3 pounds, 12 ounces.

LAKE WHITEFISH

(Coregonus clupeaformis)
Michigan average: 4-6 pounds.
Michigan record: 14 pounds, 4.5 ounces.

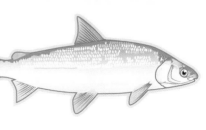

CATFISH AND BULLHEAD

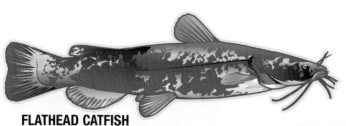

FLATHEAD CATFISH
(Pylodictis olivaris)
Michigan average: 3-8 pounds.
Michigan record: 47 pounds, 8 ounces.

CHANNEL CATFISH
(Ictalurus punctatus)
Michigan average: 2-5 pounds.
Michigan record: 40 pounds.

YELLOW BULLHEAD
(Ictalurus natalis)
Michigan average: 3/4-1 pound.
Michigan record: 3 pounds, 7.25 ounces.

BLACK BULLHEAD
(Ictalurus melas)
Michigan average: 1-2 pounds.
Michigan record: 3 pounds, 7 ounces.

BROWN BULLHEAD
(Ictalurus nebulosus)
Michigan average: 1-2 pounds.
Michigan record: 3 pounds, 10 ounces.

SUNFISH AND CRAPPIES

BLACK CRAPPIE
(Pomoxis nigromaculatus)

Michigan average: 8-10 inches.

Michigan record: 4 pounds, 2 ounces.

WHITE CRAPPIE
(Pomoxis annularis)

Michigan average: 8-10 inches.

Michigan record: 3 pounds, 6 ounces.

ROCK BASS
(Ambloplites rupestris)

Michigan average: 7-10 inches.

Michigan record: 3 pounds, 10 ounces.

REDEAR SUNFISH
(Lepomis microlophus)

Michigan average: 7-10 inches.

Michigan record: 1 pound, 15.5 ounces.

BLUEGILL
(Lepomis macrochirus)

Michigan average: 6-9 inches.

Michigan record: 2 pounds, 12 ounces.

PUMPKINSEED SUNFISH
(Lepomis gibbosus)

Michigan average: 6 inches.

Michigan record: 1 pound, 5 ounces.

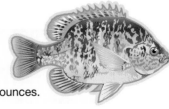

SALMON

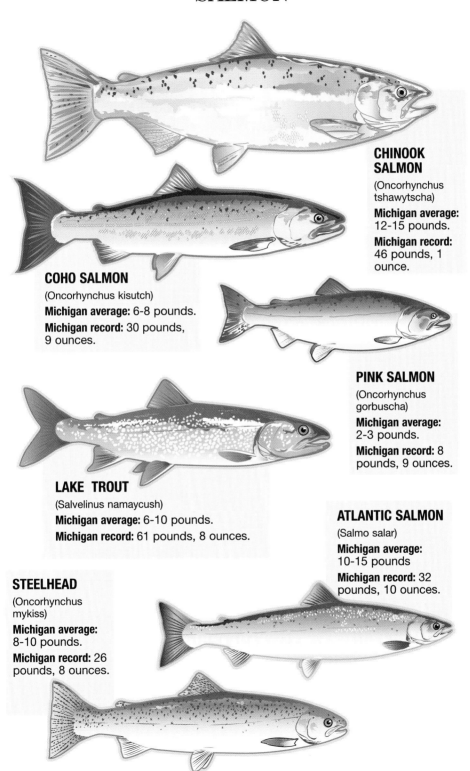

CHINOOK SALMON
(Oncorhynchus tshawytscha)
Michigan average: 12-15 pounds.
Michigan record: 46 pounds, 1 ounce.

COHO SALMON
(Oncorhynchus kisutch)
Michigan average: 6-8 pounds.
Michigan record: 30 pounds, 9 ounces.

PINK SALMON
(Oncorhynchus gorbuscha)
Michigan average: 2-3 pounds.
Michigan record: 8 pounds, 9 ounces.

LAKE TROUT
(Salvelinus namaycush)
Michigan average: 6-10 pounds.
Michigan record: 61 pounds, 8 ounces.

ATLANTIC SALMON
(Salmo salar)
Michigan average: 10-15 pounds
Michigan record: 32 pounds, 10 ounces.

STEELHEAD
(Oncorhynchus mykiss)
Michigan average: 8-10 pounds.
Michigan record: 26 pounds, 8 ounces.

CARP AND EXOTICS

CARP
(Cyprinus carpio)

Michigan average: 4-12 pounds.

Michigan record: 61 pounds, 8 ounces (taken with bow).

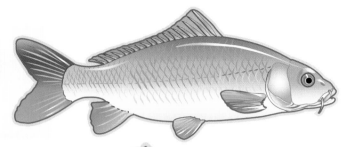

BIGHEAD CARP

Average size: 60 pounds; can exceed 100.

WHITE SUCKER
(Catostomus commersoni)

Michigan average: 1-2 pounds.

Michigan record: 7 pounds, 3 ounces.

ROUND GOBY

Average size: 4-6 inches.

SEA LAMPREY

Average size: 2 feet.

ZEBRA MUSSEL

Average size: ¼ to ½ inch.

MAJOR FISHING
Rivers

N
W—E
S

Lake Superior

Lake Michigan

Lake Huron

Lake St. Clair

Lake Erie

UPPER PENINSULA

Lake Superior
1 Montreal
2 Presque Isle
3 Carp
4 Union
5 Ontonagon
6 Portage Ship Canal
7 Yellow Dog
8 Dead River
9 Laughing Whitefish
10 Au Train
11 Grand Sable Creek
12 Blind Sucker
13 Two-Hearted
14 Tahquamenon

Lake Huron
15 St.Marys
16 Munuscong

Lake Michigan
17 Brule
18 Menominee
19 Cedar
20 Ford
21 Escanaba
22 Whitefish
23 Indian
24 Manistique
25 Millecoquins
26 Brevoort
27 Carp
28 Pine

LOWER PENINSULA

Lake Michigan
29 St. Joseph
30 Paw Paw
31 Kalamazoo
32 Grand
33 Muskegon
34 White
35 Pentwater
36 Pere Marquette
37 Big Sable
38 Little Manistee
39 Pine
40 Manistee
41 Betsie
42 Platte
43 Boardman
44 Boyne

Lake Huron
45 Cheboygan
46 Ocqueoc
47 Swan
48 Thunder Bay
49 Pine
50 Au Sable
51 Rifle
52 Pinconning
53 Saginaw
54 Black

Lake St. Clair
55 St. Clair
56 Belle
57 Clinton

Lake Erie
58 Detroit
59 Huron
60 Raisin

0   50   100
MILES

MAJOR FISHING
Lakes

N W E S

Lake Superior

Lake Michigan

Lake Huron

Lake St. Clair

Lake Erie

UPPER PENINSULA

1. Lake Gogebic
2. Portage Lake
3. Medora Lake
4. Craig Lake
5. Lake Independence
6. Lake Michigamme
7. Au Train Lake
8. Norway Lake
9. Dutch Fred Lake
10. Muskallonge Lake
11. Lac Vieux Desert
12. Chicagon Lake
13. Lake Antoine
14. Gulliver Lake
15. Big Manistique Lake
16. Carp Lake
17. Brevoort Lake

NORTHERN LOWER PENINSULA

18. White Lake
19. Croton Dam Pond
20. Hardy Dam Pond
21. Pere Marquette Lake
22. Big Star Lake
23. Tippy Dam Pond
24. Portage Lake
25. Hodenpyle Dam Pond
26. Arbutus Lake
27. Big Platte Lake
28. Crystal Lake
29. Boardman Lake
30. Glen Lake
31. Lake Leelanau
32. Torch Lake
33. Walloon Lake
34. Burt Lake
35. Mullet Lake
36. Black Lake
37. Ocqueoc Lake
38. Fletcher Pond
39. Hubbard Lake
40. Foote Dam Pond
41. Cooke Dam Pond
42. Lake George
43. Houghton Lake
44. Higgins Lake
45. Lake Missaukee
46. Lake Mitchell
47. Lake Cadillac
48. Sand Lakes
49. Lake Skegemog
50. Manistee Lake
51. Lake Margrethe
52. Otsego Lake
53. Shupac Lake
54. Wakeley Lake

0   50   100
MILES

SOUTHERN LOWER PENINSULA

56. Muskegon Lake
57. Mona Lake
58. Lake Macatawa
59. Thornapple Lake
60. Gun Lake
61. Gull Lake
62. Union Lake
63. Lake George
64. Clark Lake
65. Sand Lake
66. Wamplers Lake
67. Lake Lansing
68. Lake Ovid
69. Holloway Reservoir
70. Lake Chemung

SOUTHEAST MICHIGAN

71. White Lake
72. Pontiac Lake
73. Lake Oakland
74. Stony Creek Lake
75. Cass Lake
76. Orchard Lake
77. Kent Lake
78. Big Portage Lake
79. Ford Lake
80. Belleville Lake
81. Huron River Impoundment

Flies

ADAMS

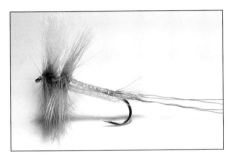

MUDDLER MINNOW

BROWN DRAKE

HEX SPINNER

HOPPER

SULPHUR DUN

ROYAL COACHMAN

TRICO DUN

Lures

PLASTIC CRAWFISH

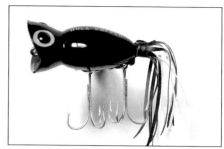

HULA POPPER

STING'R BUCKTAIL

JOHNSON SILVER MINNOW SPOON

SPINNER BAIT

ROUNDHEAD JIG

DAREDEVLE SPOON

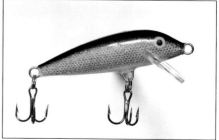

ORIGINAL RAPALA CRANK BAIT

The spirit of fishing Michigan

A solitary fly-fisherman casts in the fading light on the South Branch of the Au Sable River east of Grayling. The Au Sable is a prime trout stream.

Rick Bowen of Mason proudly displays a 17-pound, 12-ounce carp he caught during the Grand River Lunker Derby in Lansing. The event is believed to be the biggest bank-fishing tournament in the country.

As the sun rises, fishing pro Gerry Gostenik of Dearborn goes after bass in Lake Erie. Gostenik works as a guide on lakes and rivers in the Detroit area. He is a master of a technique known as the Erie drag.

Walleye tournament competitors crowd together at Lake Erie Metropark in Brownstown Township as they return from the first day of a Professional Walleye Trail event on the Detroit River. Walleye tournaments are held each year in Michigan.

CRAIG PORTER

CRAIG PORTER

Mack Dixon of Lincoln Park uses the hand-lining technique on the Detroit River. Dixon once made a hand-line reel from a windup gramophone.

Anglers cast side-by-side during a fishing derby at Palmer Park in Detroit. Events such as this often produce nice catches of sunfish.

PAUL WARNER

Catarafts have the carrying capacity of canoes and kayaks, are more stable and weigh less. This eight-footer weighs 45 pounds.

Derrick Faber of Gladwin doesn't let a downpour keep him from fishing at the Tippy Dam, a popular spot on the Manistee River. Faber has hooked a big salmon.

The yellow perch is a favorite target of anglers around the state. Perch are small, but many anglers claim they are the tastiest fish in fresh water.

ERIC SHARP

DAVID P. GILKEY

Jerry Grayton of Clinton Township checks for bites while ice-fishing on Lake St. Clair at Metro Beach Metropark in Macomb County.

Walleye pro Mark Martin of Twin Lake, Mich., right, bundles up against the cold and spray while he and other anglers scout for fishing holes before an early April tournament on the Detroit River.

CRAIG PORTER

Chapter 13

Ice fishing

THIS IS THE LIFE. THREE FAT WALLEYES LIE ON THE ICE outside my shanty on Lake Margrethe, and through the hole in the floor inside I can see another half-dozen walleyes eyeing my jig from about 10 feet away.

A portable catalytic heater keeps the inside of the shanty at a comfortable 69 degrees — and also keeps the hole in the ice open — despite single-digit temperatures outside.

Through the shanty window, I can see a tip-up I set about 50 feet away over a spot where I have caught pike in the past (and took a 27-incher this morning).

I'm sitting in a canvas armchair I bought at a discount store for $19.95. It even has a foot rest, and when the fishing slows I can read my book or switch the TV from the underwater camera to a broadcast channel. The picture isn't the greatest without an antenna, but I can still watch the Lions get beat.

The only fly in my ointment is an empty coffee thermos. I could remedy that by brewing some more coffee on a portable propane stove, but I have to go home in an hour or so, and I'm too lazy to commit myself to the required cleanup for that short a time.

Sitting in my chair, drinking the last of my coffee, I ponder my contentment and wonder why a friend ever thought of calling this "the moronic sport."

I have to admit I look forward to the arrival of ice on the lakes of Michigan, especially those first three or four weeks of ice when the fish are feeding ravenously to prepare for the lean days ahead, and the oxygen levels in the water are still high enough to keep them active.

But I'm not as passionate about ice fishing as a couple of the guys I've watched from my office window as they ventured onto Lake Margrethe early in the season.

I was sitting at the computer one morning when I saw them, wearing bright orange life jackets and pushing a small johnboat ahead of them as they edged gingerly out on a skin of fresh, black ice I knew was no more than two inches thick. (I had crept 20 feet offshore the day before.)

They got out safely to a spot where I had seen a permanent shanty set the year before, climbed into the johnboat and proceeded to drill a couple of holes through the ice on either side. Then they sat in the boat seats and started fishing.

"Guys," I thought to myself, "I guess you know what your lives are worth, but I figure mine is sure worth a lot more than a few walleyes and perch."

I had to leave shortly afterward, so I don't know if they caught fish. But I have to admit that while I shook my head over their foolhardiness, my next thought was, "Hmmm. It should be thick enough for me to get out there in a day or two."

Ice fishing is a lot of fun because: A) It can be extremely productive; B) it makes a lot of water accessible to people who don't own boats; and C) it requires less equipment than soft-water fishing.

One reason for "C" is that you can't cast, so that eliminates entire classes of lures like crank baits and buzz baits. Mostly what you do is vertical jigging with lures and/or baits, or setting baits on tip-ups that fish by themselves and signal a bite by raising a flag of some sort.

If I were just starting to ice-fish, I would buy two short rods — one fiberglass, about two feet long, with a softer tip for fishing for perch and bluegills, and the other about three feet long and stiffer carbon fiber for fishing for walleyes, pike and lake trout.

I also would buy one tip-up, preferably the newer kind you can put right down in the hole. Tip-ups are great for fishing with live bait for perch, walleyes and lake trout, and I usually prefer to set one tip-up and then fish a rod through another hole about 50 feet away. I figure that covering more water with more techniques increases my odds.

Some people like to use rods with simple plastic spools rather than fishing reels. Others like closed-face spinning reels. I would rig the softer rod with a good-quality, open-faced spinning reel and the stiffer rod with a good bait-casting reel. I've found they tend to ice up less, and you'll still need a decent drag if you hook a big fish.

Fish with as light a line as you think you can get away with. Algae blooms are at a minimum, and there's no boat or wader traffic to stir up the bottom, so water under the ice is usually as clear as it will get all year.

If I'm fishing for bluegills, I usually start with four-pound test line and go down to two-pound test if the bite is slow. For walleyes, I usually put four-pound monofilament on one spool and eight-pound on the other. I also use a three-foot fluorocarbon leader, tied to the main line with a swivel.

Rig the bait-casting rod with a braided line or one of the new super-lines, such as Fusion. I've found that eight-pound braided lines are good for everything but the biggest lake trout, and if I'm fishing specifically for lakers in a place where I might hang a 15-pounder, I'll go to 12-pound line.

Braided lines also offer an advantage in places like Higgins Lake, where anglers fish for lake trout at depths of 100 feet or more. The braided lines have far less stretch, which makes hook sets surer and easier. (Even if a monofila-ment line has a stretch factor of only 10 percent, which is low, that works out to 10 feet for every 100 feet of line.)

You can use a minnow or maggot on a bare hook for bluegills and perch, but I've found my catch rate increases if I use a small ice jig. Europeans are prob-ably the world's best ice fishermen, especially the Swedes, Finns and Russians, and the tiny jigs and lures they have used for decades are showing up in American tackle shops.

For walleyes, I've been fishing with a lot of jigging spoons for the past cou-ple of winters, especially the kind with color patterns applied holographically. You usually can catch just as many walleyes on a tip-up, but I prefer the more active style of jigging.

Another lure I've come to place a lot of faith in is an airplane bucktail jig from Northland Tackle, which has a pair of small wings at the head that make it swoop and dance as you lift and drop it. These have worked well for walleyes in the smaller sizes (about two to three inches), and the four- to six-inch mod-els have increased my take of lake trout, brown trout and rainbows.

Michigan is fortunate in having excellent ice-fishing waters from the Ohio and Indiana borders all the way through the Upper Peninsula to Wisconsin. But the mild winters that have prevailed in the past decade have meant that there has been virtually no ice fishing during a couple of years in the southern part of the state, and the ice has arrived later and left earlier in more norther-ly regions.

Saginaw Bay, especially the southern end, offers superb ice fishing for walleyes. The water is usually shallow, which means it's smart to stay quiet and not move around much. If the quality of the fish taken in a couple of walleye tournaments in the summer of 2002 is any indication, Saginaw Bay ice fisher-men should see large numbers of eight- to 12-pound fish in the next three or four winters.

If you like fishing for lake trout, Crystal Lake near Frankfort and Higgins Lake are two of the most productive inland waters. It's not for those who like a lot of action, with four or five fish constituting an excellent day, but the lake trout in these waters average about 10 pounds and often exceed 20. In addition, Crystal Lake has a good population of burbot, the only freshwater member of the cod family and one of the tastiest, albeit ugliest, fish in Michigan.

Despite getting heavy angling pressure, Houghton Lake is still one of the finest ice-fishing waters around, as evidenced by the enormous number of shanties that sprout on its surface each winter and the equally large number of anglers who come from all over the Midwest.

Houghton Lake puts on the annual Tip-Up Town celebration during two weekends in February, but the event that was built around an enormous ice-fishing contest 30 years ago has now become a snowmobile festival (and all too often a drinking festival). But Houghton Lake is well worth a visit for ice anglers who schedule their trips to avoid Tip-Up Town.

Fletcher Pond in Alpena and Montmorency counties is an excellent place to ice-fish for northern pike and black crappies, and Manistee Lake in Kalkaska County is one of my favorites for bluegills and perch. The trick on those waters is to move around until you find fish, then move again as soon as they stop bit-ing.

And every Michigan angler should try to make at least one trip to ice-fishing Valhalla — Little Bay de Noc near Escanaba. If nothing else, you'll never forget the experience of driving six or seven miles along a virtual ice highway marked with discarded Christmas trees to reach your fishing site.

A huge shanty town forms at the head of the bay, mostly because anglers can reach the shanties in a few minutes and there usually is pretty good perch fishing there.

But the more serious anglers head toward the mouth of the bay, where the catch is a mixed bag of big walleyes (eight pounds is common), perch to two pounds or more, lake whitefish and splake. The latter is as hard-fighting a fish as you'll find in fresh water, and that includes steelhead and smallmouth bass.

But if you go to Little Bay de Noc, make sure you stop in the local bait shops to learn where the safe ice is and how to get there. A tugboat often moves in and out of Escanaba Harbor, breaking the ice en route, and the safe routes to and from the fishing sites avoid places where the boat has passed.

When it comes to the question of how much is safe ice, the true answer is that no one can give you a guarantee.

About 25 years ago, I got a call from an assistant city editor at the Free Press asking me to go to Monroe, where some ice fishermen had failed to return from a trip on Lake Erie. I joined a couple of Monroe County sheriff's deputies, who went to the shoreline where the men had said they planned to fish.

Five sets of tracks went out onto the ice, but there were none coming back. It was March, and while it had been one of the snowiest winters on record, the previous week had brought a strong warming trend.

I was there when the searchers found the hole where the men had fallen through. The bodies were recovered soon after, and the track evidence on the snow suggested that two or three or them had fallen through first, and the other two had fallen in trying to rescue them.

They were members of the same family, fathers and sons and cousins and uncles, and it left an indelible impression on me about the hazards of ice fishing.

How much ice is safe ice is only a guess at the best of times. A few winters ago I saw a truck break through on Lake Margrethe in a place where the ice was about six inches thick, even though another truck was sitting on the same amount of ice 50 feet away.

And the thickness of the ice isn't the only consideration. The quality of the ice also is important. People usually can walk safely on three inches of new, black ice. But they might break through six inches of old ice that has been melted, broken up and refrozen with a lot of air trapped in it.

Then there are things like currents. On one lake I fish, a good-sized stream flows out from one end. The water in the lake moves at about a mile an hour within 200 feet of that outlet, and local ice fishermen know that if you're going to put a shanty there, you can't set it until about a week after the shanties have been set on other parts of the lake, and you have to get it out of the area about 10 days before everyone else. People like to put shanties there because the slight current seems to congregate bait fish, and they draw trout and walleyes.

Given that there are no guarantees, I usually figure that three inches of fresh ice is the minimum safe amount for a person on foot, and four inches is better.

Five to six inches is the minimum for a snowmobile (a big machine with two people aboard can push 900 pounds), and nine inches is the minimum for vehicles. Once you have 12 inches of ice, you can run just about any car or pickup truck, and the problem is no longer one of ice thickness but ice quality.

I advise new ice anglers to stay on places where other vehicles have run ahead of them, and to watch for places that look different from the rest of the ice.

For instance, if you see a dark patch in the snow, stay well away. It invariably means there is water underneath. While it might be simply the effect of the weight of snow bending the surface of the ice sheet down a bit, or slush under the snow that never froze, it might be a crack or a weak spot.

I saw a snowmobile break through the ice into three feet of water near my home one day, and when I went out to help, the two soaked riders were ready to lynch a neighbor. It seems the lakefront home owner was running water, probably from his dishwasher and washing machine, directly into the lake through a hose buried in his lawn.

That wasn't legal, but at the same time, you could see the dark patch created by his drain hose from a quarter-mile away. Yet the snowmobile driver had opted to steer right across the middle of what was obviously an unsafe area. At least it should have been obvious to anyone who was paying attention.

Early in the season, anglers should spread out and drill holes at least 50 feet from each other. Fishing in a portable shanty helps, because it spreads the anglers' weight over a much greater area. In fact, it's always a good idea to spread out people, shanties and vehicles.

I was fishing on Houghton Lake one day, about 100 yards from a couple of guys who had driven out in a small pickup truck. A few minutes later one of their friends drove up in a full-sized pickup and parked it nose to nose with the other vehicle.

Not long after that, a third full-sized pickup, this one with a snowmobile in the bed, parked next to the other full-sized truck, and now six anglers stood around the vehicles discussing how the fishing was going.

About 10 minutes after the third truck arrived, I heard a booming sound and looked up to see the small pickup drop through the ice as deep as its front axles. Then one of the big pickups did the same.

The guy who owned the third truck, the one hauling the snowmobile, jumped in it and backed it away about 100 yards while the other five people around the trucks ran for their lives.

After a few minutes, when it seemed things were at least temporarily stable, one angler walked cautiously out to the stranded trucks, looked things over and came back to report that they might be able to get the trucks out if they moved quickly.

It took a couple of hours, but both trucks eventually were saved, and both drivers told me they would never take their vehicles off dry land again.

There was a time when ice fishermen came in two flavors — those who stayed in one place in a permanent shanty and those who moved around. The people who stayed put in a shanty were more comfortable, but they were dependent on the fish coming to them, and that often meant hours or even days when not much was happening.

Of course, they could always fill in those hours or days by watching television in shirt-sleeve comfort by the stove, or even cooking a meal. (I've been in some elaborate shanties that boasted a full kitchen.)

Anglers who moved around the lake usually got more fish. But as one of those peripatetic fishermen, I can assure you there were days when I envied a Popsicle, because the freezer it was in was a lot warmer than the temperatures I had to endure.

The portable shanty has solved the dilemma, giving ice fishermen the best of both worlds. If fishing isn't good where you first set up, the shanty is light enough, and probably easy enough to erect and take down, so you can move elsewhere. Many can be moved without taking them down.

The kind and size of portable shanty you buy will be dictated by several factors. The first is the kind of vehicle you drive.

My shanty fits into the back of my pickup truck, but it wouldn't fit inside most cars or in the trunk (although it would ride in a trunk with the lip open and tied down).

Mine is a two-person model. Even though I usually ice-fish alone, I like the extra space to set up my tackle box, portable heater and sometimes even a propane stove. I also like to drill a second hole where I can use gadgets like a portable fish finder and an underwater TV camera.

I usually walk out onto the ice, so I picked a two-person model that was as light as possible, because once I load the gear on it with bungee cords, I'm dragging a load of nearly 100 pounds. I also picked one that tows easily, with molded-in runners that will handle three or four inches of soft snow.

And finally, I selected one that is easy to put up and take down, even with gloved hands or hands half-frozen. I can put up my shanty by myself in a 20-knot wind in less than five minutes. I know because I've done it more than once. A couple of friends have portable shanties that are almost impossible for one person to put up, especially in a wind.

The drawback to my shanty is that it folds so flat — it's three feet by four feet by six inches when closed — I can't stow gear inside. All of the ancillary gear — bait bucket, tackle, stove, TV camera and depth finder — has to be lashed to the outside or carried in my backpack, and a few things have bounced loose unnoticed when I was towing the shanty with a snowmobile.

Another thing that has made an enormous difference in ice fishing in the past 10 years is the fantastic winter clothing available.

I'm one of those people who has a hard time keeping his feet warm, and for years ice fishing was always a contest between how many fish I wanted to catch and how long I could stand to have my feet frozen.

Today, I have one pair of boots that claim they will keep feet warm down to 45 degrees below zero. I haven't put them to that test, but I can report that at 20 below, my tootsies are toasty with a single pair of heavy socks.

We also can buy wonderful blends of natural fibers like wool and synthetics that keep the whole body warm. And instead of surrounding myself with a down parka so thick I can hardly move, as I would have 20 years ago, today I layer-up in underwear, outerwear and a windproof shell that's as comfortable as a three-piece suit.

I only wish I could hang around another 60 years. I would really love to ice-fish in one of the suits I'm sure they will have then, one in which you set the internal temperature by turning a dial on your chest.

Now if someone would only devise a system that didn't require you to unzip to pee at 20 below, ice fishing would be the perfect sport.

Chapter 14

Hand-lining

WHERE ELSE BUT THE MOTOR CITY WOULD SOMEONE THINK to pull the guts out of an old Victrola phonograph and turn it into the most killer walleye catching rig known to man?

Hand-lining was born in the waters that were the lifeblood of Detroit, the city whose name worldwide is synonymous with mechanical innovation and expertise. And like most great inventions, it was the child of necessity.

The broad, deep Detroit River always has had a huge population of big walleyes, but it also has a strong current that makes it tough to troll plugs and spoons with conventional methods.

Enter hand-lining, which dispenses with a fishing rod in favor of a big, spring-loaded reel and a thin steel cable.

The first hand-line reels were handmade in the 1920s from the innards of a wind-up phonograph turntable, but most anglers today use store-bought models sold only around Detroit.

Anyone could have thought to use a steel cable with a one- or two-pound weight on the end to get the line down in heavy current, and some undoubtedly tried it. And anyone could have devised a system for streaming a couple of long leaders off that cable just above the weight, with a couple of lures on the ends.

But the problem was how to bring in all that steel cable, and what to do with it while you were trying to get at the leader to land a fish? If you let it fall back into the water, there was a good chance it would foul the propeller. If you let it fall into the cockpit, there was an even better chance you would end up with an unholy snarl.

The solution was the energy in that spring, which automatically wrapped the steel line around a reel as the angler pulled it in, much like the automatic fly reels popular 30 years ago. But unlike the fly reels, used only to retrieve spare line the angler stripped in by hand, the hand-lining reels used on the Detroit River work the line in and out constantly, keeping lures near the bottom and giving them an action that will attract fish.

The Professional Walleye Trail has banned hand-lining, saying it doesn't meet the definition of angling. The Wal-Mart RCL Walleye Circuit says it's legal, therefore it's as good a method as any.

Even local fishermen argue over whether hand-lining violates the ethics and spirit of angling, with some sneering at it as meat fishing and others saying that's fine, because they're out for the food. But none would argue that it is not an effective way to catch walleyes in rivers with strong currents.

Today's hand-liners use reels about seven inches in diameter, which mount on the boat's gunwales. In smaller boats, the reels usually are mounted in pairs at the stern, one on each side, because the person running the boat sits there. In bigger boats, like Robert Murray's 21-foot pursuit, reels are mounted on the gunwales farther forward, but the anglers still sit near the stern.

That's because lines are worked by the angler hanging his arm over the side and using his hand to pull the steel line back and forth a couple of feet. Some anglers wear gloves to keep their hands from getting abraded by the cable, but others buy leather tubes, called fingers, which slip over the index finger of the pulling hand. They are sold in some Downriver bait shops.

Each reel holds about 200 feet of thin steel cable. A six-foot leader — the shank — is attached to the end of the main cable, and at the end of the shank is a long, cigar-shaped weight that weighs one to two pounds (depending on the current). It bumps along the bottom of the river as the boat trolls upstream at a 45-degree angle to the current, turning from side to side every few minutes like a sailboat tacking through the wind. The idea is to use the current to slow the boat's forward progress to less than two miles per hour, the speeds walleyes usually prefer. Tacking upstream lets the angler keep the lures at the depth he figures fish are most active.

Old-timers used to use sash weights from salvaged double-hung windows, weights that weighed as much as five pounds. They were unwieldy and hung up a lot, but they were dirt cheap because they could be obtained from old buildings, with or without the owner's permission.

Today's anglers use weights designed for hand-lining rigs and weigh one-half to two pounds. The size of the weight depends mostly on the strength of the current and depth of the water.

Murray, a retired physician who lives in the Downriver community of Trenton near Detroit, fishes for walleyes in the Detroit River almost every morning.

"I'm here to catch fish to eat," Murray said. "I'm not looking for big fish, but I want to catch lots of them."

Murray clipped on a shank with brass clevis swivels and fastened a one-pound, cigar-shaped weight to a snap swivel at the bottom end of the shank.

"Most shanks are homemade," Murray said. "Hand-lining is such a specialized technique, and so local, that there isn't a big market for the stuff. But a few guys make terminal tackle in their garages."

Two monofilament leaders, one about 30 feet long and one about 20 feet, are attached to the U-shaped clevis swivels on the shank, one about two feet above the weight and the other about five feet up. Lures are fastened to the leaders with snap swivels — usually body baits like Rapalas in April and May and spoons later in the summer.

Michigan law counts all of the hooks and a plug like a Rapala as one hook, so the angler can have two lures on one hand-line. But Michigan law also limits anglers to one rod each, and the two lures fished from one hand-line are considered the equivalent of fishing with two rods. So that limits each angler to operating one hand-line, if he has multiple lures on it. And since it takes one hand to run the boat and one hand to work the lines, that works out nicely.

As Murray angled his skiff slowly up the Detroit River against the current, he said, "I love to get out here in the morning. This (overturned) bucket is my breakfast table, I drink my coffee as I watch the sun come up over the river, I catch a few walleyes, and I'm usually back in the slip by 8."

He clipped the lures to leaders and dropped them into the water. As soon as he was convinced they were swimming properly, he let the weight at the end of the shank drop toward the bottom and began pulling line off the hand-lining reel.

He pulled out line that had been wound onto the reel by the spring inside. When he felt the weight hit the bottom, Murray settled into a seat at the rear starboard corner of the boat, where he could hang his right arm over the side and work the line forward and back, imparting an erratic action to the lures. The spring inside the reel took up the slack as he moved his arm forward and gave up line as he moved it back.

"You want to feel the weight hit the bottom every few seconds," he said. "Almost all of the walleyes in the river are down in the bottom 18 inches, and they won't come up very far to get a lure."

The screen of the electronic fish finder showed no fish, only the irregular contours of the river bottom 20 to 30 feet below, although vast numbers of walleyes had started running the river two weeks earlier.

"You won't see fish, because most of them are flattened right down against the bottom," Murray said. "There's no space between them and the rocks. If you aren't hitting bottom every few seconds, then the lures aren't down far enough, and you won't get many walleyes. If you just let the weight drag on the bottom, you'll hang up all the time. There's a lot of debris down there, and the depth changes constantly. Divers have told me that the river bottom is covered with big cracks that the sinkers slip into. I think they account for a lot of the snags that we can't get loose.

"One thing you never want to do is wrap the steel line around your finger or hand. I've never seen it take a finger off the way some people claim, but if you get a hard snag, it's going to do some damage."

Murray controlled his boat with an autopilot that uses a remote control connected to the trolling motor. It allows him to fish without having to leave his position to reach the steering wheel or throttle, but most hand-liners fish with tiller-operated outboards.

"You go very slowly into the current, one to two knots," he said. "You can spend all morning covering a half-mile of water, then go back down river and cover it again."

Hand-lining is most effective in deep rivers with strong currents. It allows anglers to use heavy weights that get the bait down where it should be.

Downriggers don't work well in this situation because they keep the lures at the same depth, and if they are kept near the bottom, they will hang up if the water gets shallower.

"There are some things you have to keep in mind, though," Murray said. "You always want to work up-current. If you try to troll down-current, two things are likely to happen. One, the weight will stay on the bottom and you'll get snagged all the time. And second, you'll get your lines all tangled.

"There's a hump we know in the middle of the river that we sometimes troll around, but we always make sure that when we do the short down-current leg, it's after we've come off the hump and the water is deeper."

Murray's hand-line became taut, but instead of a fish, it was because the weight had snagged on the bottom.

"If you hand-line, you're going to get a lot of snags and lose a lot of tackle," Murray said as he steered the boat in a circle around the snagged weight until it came free. "We were lucky on that one. But I lose so many lures that I buy Rapalas by the carton."

Asked how many big sinkers he loses, Murray said, "I don't even count those."

A few minutes later the line tightened again, and this time it was a walleye. Murray demonstrated the technique he has developed for retrieving a fish on a hand-line without getting tangles.

"The key is to never let anything get into the boat but the fish," he said. "You don't want the hand-line, the leader or the weight to come in over the side. First, you pull in the main line and let the reel take it up. When I get to the shank, I wrap the main line once around this fitting" — a cleat will work — "just to hold it while I handle the leader.

"When you see which leader has the fish on, flip the other one up over your head and let it lie across your shoulders. That keeps it out of the way. Now bring in the fish" — hand over hand — "but don't let any of the line come into the boat. When you get to the end, just flip the fish, the lure and a few inches of line into the boat. That way you can take the lure out of the walleye's mouth, drop the lure back in the water and drop the fish in the fish box.

"But I've seen people bring the shank, the weight and the leader into the cockpit. Then they drop the fish in the boat, it starts kicking around, and before they know it they have a real tangled mess on their hands."

Some people have developed a technique they call pole-lining, mounting a hand-lining reel to a fishing rod built along the lines of a pool cue and then trolling with standard hand-lining techniques. It's clumsier than mounting the pole-less reels on the gunwale, but it meets the requirements of the Professional Walleye Trail and other circuits that have outlawed hand-lining. The aesthetics might leave something to be desired, but it speaks volumes for the effectiveness of this Detroit-born walleye technique.

Chapter 15
===

Lures

IN A PRETTY LITTLE CASS COUNTY TOWN ON THE BANKS OF
Dowagiac Creek in the waning days of the 1800s, James Heddon made his
living as a beekeeper and soothed his soul by fishing.

You need to keep in mind that fishing wasn't quite the respectable pastime
in those days that it is today. At least, fishing for bass with bait wasn't, which
is what Heddon did. Late Victorian snobbery dictated that killing time by fly-
fishing for trout was de rigeur, and golf was cool. (Come to think of it, early 21st
Century snobbery does the same.) But sitting on a riverbank drowning worms
was mostly an activity for town drunks or people in need of cheap protein.

Ray Scott, founder of the Bass Anglers Sportsman Society, which has more
than four-million members, said that even when he began promoting bass tournaments in the 1970s, "bass fishing was largely a pastime for the unemployed."

So when Heddon sat by the side of the mill pond in Dowagiac on that 19th
Century day, whittling a piece of wood while waiting for a friend to finish work
at a nearby mill, any proper burgher passing by probably would have noted his
fishing tackle with amusement and more than a little condescension.

When the friend arrived, legend says, Heddon stood up and unthinkingly
tossed the cigar-shaped bit of wood into the pond as he picked up his gear. It
no sooner hit the water than a big bass, undoubtedly a largemouth in that area,
came flashing up out of the depths and grabbed it.

It was one of those magic moments when something goes "click" in a human
brain. Heddon went home and began carving and painting chunks of wood to
look like minnows, hung a couple of hooks off them and learned how to use
them to catch bass. And in 1902 he was given the first patent for a fishing lure

(Pat. No. 696,433) and started the Heddon Lure Co.

In the 100 years since the Dowagiac firm was founded, fishing plugs to catch everything from bass to marlin have become a multibillion-dollar industry.

The Heddon Lure Co. was sold long ago and moved to Arkansas, but antique shops and garage sales around the country still offer the products from dozens of Michigan lure companies, big and small, that were born, prospered, withered and died mostly before the start of World War II.

The Helin flatfish is one of the longest-lived artificial baits and one of the few survivors of that great lure extinction. It's still one of the most popular lures for river-fishing for steelhead and salmon, although the Helin Co. has long since abandoned its roots in Detroit. Patented in 1936, the flatfish was the top seller of its day for virtually all fish, and Helin had sold a then-staggering five million by 1949. (Rapala now sells more lures in a year.)

But few, if any, anglers alive today remember tying on one of Turner's Casting Baits, made and sold as a sideline by a Coldwater barber around 1910; Schoonies Scooter, a lure sold about the same time by Kalamazoo carver John Schoonmaker, who gave it a grooved body that made it dart erratically like a crippled minnow; or Bolton's Bass Hog, which disappeared after World War I.

A few old-timers who still hand-line for walleyes on the Detroit River might remember the Detroit Bait Co.'s Bass Caller from the 1930s, the contemporary Cummings Minnow from Flint, and the Katy Bee, made by the Kostielny Bait Co. of Bronson.

I can remember being utterly fascinated in the 1950s by the Cat's Paw, a Detroit-made lure from the 1940s that lived in a tackle box owned by one of my father's friends. Made to cast into heavy cover, it had a spring-loaded hook that didn't flip out until a fish struck.

Today, tackle shops offer so many kinds of artificial lures that no one can keep up with them. One gigantic outdoors shop near Detroit has on display more than 500 models in various sizes — and those are just the lures we consider plugs. It doesn't include hundreds more spinner baits, buzz baits and plastics.

What I find most interesting about this plethora of plugs is that the great majority are merely variations on James Heddon's original theme. Some colors might be different, and some have subtle differences in shape, but they still embody Heddon's concept that a plug should look and act like a minnow.

The industry has grown into a $1-billion-a-year business in the United States, according to the American Sportfishing Institute. New lures of every kind hit the market every year, and most are designed not so much to catch fish as to catch the eye of fishermen.

How many remember the Banjo Minnow and the Helicopter Lure, which were heavily promoted on late-night television a few years ago? I would like to see you find one in a tackle shop today, or in the tackle box of a professional tournament angler, for that matter.

Something else that always has fascinated me is how some lures, like the Rapala silver-and-black minnow or the Zara Spook, continue to catch fish year after year, while others are like a comet, blazing briefly across the angling firmament and then dying away, never to be heard from again. Or at least not until they enjoy a revival some years later.

I've thought about that a lot and have come to some conclusions that, I'm pleased to see, are getting some support from recent scientific studies.

First, I'm convinced that some plugs, such as the original Rapala, hit just the right combination of lifelike appearance and action right off the bat. I suspect that a silver-and-black, original Rapala in one- to five-inch sizes looks real to every fish that eats prey in those sizes. And by the way, I'm talking about "real" in the way the lure appears to the fish, not the way it looks to a fisherman. Some of the attributes that make the lure look edible to fish might often be things we either can't see or haven't figured out yet.

As for those lures that enjoy 15 minutes of fame, the answer probably lies more in the fish than in the lure. Suppose that in any population of bass in a lake there are a specific number that likely will hit a green plug with purple polka dots, and many more that won't. There also are bass that learn quickly the painful results of biting a green fish with purple polka dots, and dumber bass that never figure it out and get caught by the same lure 12 times.

When the lure is introduced, someone catches a lot of those vulnerable bass with it, the word gets out and pretty soon everyone has to have a green lure with purple polka dots. Other manufacturers jump on the bandwagon with their variations, and for a few seasons anglers catch virtually every bass in the lake that's a sucker for that kind of lure.

Many of those bass go home to dinner. Others get caught so often they die of the stress at a much higher rate than others. The result is that after a few generations (at one generation a year), the gene pool in that lake has been stripped of bass that likely will hit a green lure with purple polka dots, and the smarter bass won't go near anything that looks like that.

If we wait 10 or 20 generations, you probably could use that lure with some success again, because most of the smart bass that learned about the hazard will have died, and random genetic drift will have created some bass within the newer generations that are saps for a green plug with purple polka dots.

Lures like those come and go with bewildering speed. They come because someone thinks he can make a buck off them. They go because anglers learn they don't work very well.

With fishing lures averaging about $5 today, it's irritating to waste money on something that doesn't catch fish. I went through the hard-bodied lures in my bass and walleye tackle box the other day and counted 117.

I figure I probably use about 10 lures for 95 percent of my plug-fishing, and the other 107 sometimes don't touch water for years. (They tend to get pulled out on desperation days, when nothing else will work.)

But how much do you want to bet that I'll buy at least 20 more this season?

Many fishing lures fall under the generic name "plug," a hard-bodied bait that 99 percent of the time is supposed to imitate a minnow. (A few plugs imitate crayfish or newts.) But plugs are separated into sub-categories that depend on their built-in actions, the movement the angler imparts to them and the part of the water in which they are fished.

Top-water and stick baits

Top-waters include any floating plugs that stay on the surface when retrieved. They are my favorite artificial lures because there's nothing in angling more exciting than watching a fish smash a lure at the surface.

Many, like Hula Poppers, were developed specifically for bass. A Hula Popper's dished-out face and rubber skirt is designed to mimic a wounded, dying bait fish struggling on the surface, or maybe a frog that has wandered too far from the safety of the lily pads. Other surface plugs use tiny propellers to create a constant disturbance and buzzing noise in the water.

There are some that don't do much of anything unless the angler imparts action to them. These top-water plugs are often referred to as stick baits, because they are simply shaped sticks of woods (or plastic). But they are highly effective in the hands of a good fisherman who puts them through various paces while he finds out what kind of retrieve the fish prefer.

One retrieve is called "walking the dog" and involves retrieving the lure with a series of jerks of the rod tip, letting the line go slack for a fraction of a second between jerks. When done properly, the lure will dart forward while turning from side to side every few inches.

Or sometimes an angler will retrieve a lure with a series of four to eight short jerks, then allow it to lie motionless for five seconds to a minute. Sometimes he repeats that procedure, or he might resume his retrieve by giving the lure a tiny twitch and then letting it lie still again.

Top-water lures probably offer the greatest opportunity for the angler to apply a little artistry to fishing.

Crank baits

A crank bait looks like a stick bait with a plastic lip jutting out from under its chin. Some float, some sink, but all are designed to run under the water at depths ranging from a foot to more than 20 feet.

One clue to a crank bait's depth potential is the size of the lip. Shallow-running plugs have small lips; deep divers have big lips that sometimes are as long as the lure.

These lures were named because most people cast them out and crank them in. It's a simple technique that works well, although most anglers soon learn some specialized manipulations that work better.

The easiest is to twitch the rod tip steadily as the lure is retrieved, imparting a darting action to its swimming. When using a floating crank bait, anglers often reel for a few seconds, then stop and let the bait float up a foot or two before resuming the retrieve. Many of the strikes come as the bait is floating toward the surface.

Fishing with sinking crank baits, especially deep divers, anglers sometimes reel hard enough to make the lip of the bait bounce along the sand and tap against rocks and downed logs. That's a method I've found effective with crank baits that imitate crayfish.

Some crank baits suspend, hanging in mid-water at whatever depth the angler likes. These baits often are called countdown lures, because the angler can cast them and count the seconds until the lure reaches what he thinks is the desired depth. I often use them in places where fish are hiding in deep weeds. I cast the lure, count to 10 and begin my retrieve. If I catch the weeds immediately, I cast again and count to eight. If I don't catch some weeds on the first cast, I cast again and count to 15 before starting the retrieve. Eventually, I find the countdown number that lets me bring the lure back a foot or so above the tops of the underwater greenery.

Crank baits have a huge following among anglers who troll for salmon, trout and walleyes, especially in big water like the Great Lakes. They work well off downriggers, dipsy divers, snap weights off planer boards, behind bottom-bouncer walleye rigs and on lead core and wire lines, which are enjoying a revival.

Crank baits often are trolled directly off the rod, especially on inland lakes and rivers. The key is to know how deep the lure is running. That's important to know because when one professional walleye angler did a series of tests in which divers watched crank baits being trolled at different speeds, he learned that many lures didn't run within 10 feet of what the manufacturer said they did (most were shallower).

Some walleyes hit the lures during those tests, even though the angler wasn't trying to catch them, and later examination of the fish-finder recordings showed that every fish attacked from below (and mostly from behind). Not one swam down to hit a lure.

Most manufacturers now put fairly accurate information about the depth their lures run on the package. But it's important to remember that the manufacturer's depth number is based on using the lure a certain distance back of the boat and on a certain line strength. The line diameter is the most crucial factor, and a crank bait that runs 10 feet down on a 15-pound line might run 13 feet deep on eight-pound and only seven feet deep on 30-pound.

Jerk bait

Lipless, slow-sinking hard plugs — and some soft plastic lures fished just below the surface — are usually called jerk baits. They are minnow imitators, and they dart about in response to the action the angler imparts by moving the rod.

Many of the original jerk baits were eight- to 10-inch monsters that were ripped and reeled for muskellunge, but anglers soon learned that smaller models worked well for just about any predatory fish that eats minnows.

One of the most effective developments in bass fishing has been the soft plastic jerk bait that darts about as erratically as a hard plug and also offers an enticing wiggle, a softer feel that makes fish hold them in their mouths longer. They even can be scented or flavored.

Jerk baits work best in places where the fish and the angler can see them clearly. I really like them on calm mornings, when the water is flat and you can watch the lure 60 to 80 feet away.

Spinner bait

Whoever thought of combining a rubber-skirted jig head and a couple of spinner blades on a piece of wire shaped into a shallow vee was an absolute genius.

The blades run off the top arm of the wire and create a commotion and flash attractive to bass and northern pike. The rubber-skirted jig head is fastened to the bottom arms of the wire and is almost always the part the fish tries to eat. (The hook is usually hidden in the skirt.)

Some anglers argue that a spinner bait with single or multiple blades looks like a single minnow or a school of minnows. I don't buy that. I think game fish, whose lives depend on finding the right prey and avoiding predators, would never mistake a whirling metal blade for a real fish, at least not at close range.

That belief is being borne out by new studies on the way fish see.

Spinner-bait blades seem to catch the attention of the fish. Many fish are such piscatorial omnivores that they will try to sample anything that looks vaguely fishlike in the hope it might be edible. And sometimes the lure might be an irritating thing that provokes an attack out of anger.

Buzz baits are also a kind of spinner bait, with a larger spinner designed to make a lot more noise. Some of the buzz baits are designed so the spinning blade hits a bit of metal as it turns and produces a "ka-ching" as loud as an old-fashioned cash register.

The primary difference between the forms is that the spinner bait is made to run beneath the surface to attract fish through the flashing blades and the pressure of the water it displaces. The buzz bait is made to run at the surface and draw fish through the flashing blade, the noise it makes and the bubble trail it leaves.

Jigs

A few years ago I asked several dozen excellent anglers and fishing guides this question: If you had to choose one artificial lure to fish in fresh and salt water all around the world, what would it be?

The No. 1 choice for most and top-three pick for everyone was a white lead-head jig with a rubber or hair tail.

That would be my choice, too. I've used jigs in various sizes to catch everything from char in the Canadian Arctic to peacock bass in the Amazon, and from tarpon in Florida to squirefish in New Zealand.

Jigs have a lot going for them. When you add the proper tail, they can look like anything from bait fish to shrimp to small squid. You can use artificial tails, natural stuff like pork rinds or dead minnows, or live baits like minnows, crayfish and worms.

You can work jigs on the bottom or in mid-water. You can move them steadily, hop them along, or twitch them vertically.

But while the white jig might be the universal choice, jigs now come in a variety of shapes and colors, and most no longer have the tied-on hair skirt. Instead, they use replaceable plastic tails that come in a bewildering variety of colors, shapes and sizes.

Color can make a difference, even small amounts of it. I've seen the practical result too many times when walleye fishing not to be a believer. Like most people, I often fish walleyes using a jig head with only a minnow on the hook. Many times I've been with another angler who started catching fish on a jig head of a different color while I went fishless. I started catching fish myself when I switched to the same color.

That's odd, because we know walleyes don't see color well, at least not as well as bass and pike. Walleyes evolved to feed at night and in waters where visibility is poor, so their eyes have fewer of the cone cells that register colors and more of the rod cells that discriminate light and dark objects. I suspect that walleyes and other fish perceive color differently from humans.

There are two basic types of jig heads — those meant to be worked up and down vertically under the boat (or ice), and those meant to be cast out and retrieved, usually by hopping them over the bottom. The vertical jig heads normally are round and have the eye on top. Casting jig heads usually are bullet-shaped or flattened and have the eye near the front.

Both kinds can be used with all sorts of rubber tails, but a jig head designed for use with a rubber tail normally has a small tooth just behind the head that keeps the rubber from twisting or slipping off.

There also are a lot of panfish jigs with small metal heads, chenille bodies and feather tails. These work well for crappies, bluegills and perch. But many anglers don't realize that one of the most effective ways to fish with them is not the usual cast-and-retrieve method but by putting them under a bobber as if they were a chunk of live bait.

This works best on days when there's a little wave action to move the float up and down, which makes the jig bob and the feathers wiggle temptingly.

Anglers today must learn to use one other type of jig head, those meant to be used with "creatures."

Creatures

"Creatures" is the name Southern anglers applied to the large variety of lizard-like, snake-like, squid-like, crawfish-like and just plain weird plastic lures that started showing up in big numbers about 15 years ago.

The original creature probably was the plastic worm, and to this day every serious bass angler carries this lure in a host of sizes and colors. But walleye anglers also have learned that plastic worms are often as effective as real ones when used on a crawler harness or spinner blade rig.

The fascinating question isn't why plastic worms are so attractive to fish, but why any worms are. Fish probably see some real worms in the water, especially after a heavy rain flushes them into rivers. But researchers have found that bass raised in tanks, and which had never seen a worm, just went nuts over them when some worms were dropped into the tank.

The latest trend is flavoring worms and other plastics with scents or salt. Many professional anglers think a salt-flavored plastic lure works better, even though bass in laboratory tests didn't show a preference.

Among the most useful of the creatures are tube lures, soft plastic tubes closed at one end with fringe wiggly rubber legs at the open end. The angler shoves the head of the jig into the open end of the tube until it reaches the closed end, then he pushes the eye through the plastic and ties on his line.

What the fish think these are, I have no idea. With the arrival of the round goby in Lake St. Clair and Lake Erie, bass soon began keying on tube lures that were goby-colored and looked remarkably like these little exotic invaders. The party line soon was that the bass thought the tubes were gobies.

The mimicking idea made sense until anglers learned that a sandy-colored tube lure also attracted smallmouth bass on these lakes during the hatches of the big Hexagenia limbata mayfly. They hatch in such huge numbers that the husks of their skins can cover miles of water.

It's true that the color matches the mayflies, but there's no way I will believe that a bass would mistake a six-inch-long, half-inch-thick plastic tube for a mayfly that's one inch long and maybe one-eighth inch at the thickest.

We're learning that bass and other fish have excellent close-range vision, better than ours in some ways. They can get a crisp, clear look at objects that move so quickly they are a blur to us. (If a bass looked at a movie, it would see each frame as an individual still picture.)

Now a snot-green tube lure might look like a round goby to us, but I doubt a bass makes that mistake when it's eyeing the lure from a foot away in clear water just before it strikes. And I know the bass sure as heck doesn't think a sand-colored tube is a mayfly.

The bass probably sees something the same color as something it found tasty, and has the same general shape, size and wiggly bits as other things it also found tasty in the past. So the fish figures that with all of those things going for it, the lure probably will be just as good.

Tube lures have proven so effective, especially in bass fishing, that manufacturers offer them in a variety of sizes ranging from about one to eight inches long. I've been using small tubes a lot in the past couple of years for sunfish. Sometimes they work better than flies or bait. Sometimes they don't.

Big creatures work well for bass and walleyes (especially on inland lakes), and they come in a host of shapes. Many are designed to suggest a crayfish, which anglers and game fish see often and are a good natural bait.

Others look like salamanders and mud puppies, which anglers don't see often but the fish probably do. Still others look like creatures from outer space, but the fish still seem to like them.

By the way, research has shown that creating an exact replica of a natural bait in a plastic lure isn't necessarily the way to go. In one test, plastic crayfish with exaggerated features like oversized claws and antennae drew more strikes than exact plastic replicas. But the most successful version didn't have claws, antennae or legs, just a crayfish-shaped body.

Spoons

The first spoon supposedly was made by Julio Buel of Whitehall, N.Y., in 1821 after he dropped a teaspoon into the water during a picnic and saw a fish flash at it as it wobbled toward the bottom. (Sounds suspiciously like James Heddon's plug invention story, doesn't it?)

The first spoons apparently were made by soldering a hook to the flattened bowl of a teaspoon, and a number of killer spoons on the market today are pretty much the same.

But leave it to fishermen to make the simple complex. Today spoons have evolved into three basic forms — casting spoons, excellent for almost every kind of game fish in the proper size; jigging spoons, good in vertical presentations, especially through the ice; and trolling spoons, which have become the standard lure all summer for salmon, lake trout, steelhead and walleyes on the Great Lakes.

Every angler's box should include a few casting spoons in a couple of sizes. Silver models in one- and three-inch sizes will take everything from brook trout to northern pike. If the pike don't want silver, try a red-and-white-striped spoon about three to five inches long. And for casting to salmon from piers or in rivers, my favorites are green and silver, blue and silver, and orange and silver, again three to four inches long.

Casting spoons come with feathers and rattles, holes that create weird sounds as the water flows through, and lifelike fish-scale patterns and eyes painted or molded into them.

They also come in different weights for different fishing situations. Light spoons are good for shallow, weedy waters and allow the anglers to skim them just over the underwater greenery. Heavy spoons will go a lot deeper.

We apparently have entered an era when you can't be too rich, too thin or have too many trolling spoons. Serious salmon and walleye anglers I fish with often own hundreds, and it's really interesting how a color that works well in Lake Erie — the elegantly named Monkey Puke, for example — won't take many fish in Lake Huron.

The truth is that when it comes to selecting trolling spoons, the answer is to talk to local fishermen and tackle shops to find out what's working in the immediate area.

Spinners

Spinners might be the single most popular lures for freshwater fishing around the world. I mostly use them in streams for trout, salmon and small-mouth bass.

In these lures, the spinner blade revolves around a central shaft. In most spinners, one end of the blade is fastened to the shaft with a clip or a small device called a clevis. In weight-forward spinners, the shaft protrudes through the top of the blade.

Both kinds work equally well, and spinners are among the best lures to use with ultralight spinning tackle because they can be cast easily and produce a lot of flash on the retrieve.

While spinner blades come in a variety of colors, I tend to stick with the plain brass or silver blades, using the brass in cloudy water and silver in clear.

The most effective way to work spinners is to cast across or slightly upstream in a river, let the current bring the lure down on a tight line until it is slightly downstream from you, then retrieve it as slowly as you can without hanging up on the bottom.

If you let the current do the work of turning the blade, you can keep the lure in the water longer and put it in front of more fish.

That's a synopsis of most of the lures that freshwater anglers use and how they use them. But while a book can offer information to get you started, the only way anyone becomes a fisherman or fisherwoman is by fishing.

Chapter 16
===

Tackle

T HE OTHER EVENING I WAS FLY-FISHING ON A SMALL STREAM near my home, a tight, brushy little creek where there's not a lot of room for a back cast. So I fished with a six-foot, four-weight bamboo rod my wife, Susan, bought me as a Christmas present years ago when we couldn't afford such an extravagance.

She had seen me handling the rod and mooning over it at what was then Dick Pobst's Orvis shop in Ada, like a 10-year-old staring at a train set in a shop window and trying to convince himself that he still believed in Santa Claus. We had a new baby and not a whole lot of anything to waste in those days, but somehow she squeezed the money out of the weekly budget, and every time I fish with that rod I can feel the love flowing from the handle and strengthening my undeserving arm like a magic spell.

As I cast a sulfur dun to brook trout rising in the gathering dusk, I thought about how I wanted to lay out this chapter about the gear we anglers use. And the more I thought about it, the more I realized the importance of the connection between our tackle and the technological roots of our ancient sport.

There are four basic kinds of modern sport-fishing tackle — fly, bait-casting, trolling and spinning. All work well in certain situations, but only spinning tackle can claim to be an all-around fishing system.

I used the word "modern" in the previous paragraph because angling for sport was around long before fishing reels and rods with line guides. Egyptian tomb scenes painted 4,000 years ago show people who seem to be fishing with a line tied to the end of a rod, and perhaps even using flies. The Chinese sage Confucius was an enthusiastic angler about 500 B.C., praising the moral virtues of the rod over the net, and the Greco-Roman historian Claudius Aelianus wrote in the Second Century A.D. about Macedonian anglers who fished with flies in fast streams for "the fish with speckled skins," almost certainly brown trout.

But it wasn't until about 1000 A.D. that the first fishing reel appeared in a Chinese painting, mounted on top of the rod, and by about 1400, Europeans were using primitive reels, called "winds" or "wynds," to store line.

English and Scottish artisans produced rude versions of modern fly reels by the late 1700s, some of them multipliers in which the spool turned several times for each turn of the reel handle, like a modern bait-casting reel.

But it was in the United States that a Kentucky watchmaker named George Snyder brought skilled craftsmanship and jeweled bearings to the mix and started the reign of the famed Kentucky reel, a product that was improved by other southern American craftsmen like the brothers Benjamin and Jonathan Meek and B.C. Milam, and New York manufacturers like Conroy and Krider.

The drawback to these reels was that they were as beautifully made and expensive as a fine watch, which kept them out of the hands of the masses. But American ingenuity, determination and the desire to make a buck being what they are, much cheaper mass-produced versions turned America into a nation of anglers after the Civil War.

When the 19th Century began, the British were still the world's best rod makers. The Royal navy and British merchant fleet ruled the waves, and colonial possessions in the Empire on Which the Sun Never Sets provided scores of exotic woods that were tried in rod-making (including hickory from the former American colonies).

British craftsmen pioneered such techniques as making multipiece rods that used different materials for different sections, perhaps stiff deal — a kind of wood — for the butt section, softer hazel for the mid-sections, and a top section of flexible yew tipped with a foot-long piece of tortoise shell or baleen, the springy whalebone also used for corset stays.

Brits also made the first strip-built bamboo rods, but they failed to develop this technology properly. American craftsmen then were much like the Japanese of 150 years later, and the Yanks looked at what the English had done, figured out how to make it better and perfected the six-sided, bamboo strip-casting and fly rods that were the best available until the invention of carbon fiber more than 100 years later.

The early British rods were remarkably long by modern standards, usually 15 to 21 feet, and they often weighed a couple of pounds. Today's anglers, accustomed to an eight- to nine-foot graphite rod that weighs four or five ounces, would find them exhausting.

Until the middle of the 19th Century, there really wasn't much difference between fly rods and bait-casting rods. With easy access to woods like ash and yew (rare in Great Britain by 1850), Americans made rods that were cheaper and cast better. And when they combined them with their fine-casting Kentucky reels, the Americans were able to bring down the length, as well.

In the late 1800s, James Henshall, one of the patron saints of late 19th Century American angling, introduced a revolutionary, one-piece wooden bait-casting rod that was only eight feet, three inches long, and by 1900 many companies were selling bait-casters as short as six feet.

Something similar was happening in the fly-fishing industry, based in New

York City and New England. Rod manufacturers like Samuel Phillippe, Charles Murphy, H.L. Leonard and Charles Orvis so far surpassed the English makers that the Americans by 1900 were turning out split bamboo fly rods that weighed half as much as English rods and cast 50 percent farther.

It was a tradition that flowered in the 1940s and '50s under individual masters like Paul Young, whose Detroit shop was part artisan's atelier, part cracker-barrel store; and Lyle Dickerson, Wes Garrison and Ed Payne. It reached its zenith in the 1960s, when semi-mass marketers like the Orvis Co. and Thomas & Thomas turned out thousands of fabulous cane rods that might not have had the cachet of a Garrison or Young but cast just as well.

The tradition continues to this day, with brilliant rod makers like Bob Summers of Traverse City and Leon Hanson of Plymouth turning out handmade masterpieces that bamboo fanatics will wait two or three years to receive and consider a bargain at $1,500.

But few anglers use bamboo or wooden rods of any kind now. In fact, even the cheapest rods are usually made from carbon fiber (graphite), usually mixed with varying amounts of fiberglass.

I was about four years old when Shakespeare Co. introduced the first fiberglass rods in 1947. They were one of fishing's greatest success stories, and they were so cheap to produce that soon after we moved to this country from Scotland I was the proud possessor of two — a fly rod and a bait-casting rod.

For an 11-year-old who would ride a bike three hours to fish for one, the glass rods were magic. They didn't break like bamboo or kink like metal, and they wouldn't rot or rust if you left them underwater for 10 years. They were top-heavy, flexed miserably by today's standards and took some getting used to, but they were far superior to everything except handcrafted rods I never could have afforded anyway.

The good news for today's anglers is that the rods they can buy for $20 are as far ahead of those old Shakespeare Wonderods as the Wonderods were ahead of the stuff they replaced. And on a corrected-for-inflation basis, today's rods cost a fraction as much.

But relatively few fiberglass rods are sold today. It's one of the ironies of our sport that fiberglass casting, spinning and fly rods, which helped get the masses fishing, are now mostly dime-store items for small children, or come from specialty makers who get premium prices for one.

When it comes to fishing rods, pure fiberglass has gone the way of the vinyl record, and the graphite rod is the fishing equivalent of the music CD. And it looks as if graphite will be the material of the future, largely because it works so well that it's hard to see why we would want to use anything else.

I remember when manufacturers tried to get us to abandon perfectly good carbon-fiber rods in favor of new stuff called boron. Every major rod maker jumped on the bandwagon and came out with a boron rod that cost 50 percent more than the previous top models.

These cannons would blast a fly line out 100 feet and a lure 200, but they had all the delicacy of a broomstick. Despite the hype, anglers recognized that these things just didn't feel right, and it took only a couple of years for boron to go away.

What's next? I'm not sure there will be a next for a while. I thought matrix material — ceramics laid in a graphite base — might make a move, but the graphite rods are so light that there's not much point in going to a far more expensive material. (Light weight is why matrix materials are getting so much attention from bicycle and automotive manufacturers.)

Meanwhile, I'll fish my carbon-fiber spinning, bait-casting and fly rods most of the time and delight in their lightness and efficiency. But every now and then, I'll take that little Orvis bamboo rod out of its aluminum tube just to feel the magic.

Bait casting

We'll start with bait-casting equipment, because it's the most American of currently used angling techniques.

Bait-casting tackle was named back in the early 1800s when reel makers like George Snyder and the Meek brothers started turning out finely machined reels that could throw live baits like worms and frogs long distances without killing or dismembering them.

Today, bait-casting tackle is used to cast artificial lures like plugs and plastics 99 percent of the time, but the lures are still called baits and the reels bait-casters.

Bait-casting reels also are called revolving spool reels. The line is stored on a horizontal spool, and the spool revolves as the lure or bait is cast or retrieved. Even the cheapest reels today are level-wind models, with a small guide at the front that shuttles back and forth as the line is retrieved, laying the line on the spool evenly and preventing it from piling up in one spot.

Bait-casting rods have undergone more changes in length than women's skirts. Back 120 years ago, people routinely used bait-casting reels on 10- to 14-foot rods. Twenty years ago the fad was for short rods, five- to six-footers that had all of the sensitivity of a pool cue. Today, most anglers use six- to seven-foot bait-casting rods, which offer the advantages of longer casts, increased leverage when playing a fish and more forgiveness for errors on the part of the fisherman.

Bait-casting rods have smaller guides than spinning rods. That's because the line comes straight out of the small opening (usually less than a half-inch in diameter) on the reel's level-wind mechanism. By comparison, the line comes off a spinning reel's fixed spool in big loops. The first couple of guides on a spinning rod are often one inch in diameter to gather the line and lead it up the rod.

The bait-casting system requires the angler first to overcome the inertia of the spool at rest, and the small line guides produce a lot of drag. The result is a rod and reel that will cast a lure of a given weight a considerably shorter distance than a spinning rod, although bait-casting reels made in the past 10 years are so wonderfully machined they can cast about twice as far as many earlier reels.

Bait-casting rods usually have a shorter handle than spinning rods. That's because the angler normally wraps the hand on his casting arm around the reel and the rod grip while retrieving line and playing a fish.

A big change in bait-casting reels in recent years is the introduction of low-profile models that fit the hand much more comfortably. Most of my bait-caster reels are Ambassadeurs from Sweden that have the old high, round shape. I have fairly large hands, so I never gave the profile question much thought. But after recently using a new Cabela's low-profile model for a week and a similar Pflueger Trion, I found them lighter, a lot more comfortable to hold and less tiring on the hands.

Bait-casting gear lost most of its popularity when European spin fishing tackle was introduced to the United States after World War II. Bait-casting equipment required some hours of training, and even experienced anglers occasionally created horrible bird's-nest snarls when they let their attention wander. Most people could learn to cast a spinning rig in five minutes, and even if they made mistakes, serious tangles were rare.

But bait-casting rigs maintained a strong following among bass anglers because they can cast a lure with pinpoint accuracy, throw big artificial baits with relatively short rods, and their big gear ratios (as much as 6:1) give anglers a lot of power to crank in a fish and retrieve line quickly.

In addition, manufacturers devised internal magnetic braking systems that make the spool slow down much more smoothly and greatly reduce the odds of an overrun. The angler can set the magnets at a high level to start, which cuts the casting distance but can make the chances of a snarl so unlikely that it's not necessary to keep a thumb on the spool (to stop the spool spinning as soon as the bait hits the water.)

As he develops expertise and becomes more confident, the angler can dial down the magnet settings — moving the braking magnets away from the spool end — and make longer casts.

I still keep three or four bait-casting rods rigged up, six- to seven-footers I prefer for throwing spinner baits, buzz baits, pike spoons and deep-diving, big-lipped plugs that put a lot of strain on the line. I also use them anytime I fish in heavy cover like thick weeds or downed timber, and they double as light trolling reels.

Less than 10 years ago, the most expensive bait-casting reels cost about $60 and the top rods were $50. Then tackle companies realized that an angler who will drop $35,000 on a boat and motor also will spend a lot of money on other gear, so we have been treated in the past few years to a seemingly non-stop introduction of $150 to $400 bait-casting reels and $200 to $400 rods.

That kind of tackle is nice but not necessary, and there are a batch of excellent rods and reels in the $50 to $100 range that will last the average angler for life — or until he gets the bug to buy something new.

Spin fishing

Most casual anglers own one or two fishing rods. If I were one of those people, it would be a $30 to $50, six-foot carbon-fiber spinning rod designed to cast four- to 10-pound line. I would mate it to a $30 to $50 spinning reel that came with two spools, filling one of the spools with four-pound monofilament line I would use for bluegills, perch and walleyes in open water, and the other with eight-pound braided line I would use for bass, pike and jigging.

When the French-made Airex and Mitchell spinning reels were introduced to the United States in the late 1940s, they revolutionized angling. Suddenly, people who couldn't cast 10 feet without creating a tangle that could only be fixed with a machete could join their expert friends in the fishing boat and enjoy the trip.

Open-faced spinning reels have been around since the early 1900s, when British angler and inventor Alfred Illingworth came up with the Illingworth reel, which apparently was derived from the fixed-bobbin spindles in cloth spinning factories.

The factory systems were designed to let thread pull off a fixed (non-revolving) spindle by the shuttle of a weaving loom. Illingworth realized that by adding a revolving pickup arm, he could also wind line back onto the fixed spool.

The problem in the early days wasn't with the reels but with the lines, mostly made from braided cotton or linen. They could make long casts with light lures and natural baits using very fine lines, but when it came to the bigger lures used by American anglers for bass, walleyes and pike, the spinning reel wasn't much good.

Then came the invention of nylon line, the progenitor of today's monofilaments, and suddenly spinning reels could not only cast tremendous distances, they could cast amazingly tiny and effective lures called spinners for everything from bluegills to salmon.

Walk into any tackle shop today and you'll see five or six spinning reels for every bait-casting reel, and anglers can drop $500 to $800 on top-quality saltwater spinning reels made to handle marlin and tuna. But superb reels can be had for $40 to $80 (I have been particularly impressed by the Pflueger Trion, Abu Garcia and Metaloid reels), and a few dollars more buys a spare spool that can be loaded with a different-weight line and put on the reel in a few seconds.

Illingworth's original reel, and several that were turned out by competitors, used a small metal arm that revolved around the spool. The angler lifted the line off a notch in the arm to cast, and after casting, he used his index finger to lift the line back into the groove. As he turned the reel handle, the little arm spun around the fixed spool and wound the line on it. Manufacturers later replaced the notch arm with a U-shaped piece of metal call a bail, which was fixed at both ends to a cup that surrounded the base of the spool.

They added a couple of gears and cams, and now the angler could pull the bail back until it locked against a spring. After he cast, he merely had to turn the reel handle to make the bail flip back to a position where it automatically picked up the line and laid it on the spool.

Interestingly, a top-of-the-line spinning reel that sells for more than $700 and is made for big saltwater species has dispensed with the automatic bail and gone back to Illingworth's old notch-and-finger system. The manufacturer says the simpler system eliminates several mechanical bits that could break and cost the angler a trophy fish.

I suspect bait-casting rods will continue to lose their popularity, largely because there is less reason for using them. While bait-casting reels once had decided power advantages, modern spinning reels come in such a huge variety of sizes and gear ratios that they have largely eliminated the difference.

In addition, given similar line and lure weights, a spinning reel will out-cast a bait-casting rig by a considerable distance, especially spinning reels with the new, tapered, long-cast spools. They look amazingly like the tapered factory-thread bobbins that gave Illingworth the idea in the first place.

The ascent of the spinning rig is perhaps best illustrated by looking at the touring bass pros. Twenty years ago, many didn't have a spinning rod on their boats and looked at spin fishing as something fit only for kids and effete Yankees. Today, every pro has a full complement of spinning rods alongside his bait-casting tackle.

Spinning rods also have evolved with the reels. There was a trend about 20 years ago to shorter and lighter sticks, but that turned around in the 1990s, and most rods now are six to eight feet long, with a growing trend toward nine- to 10-footers like those popular in Europe. Good spinning rods are available at even cheaper prices than good bait-casting rods. While I own several spinning rods that sell for more than $200, the ones I use most days average about $60.

I own a batch of spinning rods in lengths ranging from four to 12 feet. I use the four-footer to fish small, brushy streams for trout and bass. It's designed to cast two- to eight-pound line and works perfectly in places where the tree branches are sometimes only a foot over my head.

I use the 12-footer to fish from the shores of lakes, mostly for big carp but sometimes for bass and pike. Designed for eight- to 20-pound line, it will cast a two-ounce lure or bait 100 yards without much effort, allows me to cover an immense amount of water and has the muscle to drag a large fish out of a weed bed 50 yards away.

But one of my favorite rods is a slender 10-footer designed for four- to 10-pound line. It's much stiffer than the Michigan-developed noodle rod, which means I can cast with it fairly well.

Rigged with a spinning reel loaded with four-pound line, it's a wonderful rod for steelhead. I can fish good holding lies while wading by reaching out, dropping the lure gently into the water and holding the rod tip over the lure as it drifts downstream.

And yet this is also one of my favorite rods when wading the shorelines of lakes for bluegills and perch. Once again, the 10-foot length lets me reach out and lay the lure gently into openings in the weeds, and it is sensitive enough that I can feel the most subtle takes.

For bass and walleyes, I usually pick a six- to seven-foot spinning rod, and I base the selection on the kind of cover we'll be fishing. If it's dense weeds or around underwater snags where abrasion is a problem, I want a stout rod designed for 14- to 20-pound line. In open water, I choose a rod that lets me cast eight- or even six-pound line.

Spin cast

Spin-cast reels came along in the 1950s, and I suspect they were born not out of need but from the craze for anything push-button that symbolized modernity in that era.

Spin-cast reels try to combine the above-the-handle feel of a bait-casting system with the simplicity of a spinning rig, and as is usually the case in such forced marriages, the result isn't very pleasant.

The popular theory seems to be that spin-cast reels are good for children because all they have to do is push a button, hold it and let the button go as they bring the rod forward to cast. I've found that most kids older than about seven can learn to use an open-faced spinning reel just as easily, but a lot of spin-cast equipment has a place among small children.

Most spin-cast reels I've owned — and seen other people use — seem to have more problems with line that gets tangled around the inside components than do open-faced spinning reels.

Trolling

Trolling reels and rods look like oversized bait-casting rigs, but they are not meant to be cast.

Instead, the angler flips a switch on the side of the reel, which allows the spool to spin freely, and lets the weight of the lure and the current caused by the boat's forward motion pull out line to the desired distance.

Today, that's a lot easier to figure out because many trolling reels are equipped with digital or mechanical line counters that make the angler far more efficient.

For example, an angler can let out a spoon on 50 feet of line on one rod, 40 feet on another and 30 feet on a third. He can send those lines out to the sides of the boat on planer boards. If he consistently gets hits on the spoon 30 feet back, he can set the other lures at the same distance simply by looking at the counter.

Line counters also are handy when bringing in fish to the net. The angler knows at a glance how far off the fish is, and the closer it gets, the more cautious he knows he has to be.

Trolling rods tend to be more flexible than bait-casting and spinning rods. That's because they must absorb the impact of a large fish that might hit the lure at high speed while moving in the opposite direction of the boat. A more flexible rod helps absorb the shock and prevent the line from breaking.

Because of that need for flexibility, the trolling market is one place where all-fiberglass rods are still held in high esteem and used for everything from chinook salmon to walleyes.

Many anglers like trolling rods seven to eight feet long, which helps control a big muskellunge or salmon as it's being led alongside the cockpit to be netted. That's especially important in boats with a high freeboard.

Fly tackle

It's one of the most discouraging sights I know: I'm sitting at a sports show or fishing lodge, and I see a man coming toward me with a small, narrow wooden box he cradles with all the reverence of a medieval monk carrying the bones of a saint.

I know what he's going to tell me next: His grandfather/father/Uncle Harry brought this delicate bamboo fly rod back from World War II, and since he has read that old bamboo rods cost so much, could I please tell him the value of this rare gem.

When I answer that it's worth about $2.95, assuming the hinges on the box aren't broken, I know what's coming next: a look of terrible disappointment, for which I'm to blame, or a look of disbelief and disgust aimed at someone who is obviously trying to rip off an objet d'art — namely me.

It's true that some old bamboo rods sell for more than $2,500 and a few for more than $5,000, but only those made by the greatest of the American masters in the heyday of bamboo rod-making, which ran from about 1930 to about 1960. A porcelain Easter egg handmade by Faberge in 1880 for a Russian nobleman is worth more than $1 million. A plastic Easter egg turned out by the millions by the American Widget Co. in 1957 might be worth 98 cents.

The same is true of bamboo fly rods. A rod handcrafted by a maestro like Lyle Dickerson in his Detroit shop in 1939 might go for $5,000 or more. A crude imitation turned out by the thousands at the Yokohama Fly Rod and Chopstick Co. in 1953 for sale to gullible American GIs is virtually worthless.

Like George Orwell's pigs, not all bamboos are equal. High-quality fly rods are made from Tonkin cane, which grows only in a relatively small part of China. Those cheap Japanese rods are made from stuff that will convince even the most casual observer that bamboo is indeed a member of the grass family.

Even fine European rods made by Hardy of England and Pezon et Michel of France from Tonkin cane are usually worth only a few hundred dollars at most, often less than the angler paid for them new.

But few anglers fish with bamboo fly rods anymore, even those who can afford them. The reason is simple: As a fishing tool, they are inferior to a top-quality graphite rod.

I know this will sound like heresy to some, but as the owner of a half-dozen superb bamboo rods, I know they don't cast as far, don't signal strikes as well and can't match the pinpoint accuracy of my good graphite rods.

I still fish with bamboo sometimes because there is a feel to it, a delicacy that graphite can't match. But I stopped pulling the wool over my own eyes a long time ago, leaving that for the tackle makers who never stop trying to convince me to dump perfectly good rods and reels and buy new ones I neither need nor want.

Graphite is wonderful stuff. This is something else the British invented, but the Americans were first off the mark when using it for fishing rods. It wasn't until about five years ago that the Brits started selling carbon-fiber fly rods as good as our models. (And that technology came out of the British coarse fishing industry, where anglers will spend $1,000 for rods designed to catch carp and a lot of small fish that all look like suckers to us.)

Fly-fishing has long suffered from innate snobbery. In the early years of its American flowering — the late 19th Century — it cost a lot of money for decent tackle and to travel to places trout lived. Early American fly anglers also imitated their peers in England, where only the elite were allowed to fly-fish for salmon and trout, and the hoi poloi had to make do with such lowly critters as tench and rudd.

Michigan doesn't fit that mold, probably in large part because blue-collar workers here were among the first in the nation to be paid so well that they could not only afford the occasional trip to trout country, they could afford summer homes there. Michigan also has long offered exceptional public access to thousands of miles of trout streams, something that isn't true in most states.

That's why some of the best-known American trout flies were invented here, the Adams and the Roberts drake and the Madsen skunk, and why we have far more fly anglers than any other state (although they still comprise only about 15 percent of the angling population).

If you want to become a fly angler, you couldn't live in a better state. Even people who live in Detroit can be fishing for trout in Paint Creek in Oakland County within 45 minutes of leaving home, and numerous streams in southeast Michigan offer superb fly-fishing for smallmouth bass (the Huron is probably the best).

If I were going to fly-fish in Michigan and could have only one rod, I would buy a nine-foot, seven-weight graphite. A whole batch of superb rods like this are available for about $60, and if you have $100 to $125 to spend, you can buy a rod from Temple Fork, Redington, St. Croix, Orvis and a dozen other companies that will outperform rods we paid $350 for 10 years ago.

My personal feeling is that a seven-weight is a little heavy for most trout fishing, but novices usually find it's easier to cast a heavier line like a seven-weight than a light line like a four-weight. If you overload the rod slightly with an eight-weight line, it will toss a big, air-resistant bass bug pretty well, and that's also a good line for fishing steelhead and smaller salmon (although you had better have some expertise to tackle a 20-pound chinook with one.)

You also can have a good time with that rod by taking it to the local county or city park and tossing poppers at sunfish, one of the best ways I know for anglers to develop the timing needed to set the hook on a trout.

Once you develop some casting skills, you might want another rod. My advice is to go lighter, say a seven-foot, four-weight that will turn 12-inch brown trout, nine-inch bluegill and 12-inch smallmouth bass into raging monsters.

The problem most fly fishermen face is that they don't fish enough to develop real casting expertise. I was fishing recently at a place in Canada where Joe Arterburn, a Cabela's PR guy, brought one of that company's new 10-weight rods.

We took it on the lawn where Bryan Watts, a full-time redfish guide and professional tournament fisherman from Florida, and Bill Buckley, a photographer from Bozeman, Mont., and I were soon laying out 90- to 100-foot casts.

It was fun to watch Watts and Buckley casting, but they cast so well not because they have superior reflexes or musculature, but because they love to fly-fish, and there have been periods in their lives when they did more casting in a month than the average angler does in five years.

My home lies between the headwaters of the Manistee and the Au Sable rivers, and I can be on either stream or a half-dozen smaller ones in five to 15 minutes. I also carry a couple of fly rods in the car as I travel around the state. As a result, I probably get to fly-fish an average of three days a week from April to October.

Some days I can get out only for an hour or so, but it adds up to more than 80 excursions a year, and when you get to put in that much practice, you have to develop at least a modicum of ability. A lot of fly-casting is simply timing and muscle memory, and the more you do it, the better you get.

But what anglers need to learn is that fly-casting is only one part of fly-fishing. There's also stream craft, which includes learning how to get into good casting position without spooking fish, learning where fish are likely to lie, and figuring out what fly they are most likely to eat.

When you buy a rod, you'll also need a line and something to hold it while you're fishing.

Fly lines are expensive. They also are far more important than the line in other forms of fishing. For example, one of my favorite spinning rods casts almost as well with four-pound line as with 10-pound. But if I were to replace the five-weight line on one of my favorite fly rods with a 10-weight, the thing would be almost unusable.

Fly lines aren't measured by their breaking strain but by the weight of the first 30 feet of line. The first 30 feet of a four-weight line weighs 120 grains, a six-weight weighs 160 grains and an eight-weight weighs 210 grains.

That might not seem like much in absolute terms. The 90-grain difference between a four-weight and eight-weight is only two-tenths of an ounce. But in relative terms it's a difference of 75 percent, which makes an enormous difference in the way the rod performs.

Line weight is so important in fly-fishing because while we say we are casting a fly, what we really cast is the line. The fly on the end of the leader just goes along for the ride.

My advice to novices is to start with a weight-forward line, which cheats a bit by concentrating a little more weight in the first 30 feet. That small additional weight, swung back and forth at the end of a nine-foot rod, helps load (bend) the rod and build kinetic energy in the graphite fibers that make it up.

When those fibers straighten out, the line is shot forward and backward. (Remember, fly-casters make false casts in both directions to build up line speed and kinetic energy.) The angler has to coordinate that bending and straightening of the rod to put as much energy as possible into the job of sending the line and fly where he wants it to go.

Another piece of advice I give novices is to get out and cast at their homes (on the grass, not on the concrete or asphalt driveway, which will eat up the coating on a fly line). As in any other finesse sport, practice makes perfect. Exceptional casters have the basics down so well they can pay little attention to the mechanics of casting and concentrate instead on the fish they are casting to and the place they want to drop the fly in the current.

Finally, there's the question of a reel on which to store the line. Years ago, people argued that there was no point in spending a lot of money on a reel because it's only a place to store the line you aren't using to cast.

There was some truth in that, because even large trout usually don't make long runs. (By large in Michigan, I mean fish bigger than two pounds.) So a high-quality drag like those on reels used for saltwater species like bonefish, which can smoke off 100 yards of line faster than an Olympic track star, weren't deemed necessary.

But then Michigan anglers began fly-fishing for salmon, and they learned that a big chinook can melt line off a reel so fast the drag becomes useless, and without a working drag, it's really tough to stop a big, powerful fish.

If you're going to fly-fish mostly for species like trout and smallmouth bass, fish that don't make big runs, there are a lot of excellent reels on the market starting about $25 and running to $75. My advice to most newcomers with limited budgets is that if it comes down to a choice, buy a cheaper reel so you can put a little more money into a better line.

If you're willing to shell out $100 to $120, you can buy reels that will stand up to anything you'll find in Michigan, or in fresh water anywhere, for that matter, and a lot of smaller saltwater species as well (bonefish included).

And remember, it's fun to talk about fly-fishing, but it's a lot more fun to do it. I regularly get calls from people who say they are about to spend $500 on another rod and want my advice on which brand they should select.

I've ticked off more than one by suggesting that they spend $150 on a nice Temple Fork or Redington and use the $350 they save to take a fishing trip to the Pere Marquette, Manistee, Au Sable or some other river where they might actually learn to catch some trout.

Spinning and bait-casting lines

The first fishing lines I can remember were made of black cotton. Nylon lines were available, but no one would spend that kind of money on fishing tackle for a kid.

The cotton lines were so thick they cast miserably, snarled if you looked at them wrong and exhibited the tensile strength of a spider web if you forgot to dry them before putting the reel away for the winter.

Nevertheless, we caught fish on those lines, lots of them, and I think the limitations imposed on us by our lines and rudimentary gear helped make us better anglers by teaching that strategy and stealth were more important than tackle.

Today, when I walk into a place like Lakeside Fishing Shop in St. Clair Shores or the huge Cabela's or Bass Pro Shops, I see entire walls of fishing line, and I'm amazed not just by the number of brands available but by number of materials we can choose from.

Cotton is gone, but Dacron is still there for anglers who like to use it as backing, or even for trolling in some offshore saltwater applications. There are nylon monofilaments, braided lines, fused lines and some that apparently will scale and fillet the fish before they get into the boat, if you go by the superlatives on the boxes.

Let's try to clear up some of the confusion for people who wonder what all the hype is about.

Dacron has been around for about 60 years, and today it's mostly used as backing for fly lines and for offshore trollers who target species like marlin and tuna and need to fill a reel with 1,000 yards of something.

In each of these instances, the Dacron is used because it's cheap, and the business end of the fishing rig is something else, either 35 yards of fly line with a monofilament leader, or 250 to 300 yards of mono on the trolling rig.

Monofilaments have been around since DuPont made the first nylon line 60 years ago. Nearly all are still made from nylon, and today's monofilaments can be bought in line strengths ranging from one pound to more than 150 pounds and in densities ranging from super-limp to super-stiff.

Monofilaments are the line of choice for most people and most kinds of fishing. They work well on spinning or bait-casting reels, they're cheap (especially if you buy bulk spools of 500 yards or more), and the new fluorocarbon monofilaments are almost invisible underwater.

Many people are surprised to learn that high-quality monofilament lines used by anglers who try to set world fishing records are guaranteed to break under a pressure that is no greater than the rated strength of the line.

That's because the angler has to send a sample of line to the sanctioning organizations, the International Game Fish Association or the National Fresh Water Fishing Hall of Fame. If a line that's submitted for a two-pound test record is shown to have a breaking strength of 2.4 pounds, the catch is bumped up to the four-pound class, where the fish might not beat the existing record.

Braided lines are made from multiple modern fibers like Spectra or Kevlar, stuff that pound for pound is stronger than steel. They are very supple, and one of their benefits (the one most anglers don't talk about) is the ability to remove snarls in bait-casting reels much easier than with monofilaments.

Braided lines are getting competition from cheaper fused lines, which are made from the same fibers as braided lines but are fused into a single strand that is basically a super-monofilament. Braided lines and fused lines share one drawback: Both are susceptible to abrasions and nicks far more than most monofilaments. If even a couple of strands of a braided line are cut, or the exterior skin of a fused line, it loses a great deal of strength.

People use braided or fused lines mainly because they are much thinner than monofilament of equivalent breaking strain. It's common to see a package of braided line marked with a phrase like "eight-pound test, two-pound diameter," and the small size of braided lines has made the whole issue of line test a bit confused.

I would like to see us adopt the European system in which lines are measured not by their breaking strain but by their diameter. Fly-fishermen have used this system for years to describe the size of their leaders, listing them from 0X to 8X diameter rather than listing them in pounds of breaking strength, which is really of importance only to people who seek records.

That's because fly-fishermen know that the most important factor often is how visible the end of the leader is to the trout, and that changing to 6X leader can bring strikes from fish that have ignored flies tied on with 4X. And through the years anglers learned that 2X leaders were usually about 10-pound breaking strain, 4X about five pounds, 8X about one pound. That's changed a bit in the past 10 years, with many 4X leaders offering seven to eight pounds of strength as leader manufacturers got access to monofilaments manufactured by new processes. But the key is still diameter, and I would much rather fish a 6X leader that tests two pounds than a 4X that tests eight, if the former draws more strikes.

Smaller lines not only are harder for fish to see, they cast lures farther, and they let a lure sink faster and deeper. A lure that runs 10 feet deep with a 10-pound test braided line might only get down six feet if the angler uses 10-pound monofilament that's twice as thick.

The thinner diameter of braided and fused lines means it takes more line to fill the spool, and since braided and fused lines cost two to four times as much as monofilament, that could get expensive. That's why many anglers fill most of the spool on big spinning reels, which might hold 250 to 350 yards of line, with a cheaper monofilament and top it off with 100 to 150 feet of braided or fused line. Bait-casting reels usually hold much less line than spinning reels, so anglers often fill them completely with braided line to lengthen their casting distance.

Some argue that braided lines aren't really more expensive in the long run, because one spool of braided line usually lasts three or four times as long as monofilament, at least for anglers who change line as often as they should.

Let's talk about line stretch. A low-stretch, premium monofilament line stretches about 10 percent at maximum load when wet. Many inexpensive monofilament lines will stretch 20 to 25 percent. That means if you cast out 100 feet of 10-pound test mono with a 10-percent stretch factor, it will elongate to about 110 feet before it breaks. If it has a 20-percent stretch factor, it will stretch to about 120 feet.

You'll sometimes hear people say this inherent stretch factor results in a lot of lost fish when the angler tries to set the hook, but most of the time that isn't true.

First, an angler who pulls back on the rod to set the hook on a strike rarely comes anywhere near the maximum breaking strain of the line.

If I give a quick upward jerk on the rod when I feel a four-pound bass hit a spinner bait, I probably put a pound or so of pressure on the line. If you don't believe me, tie a good fish scale to a door handle, loop the line around the hook on the scale and see how much pressure you have to apply to make it read one pound.

Most of the time the bend in the rod will exceed the amount of stretch in the line. And a small amount of stretch is often a good thing, especially when trolling, because it greatly reduces the odds the line will break.

Second, most of the quarry we fish for are relatively small, less than 10 pounds, and the impact of the strike will move the fish a couple of feet through the water even if the angler manages to apply only a couple of pounds of pressure.

Third, if I'm trolling for salmon or steelhead in the Great Lakes and a big fish hits my lure while going 15 to 20 miles an hour in the opposite direction from the boat, there had better be some give in that line and bend in the rod, or the line will snap like sewing thread.

But there are occasions when stretch is bad. For example, if I hook a 20-pound salmon with 50 feet of 12-pound line while wading the Au Sable River, and that fish decides to head downstream, there's no way I can stop it by screwing down on the drag. The fish would break the line, so all I can do is apply about 11 pounds of pressure and hope it's enough to convince the fish to stop or turn.

But if that line has, say, 20 percent of stretch, the salmon will gain another eight or 10 feet when I use the reel drag and my thumb on the spool and push the line near its maximum breaking strain. That might be enough for the fish to wrap the line under or around a snag. So for this kind of fishing I'll probably go with a low-stretch mono behind 100 feet of fluorocarbon, which is not only less visible but stretches less than standard monofilament.

Another place I don't want to see stretch is when fishing for bass in thick weeds. This kind of fishing usually involves heavy line, 20- to 30-pound test, because the trick to landing fish is to stop them from going anywhere as soon as they strike.

If I hook a four-pound bass in this situation, usually while fishing with a six- to seven-foot bait-casting rod, I'm going to rear up and back with that rod as hard as I can, trying to get the fish to the surface before it can wrap up in the greenery. If the fish can gain a couple of feet of line from stretch because I'm pulling against the weight of the weeds as well as the weight of the bass, chances are it will get farther down in the vegetation and wrap the line around the bases of the plant stems or some other underwater obstacle where I'll never get it out.

In that case, I'll use a braided or fused super-line, and I won't be surprised if I occasionally break a rod.

Low-stretch lines also are handy in places where anglers can take advantage of another factor that usually accompanies low stretch — extreme sensitivity.

I like braided lines for jig-fishing for walleyes in places like the Detroit River, where these super-lines not only telegraph subtle takes by fish but help me feel the movement of the jig on the bottom and even determine whether it's on rocks or a soft substrate.

Chapter 17

Gadgets

ONE OF THE REGULAR QUESTIONS PEOPLE ASK OUTDOORS writers is, "What kind of GPS should I buy?" And a lot of people seem surprised when I say that the first thing they should look for in an electronic navigation unit is simplicity.

Let me give you an example why. A friend and I were fishing in his boat and found a little hump on the bottom of Lake Erie where the walleyes were as thick as fleas. Sonar showed that it was a tiny ridge of rubble, about two feet high, six feet wide and 40 feet long, on what was otherwise an almost featureless sand flat in 21 feet of water three miles from the nearest land.

There were lots of walleyes, something we confirmed with an underwater television camera, but we couldn't get them to bite.

We marked the spot, then left and fished elsewhere for a couple of hours with no success. Then we got a hit and landed a three-pounder. In the next 30 minutes, one of us caught a fish almost every time we spotted a couple of hooks on the fish finder. It was obvious the mysterious voice that suddenly tells fish, "Hey, it's time to eat," had spoken, and we turned to each other and said at the same time, "Let's get back to that hump."

My friend fiddled with his global positioning system for a few minutes, then turned and said with obvious embarrassment, "You know, I can never remember how to use most of the features on this thing. I marked the spot where the hump was, but now I can't remember how to bring the numbers up again so we can run back to it."

He fishes only a couple of times a month, and the GPS required a few steps to bring up the way point we had marked, and he couldn't remember the sequence.

Finding that hump without a GPS would have been nearly impossible. Even if we had some bearings on day marks or shore-side landmarks (which we didn't), it could have taken hours to locate it by using the depth finder.

Fortunately, his GPS was made by the same company that made my hand-held GPS, and by playing with some buttons I found the missing way point so we could return to the hump. We had an excellent evening and caught a couple of dozen walleyes in less than two hours.

Virtually every GPS sold today will give you an excellent position number. Most will be within 30 feet of where you are or want to go, and even the most rudimentary will get you within 100 feet.

But think about some of the other gadgets you own that have features you rarely use. How many of you could program the time on your VCR or DVD player without looking at the manual? How many of you can change the ink cartridges on your computer printer without looking at the cheat sheet pasted inside the little door?

The best GPS in the world is useless if you can't remember how to make it function. And for most people, simplicity of operation is far more valuable than gee-whiz stuff they will never use (like the ability to plot the effects of current off the coast of Alaska).

This is a good moment to emphasize that a GPS must be used in conjunction with a far more ancient navigation device — a map or chart, even if it's an electronically generated map or chart stored inside the GPS or electronic chart plotter.

Suppose your GPS shows that you are at Point A in Lake Huron, 15 miles from the nearest land and 21 miles from the place you want to go. But that doesn't tell you what's under your boat, or any obstacles, ranging from a floating buoy to a shallow sandbar to a mile-long point of land, between you and your destination.

I once towed in another boater who had smashed up his out-drive by running over a shallow rock reef. He was relatively new to boating and new to the Detroit River. When he decided to run across to Canada, he had plotted a straight course from A to B on the GPS.

Unfortunately, that course took him right across one of the most notorious rock piles in the Downriver area. But he didn't have a chart on board, so he never looked to see if the water along his beeline were deep enough for his boat. As I said earlier, a GPS can show you where you are and where you want to go. But unless you have a chart to plot those positions, you can't tell if they are in the middle of Lake Huron or on the brink of Niagara Falls.

Today, for $100 or less, you can buy a satellite-based, hand-held GPS that not only shows latitude and longitude (in two or three user-selectable formats), it reveals your speed, heading, bearing to where you want to go, bearing to your starting point, distance to the target, distance you've come and a batch of other data you will rarely, if ever, use.

For less than $300, you can buy hand-held or mounted units that not only display those numbers but have maps — or charts if you're on the water — that mark your position with a little arrow or a cursor.

On the Magellan Gold hand-held I'm using, I can zoom out or in on the map to display my position in a state, or a country, for that matter. That's handy on a long driving trip, or for the last 100 yards to my deer stand, when I would be trying to find the right darned tree in the dark.

In addition to the land-based maps, my Magellan unit shows the buoys, lights and day marks for all the coastal and inland waters in the United States, although it doesn't have true marine charts that show water depth.

But I can get those from CDs or the Internet, or I could buy a specialized Magellan hand-held marine GPS that has all of the marine charts in its memory.

You don't even need a dedicated GPS anymore. I like the Magellan Gold because of its map display, water-tightness, rubber-armored body and many other features, but I also own a Magellan unit that plugs into my Handspring Visor PDA and turns the Visor into a GPS.

It sells for about $150 and is a great unit for people who mostly want to find their way in a car. Several times now, friends have given me the GPS coordinates of their hunting camps or hard-to-find homes on country roads. Instead of counting driveways from the last right turn or looking for the two white birches, I just let the Visor-Magellan be my guide. And as a bonus, the screen on the Visor is much larger than the screen on most hand-held GPS units, almost as big as the screen on many mounted units.

So if you can buy a good hand-held for $100 to $350, why spend as much or more for a unit you mount in your boat? The answer is easy — features. First, the bigger screens on mounted units are usually easier to read and display information in better detail. Second, you can run a color screen without worrying that it will eat up your batteries (nearly all of the hand-helds use replaceable AAs). And third, the bigger mounted units have a lot more memory, which means more and better maps.

Units sold these days come with 12 channels. They can pick up signals from as many as 12 satellites at the same time, although it's a rare day when more than six are on your side of the planet and high enough above the horizon for your unit to recognize them.

A 12-channel unit uses three or four satellites at a time to get a fix — one to coordinate time signals and two or three to plot bearings. If it can read four channels, you can get a reading that includes your altitude. If it can read only three, you get ground position. The GPS chooses the three or four best signals from all of the satellites it is reading.

It's hard to imagine that it was less than 20 years ago, but I once navigated a boat for the legendary Bob Magoon, a former world champion offshore powerboat racer, in an effort to set a Miami-New York speed record.

I don't like to think of that trip very often. Suffice it to say, the weather bureau got the prediction very wrong, and at one point we were driving the 45-footer so hard through six- to eight-foot seas at 70 miles an hour that we shattered the half-inch lexan cockpit cover. (I still remember staring out into the dark Atlantic 80 miles off Jacksonville, Fla., bracing as each big wave broke and listening to Magoon standing at the wheel and humming the theme from "Chariots of Fire.")

The jagged, broken pieces of the cockpit cover were threatening to decapitate us, so we stopped while Bob Saccenti, another world champion driver, and I climbed onto the foredeck and cleared away the wreckage. Needless to say, the loran unit had packed it in under the pounding about two hours into the trip, and the barrels of water that poured into the boat with every wave found their way through numerous cracks in the decks and shorted out all of our radios. (This was before GPS was available.)

Magoon, ever the optimist, looked at me and said, "That's OK, we have to refuel anyway. We'll just run into Wilmington, N.C., and gas up there. Which way to Wilmington?"

I stared at him in disbelief, but fortunately, I was able to get down on my hands and knees and pull from a locker the remnants of a soggy marine chart on which I had plotted a dead-reckoning position every 15 minutes as a backup to the electronics.

I pulled my dividers from my pocket, made a couple of measurements, then waved my arm in a northwest direction and said, "That way, 70 miles. 283 degrees." By the time we got to shore, it was obvious we had fallen too far behind on time, so we abandoned the effort and returned to Miami. (Five years later, when I went through Wilmington again, the battered boat was still sitting in a storage yard.)

The point of that long yarn is that knowing where you are isn't enough. You also have to know where you're going and be able to plot a route to get there, and that requires a chart. Another point is that electronic instruments aren't foolproof, and a smart navigator keeps a backup, at least in his head.

But I have to admit that today's electronics are amazingly tough. I once was riding with a pro bass angler who wanted to show off how well his new 20-foot boat took big waves. We were battering along through four-footers when we launched off the top of one wave like a missile and shot 10 feet in the air before slamming back down with a crash so hard it shut down the outboard engine.

We scrambled around for a couple of minutes grabbing gear that had flown out of every locker, and as I picked up the chart plotter, which had broken off its mounting, I was surprised to see that it was still running perfectly.

Many, if not most, serious fishermen, at least those who fish enough different waters that they can't remember them all, now carry their charts in the form of an electronic chart plotter. The device, about the size of a mounted GPS unit, looks and works like a paper chart.

Antennae and such

Before we talk about some of the other electronic marine marvels we can buy today at such great prices, let's discuss a couple of practical points that play a crucial role in how well those gadgets work.

First, most of these things need a way to contact the outside world. That's an antenna in the case of GPS, radio or radar, and a transducer in the case of the fish finder.

Using a GPS, radio or radar with the wrong antenna drastically degrades its accuracy. And the transducer you used with your former fish finder might not work with the new one, or even worse, give you false readings, even if it's from the same maker.

Not only do you need to connect the proper signal sensor to each device, it has to be mounted properly and in the right place. If you don't know how to do it, have it done by an expert.

Second, you might be surprised to learn that most of these devices can talk to each other and do even more in concert than they can individually. But before you buy, say, a fish plotter, make sure it's compatible with your GPS and speaks the same electronic language. That doesn't mean it has to come from the same manufacturer, although that's usually the easiest way to ensure compatibility.

Chart plotters

Chart plotters start at about $250 and run to more than $2,000. The more expensive models have bigger color screens and often are a combination plotter-GPS, or plotter-fish finder. Let's think about those combo units. They are functional and take up less space in a small boat. But it means that if the GPS fails, you also lose your chart plotter while you are waiting for the unit to come back from the repair shop.

It's also important not to let yourself get overwhelmed by the gee-whiz factor when you buy electronics. It's pretty neat that one small unit can hold all of the marine charts for North America, but ask yourself, "When am I going to run my boat in Alaska?" Or even South Dakota, for that matter.

Some people will give up a color screen to get a bigger one. And remember, a color screen that looks good in the artificial light of a marine equipment store can be hard to see in bright sunlight. You might need to install the unit inside a wheelhouse or under a roof of some kind, or pick a more expensive one that does show up in daylight.

Other people, especially tournament anglers, want the memory capacity to store routes to hot spots at lakes all over the country, or store complex trolling patterns that were productive.

Chart plotters can make you lazy. They do nearly all of the work, and all you have to do is move a cursor around the screen. The most elaborate units will do the course plotting for you, working out a route from Points A to B to C that avoids, say, any water less than five feet deep, or more than 100 feet, or anything else you want to specify.

That's great for commercial fishermen and big-boat owners, but most anglers don't need those features and would be better off buying a simpler chart plotter and using the savings to buy other gear.

Fish finders

Fish finders, or sonar units, are even more common than chart plotters on most of today's fishing boats. I saw a perfectly functional one, albeit a basic model, on sale in a big-box store the other day for $79, and $200 will buy a unit so sensitive it will differentiate between the bottom and a walleye plastered flat against the bottom.

Again, there's a huge price range, and color-screen units now have dropped below $500. Some anglers say the color screen lets them differentiate among fish of various species, and I've seen enough demonstrations to believe that in some cases it's true.

Most fish finders are the screen type, offering an electronic representation of the water column, bottom topography and the fish, rather than the flasher types that appeared on the market 60 years ago (and are still around). Looking at a modern fish finder is sort of like watching television, or maybe a video game. But anglers need to remember that what they see isn't necessarily all that's there. Less-expensive units often won't discriminate between fish and inorganic structure when the two are close together (such as a walleye hunkered down on the bottom), and they sometimes won't show whether the angler is looking at a bass or a small group of bait fish.

Most units use LCD screens, which operate at lower voltage than a cathode ray tube system (television) and are a lot easier to waterproof. And LCD screens have improved to the point that they are just about as readable as the TV systems.

Years ago, people had to choose between 50-kilohertz units, which were good for reading deeper water but not so good at seeing little things like bait fish, and 270-khz systems that were the opposite. Today, most units include both frequencies, and some can be tuned to in-between frequencies. That keeps the screen from going haywire when you pass near another boat using a fish finder. (It's fascinating to see the same thing happen when you pass near echo-locating dolphins in the ocean.)

Just as important as the unit is the type and placement of the transducer that sends out the sound pulses reflected back to the boat and represented on the screen as fish, rocks, mud, weeds or water.

A bass or walleye angler, who usually fishes in relatively shallow water, wants a transducer that displays a wide angle. That's because the transducer sends out sound pulses in a cone shape, and the farther the sound gets from the boat, the wider the bottom of the cone. A transducer with a narrow angle might show an area only five feet wide at a depth of 20 feet. But a wide-angle transducer might show a 20-foot wide chunk of bottom in the same depth.

That's important for someone like a bass angler who does a lot of his fishing close to the boat. Salmon anglers typically fish much deeper. They consider 50 feet shallow, and most of the time they are fishing in water 100 or more feet deep (even if the fish aren't that far down). They want a transducer with a narrower beam, because by the time the sound pulse gets down to where the fish are, the bottom of that cone is wide enough to let them see what's passing under them in the crucial areas where they are likely to get a strike.

A narrow-beam unit like that usually doesn't discriminate as well among small objects, say a bluegill and a bass, as a sounder with a wider beam. But a person fishing in 100 feet of water usually doesn't worry much about little fish except those salmon eat.

Some units allow the user to switch between narrow and wide beams. Others have side-scanning or forward-looking sonar that allows anglers to see fish off to the side or ahead of the boat. Side-scanning has been more useful to offshore saltwater anglers, who often scan vast areas of relatively empty water for big fish like tuna and marlin and then go over to them. It's less important for freshwater anglers, who usually are more concerned with locating the structure where fish like to live than in seeing the hook shapes that mark fish on the screen.

Many freshwater fish move out of the way as a boat passes and never show up on the fish finder, but they still get caught because the angler is casting to the sides or trolling lures off to the sides on planer boards.

Forward-looking sonar is something else. I've used it on a few big boats owned by friends, and it's like having underwater radar. We once navigated a tricky channel at night by using the forward-looking sonar to stay in deep water.

We should mention flashers, the little round units that preceded these with an LCD screen. In these simple devices, a little flashing bar of light moves around a dial to show the depth. Other thinner bars that appear above it delineate fish.

Many anglers who have used flashers for a long time can tell from the quality of the light not just how far down the bottom is but whether it's muddy, weedy or rocky. They also can see fish moving up and down the water column in real time, something they say is especially important in ice fishing because it helps determine how to work the lure. One walleye pro I know is so worried that the flasher will go the way of the vinyl record that he has a dozen brand new ones stored in his garage.

Underwater TVs

Two years ago, I got a black-and-white Vista Cam underwater camera system. The only problem is, once I start looking at what's going on below, I often get so fascinated by watching critters that I forget to fish.

This is another item that has dropped below $300 for black-and-white systems and $400 for color. I've used both and have come to the conclusion that in the limited visibility of most freshwater fishing, color isn't that much of an advantage.

While I use my camera in the summer in boats, and sometimes when I'm wading streams (you should see the stuff that's under some of those piles of dead trees), I probably use it most often while ice fishing.

It sure has increased my take of whitefish. Watching on the camera has taught us that whitefish often won't touch a jigged minnow, but it you let the lure and bait lie on the bottom for a few minutes, they'll often pick it up.

But they will do it so gently you will never know you had a bite. Several times I've watched on the television screen while a whitefish picked up a minnow and spat it out several times without my feeling so much as a tremor through the rod.

I watched until the fish had the bait in its mouth, then set the hook. It's weird to see the fish suddenly shoot up and off camera as you lift the rod, but it works.

Most bass and walleye pros I know own camera systems. They use them not simply to confirm that the fish they see on the fish finder are the proper species, but that they are the right size.

What has surprised me is how often we see fish even when the water is so muddy it looks like coffee. Fishing in the Chicago River in downtown Chicago, we lowered the camera, dropped some corn next to it as chum and were delighted to see carp shoving their noses into the lens in visibility less than a foot.

I like the Vista Cam system because it uses a regular nine-inch portable television rather than the smaller screens used by some systems. One neat advantage is being able to switch the TV to a football game when I'm sitting on the ice in my portable shelter.

VHF radio

Something that always amazes me is the number of people who motor away from the dock or launching ramp in a boat that has a $1,000 stereo system, complete with CD changer, but doesn't have a $150 VHF marine radio.

I've heard people argue that VHF is outdated in these days of cell phones. Don't believe it. The U.S. Coast Guard doesn't call you on the cell phone to tell you a vicious blow is headed your way. You can hear that information on general broadcasts on VHF.

And many people don't realize that rescue vessels often find and go to a boat in trouble by running down the VHF signal. I don't know if they still do it, but many charter and commercial skippers used to carry a radio direction-finding antenna so they could locate another boat that made the mistake of announcing a good catch on the radio.

The signal gave you a bearing to the other boat, and though it didn't give the distance, you knew he probably wasn't more than a few miles away because of the line-of-sight limitation of VHF.

VHF is a good way for groups of boats to keep together and stay current on what's happening, as in a fishing tournament or group cruise, and it's still the best way to call for help when you need it. Unlike a cell phone, you don't have to know the other guy's number. Just get on Channel 16 and put out a mayday, and it will be heard by everyone tuned to it.

If you have a VHF radio, spend a little time learning what the different channels are for — many are not supposed to be used for idle chatter — and about radio etiquette. Every experienced skipper can give you a story about inconsiderate jerks who hog limited frequencies discussing where to go for dinner.

Radar

Radar is just coming into the purview of the small-boat angler. Costs are realistically under $1,500 for a complete setup, and perhaps even more important, antenna systems have been developed that are practical on boats less than 25 feet.

Most small-boat radars are 1.5- to two-kilowatt units that have a maximum range of 16 miles. Part of that limitation is the 16-inch-diameter antenna, which is usually hidden inside a radome. (A 24-inch antenna will give a range of about 25 miles.)

But don't worry about that 16-mile number. You usually don't waste time trying to spot anything that far away. To see something 16 miles away, it must be 256 feet high, or you need a much higher antenna than you can carry. Like human eyes, radar is line-of-sight, and for a six-foot person standing on the deck of a small boat, anything more than about 2.5 nautical miles away (2.85 land miles) is hidden below the horizon.

Where you really use radar is at much closer ranges. Many skippers who run at night set an alarm that goes off if the radar picks up anything within a circular area that extends two to four miles from the boat. It's a great safety feature that warns you if anything is coming your way or if you are running toward another object.

We saw an example of that recently on Lake St. Clair when we were returning after dark from Canadian waters. The radar showed a small, weak signal at about two miles. At a quarter-mile, we saw nothing, but we altered course, leaving the object a couple of hundred yards to starboard. After it was behind the beam, I could see it was a small boat, maybe a 16-footer, whose red port running light was out. As we ran by him and changed the angle, I could see his green starboard light and through binoculars could even make out two people sitting in the cockpit holding fishing rods.

I've used radar to follow a channel between a line of unlighted day marks — posts sticking above water — and to spot canal and marina openings on shore-lines when all our eyes could pick out were a lot of bright lights. Radar also was useful in places so dark that all we could see was the thicker darkness of the shore-side vegetation against the slightly lighter darkness of the sky.

Radar is great in rain and fog, although units with two kilowatts or less often can't penetrate heavy rain more than about a quarter-mile. But radar probably is close to a price revolution similar to the one that happened in GPS. Not that long ago, the cheapest GPS units cost more than $1,000. The big difference is that while GPS is always useful, radar comes into its own at night and in bad weather, times when most small-boat skippers are off the water.

Other stuff

Most anglers know that temperature plays a key role in determining where to find fish. And most probably don't realize that temperature often is more important than they realize.

Many boats have temperature meters mounted in the hull, the bottom of the trolling motor or on the GPS or fish-finder transducer. That's handy when fishing for species that mostly live in shallow water, such as bass and pike, but it doesn't help in figuring out what's going on with species that spend most of their lives 20 or more feet below the surface.

One option is a temperature sensor that mounts on the downrigger. (People who fish that deep usually use downriggers.) But there also are excellent, inexpensive weighted thermometers that you attach to a line, toss over the side, let sink to the desired depth and then read when you pull them to the surface after a couple of minutes.

They work surprisingly well, and I have one that I often use for fishing for walleyes in inland lakes. But if that isn't high enough tech for you, several manufacturers offer similar units that send the depth and temperature readout to a hand-held LCD display.

I've also seen several pH meters offered, which read the acidity or alkalinity of the water. That would seem to be valuable information to anglers, since most game-fish species have preferred pH levels, and finding the ideal level should result in more strikes from active fish.

Unfortunately, the kind of pH meter that can be built into a boat hull is so crude that the results are not very accurate, fisheries scientists say. In addition to that, pH levels can vary dramatically within a few feet, affected by factors like metals and other materials in the water, so the only way to get a usable pH reading is to take the average of hundreds.

Chapter 18

Exotics

EVERY SHIP THAT LEAVES THE OCEAN FOR THE SWEET-WATER inland seas of the Great Lakes is a potential ecological troublemaker, a Typhoid Mary on an epic scale that could be carrying the seeds of harm in its bowels.

In the past 100 years, nearly 150 species of exotic fish, invertebrates and plants have established themselves in the Great Lakes watershed. But the rate of exotic introductions has skyrocketed in the past two decades, largely because of an increased number of ocean-going vessels from many places that bring the intruders with their ballast water.

Some exotics, like Pacific salmon, brown trout and rainbow trout, were brought in deliberately by man and are valued as sport fish and for their ability to control alewives, another exotic fish that man introduced inadvertently by opening the Welland Canal.

Others, like sea lampreys and zebra mussels, have become costly nuisances. Lampreys nearly wiped out native lake trout, and mussels clogged water intakes and other man-made underwater structures.

With no natural enemies in the Great Lakes, zebra mussels reproduced at a rate up to 1,000 times higher than in their native waters. Billions of the dime-sized, filter-feeding mussels have brought an enormous increase in the clarity of the Great Lakes and created at least a temporary boom in the populations of native sight-feeders like smallmouth bass, pike and muskellunge.

But many scientists worry that the mussels are sucking too much plankton from the bottom of the food chain, food that's also needed not just by small prey fish and juvenile game fish but by the even smaller creatures tiny fish feed on.

The Great Lakes could become so clear that they won't support the tens of millions of sport fish — from perch to chinook salmon — that have made sport-fishing a $1-billion-a-year industry on the lakes. Anyone who wonders if that could happen need only look at walleye numbers in Lake Erie. The lake held more than 100 million walleye in 1990 — when the average underwater visibility was about three feet — and 35 million in 2002, when underwater visibility had increased to about 12 feet.

Scientists say the walleye decrease is a direct result of the decrease in alewives and other prey species, which in turn is a direct result of a dramatic decrease in the plankton base.

Sea lampreys didn't get a foothold until man opened canals that allowed them to swim in from the Atlantic Ocean. Most sea lampreys come into fresh water only to spawn, but like Pacific salmon, the lampreys that reached the Great Lakes discovered they could live happy and fulfilling lives without returning to the sea.

Lampreys feed by attaching round, sucker-like mouths filled with rows of hooked teeth onto the side of a big fish, usually a lake trout. Then they drill a hole in the fish with a tongue like a file. They suck the fluids from the laker until it is too weak to swim, at which point the lamprey abandons the dying lake trout and seeks another.

By the 1950s, lamprey eels had almost wiped out lake trout, the original top predator in all of the Great Lakes. The loss of the lakers was the reason Pacific salmon were introduced in the mid-1960s. The federal and state governments around the lake have spent tens of millions of dollars to re-establish lake trout and eliminate the sea lampreys — with limited success.

As the new century unfolds, it seems that sea lampreys are finally being controlled thanks to the discovery of a new chemical, granular Bayluscide. It can be used in breeding hot spots in the St. Marys River near Sault St. Marie without killing everything else on the bottom.

That's good news, because the sea lamprey experienced another population boom in the 1990s that threatened to undo all the previous eradication efforts. By 2000, lampreys had reached such proportions in northern Lake Huron that biologists estimated that every lake trout was killed by lampreys before it reached breeding age.

Ironically, the primary reason for the lampreys' rejuvenation was man's 30-year effort to treat pollution.

It began with an event that in retrospect proved to be the final straw for the almost-uncontrolled dumping of pollutants into the Great Lakes. In 1969, a welder was working on a bridge in downtown Cleveland when his torch set the Cuyahoga River on fire.

The incident started jokes that called Cleveland "the mistake on the lake," a place so environmentally fouled that even the water would burn. And just as important, it happened in an era when television networks could broadcast to the nation a news event so horrific and mind-boggling that it was almost laughable.

Those kinds of incidents led to the creation of the federal Environmental Protection Agency, and politicians in states and cities all around the lakes found themselves under pressure from citizens outraged by the mess and embarrassed at being tarred by association. Even if their water wouldn't burn, in many places it was so laden with chemicals, algae and bacteria that it looked like pea soup and smelled like a sewage lagoon, worthless for swimming or fishing.

Congressmen were spurred to action and passed clean water laws. And while crews were cleaning out the stuff that burned, environmental regulators imposed stringent bans on things like high-phosphate detergents and other nutrients that over-enriched the lakes' plant life, including algae.

In the next 20 years the Great Lakes and the rivers that feed them underwent a transformation that, while far from perfect, was an amazing improvement. But the cleansing of many rivers, especially the St. Marys, had some side effects. One gave sea lampreys a new lease on life.

It turned out that lampreys are almost as susceptible to pollution as trout, and lamprey numbers largely had been held in check not so much by lamprey controls as by man's practice of fouling his own nest.

In addition, lampreys found plenty of prey in the vast numbers of salmon and lake trout that had been introduced or reintroduced. More lampreys survived to spawn in those cleaner rivers, and they produced even more lampreys.

In the late 1990s, U.S. Fish and Wildlife scientists developed a way to use Bayluscide to treat lamprey breeding areas in the St. Marys, which produces more lampreys than all other Great Lakes tributary streams combined. By 2001, the program appeared to be working.

But despite some improvements in the Great Lakes, many biologists are worried about the future. No one knows what the long-term effects will be from the introduction of round gobies, a six-inch, bottom-dwelling fish from the Baltic. Gobies have proved so popular with smallmouth bass that the bass population is exploding in many areas, and tackle manufacturers are making baits that look like round gobies.

But biologists also know that round gobies can suck a fish egg out of three inches of gravel. Massive numbers of gobies now prey on eggs and compete with the young of valued species for a limited food supply.

Despite scientific evidence, increasing public awareness of the threat from invasive species, and the enormous biological and physical costs such invasions can entail, the arrival of exotics continues almost unchecked.

A major problem is that the remedies are based on science, but the decision to apply those remedies is political, and those with a vested interest in avoiding solutions have a lot of clout in the political arena.

Many scientists who study the Great Lakes agree that something must be done to prevent the continued importation of exotics in the water ballast of ocean-going ships. Several proposals have been made that would require ship owners to treat ballast water with chemicals or heat to kill anything living in the tanks. But those solutions would cost the shipping companies money; the compromise is a requirement that ships empty their ballast tanks and re-flood them with salt water before entering the Great Lakes system.

But many organisms, from bacteria on up, won't be killed by this process. And the U.S. government doesn't inspect ships to make sure they have complied.

A list of invasive fish in Lake Erie, put together by the Point Pelee Natural History News at Canada's Point Pelee National Park, includes gizzard shad, which showed up about 1846; goldfish, 1878; common carp, late 1800s; sea lamprey, 1921; white perch, 1950; and tubenose goby, the latest in 1996.

But the list also includes glamour species introduced by man as sport and food fish. Although these fish didn't establish breeding populations until the large stocking programs of the 1960s and '70s, they were seen in Lake Erie some time before. They include chinook salmon in 1875; rainbow trout, 1876; brown trout, 1913; and coho salmon, 1933.

Some people might be surprised that Lake Erie could support salmonids, because it is the shallowest and warmest of the Great Lakes. They would be more surprised to learn that when Lake Erie was the world's most productive commercial freshwater fishery in the five decades before World War I, the bread-and-butter fish were three cold-water species — lake trout, whitefish and lake herring. Today's primary commercial species, walleyes and perch, were largely an untargeted by-catch.

The roles economics and politics play in exotic species problems were well illustrated in the summer of 2002, when the U.S. Army Corps of Engineers turned on an underwater electrical barrier in the Chicago Sanitary and Ship Canal a few miles below Lake Michigan.

The barrier was designed to keep three new species of Asian carp out of the Great Lakes, but many scientists feared it was too little and too late. If the new invaders already had reached the lakes, they could make the zebra mussel problem look like small potatoes.

Weighing 50 to 100 pounds, these species of Asian carp reproduce so quickly that the Australians nicknamed them "river rabbits." In addition, they can suck down two or three times their weight in plankton or mussels every day, and one of them, the silver carp, can leap six feet into the air and jump over barriers that would stop a salmon.

Bighead and silver carp were imported in the 1970s as biological controls on plants and algae in Southern fish farm ponds. The first black carp probably were mixed in accidentally with fingerlings of the other species. But because black carp eat mollusks like snails, clams and mussels, more were imported by the fish farms in the 1980s to control a catfish parasite that used snails as an intermediate host.

Since then, the new Asian carp have spread into Midwestern river systems.

Jerry Rasmussen, a U.S. Fish and Wildlife Service biologist at Rock Island, Ill., said: "In some places on the Mississippi and Illinois rivers, there are so many Asian carp that commercial fishermen gave up trying to fish those pools. There are so many that when we took people on a sight-seeing tour on a barge that had a table and umbrella on the deck, a silver carp jumped out of the water and landed on top of the umbrella. Some of our staff have been hit multiple times by big carp that landed in research boats."

Fish and Wildlife Service biologists netted no Asian carp when they sampled the Mississippi and Illinois rivers in 1990. Ten years later, Asian carp made up 97 percent of a large fish kill in a Mississippi slough south of St. Louis.

Silver carp can weigh up to 60 pounds, and bighead can top 100. Widespread in the Mississippi and Illinois systems, they were found in the Chicago Sanitary and Ship Canal only 11 miles below Lake Michigan. Black carp escaped to the wild in the 1990s, and biologists fear they also might become a threat.

"Both the bighead and silver carp feed on plankton, but the silver carp is a major filter-feeder, just like a vacuum cleaner," said Bob Kovetsky, Great Lakes biologist for the U.S. Fish and Wildlife Service in East Lansing. "The question is whether the plankton is concentrated enough in the Great Lakes to support large populations of these fish."

If the carp reach the Great Lakes, the fear is that they will compete for food not only with juvenile game fish but all the bait fish fry and fingerlings near the bottom of the food chain.

Fish farmers say carp escape to the wild accidentally when rivers overflow their banks and flood farm ponds. Rasmussen isn't so sure.

"We have good reason to think that when they pull the nets, they just take carp they don't want and throw them over the levees" into a river, he said. "We know our netting surveys find an awful lot of Asian carp in the rivers by the fish ponds even when there hasn't been a flood."

Rasmussen would like to see the importation of Asian carp stopped, but his stance is not popular with fish farmers.

Hugh Warren, a spokesman for the Catfish Farmers of America in Indianola, Miss., disputed Rasmussen's arguments.

"He says a lot of things," Warren said, "but having facts is something else."

Warren said fish farmers use Asian carp in their ponds because other controls aren't economically feasible. The farmers base their practices on "the findings of sound science," he said. Fish farmers don't deliberately release Asian carp and go out of their way to avoid carp escapes "because obviously you don't want that to happen," Warren said.

No matter whether Asian carp enter streams through natural flooding or negligence, they represent a potential threat to the Great Lakes.

"If you don't try to stop them, you're playing Russian roulette," said Craig Czarnecki, field supervisor for the U.S. Fish and Wildlife Service's East Lansing office. "Do they represent a threat? We can't say 'yes' for sure, but why take a chance? Maybe we can stave off an introduction for decades. Anytime you have a new neighbor move into the neighborhood, you don't know what kind of effect it will have, or the kind of cascading effects you can get over time."

The species are called Asian carp to differentiate them from common carp, another Eurasian fish the U.S. government imported via Germany in 1877. It also created environmental problems soon after it was introduced.

A fourth Asian species, the grass carp, reached some parts of the Great Lakes in the past decade. Scientists don't think it will become too populous because it feeds on rooted plants in short supply in the big waters.

The only Asian carp found in the Great Lakes by mid-2002 were two bigheads netted in Lake Erie and one taken from a fountain in Toronto on the shores of Lake Ontario. Czarnecki thinks those fish didn't swim in but were introduced through an Asian religious practice.

"Many Asians believe that they increase their karma by releasing a fish for every one they eat," Czarnecki said. "Asians eat bighead, silver and black carp, and we think that's the source of the three found so far."

One of those Lake Erie bigheads examined at the University of Guelph in Ontario weighed nearly 40 pounds and apparently had been in the lake for a few years.

The Chicago Sanitary and Ship Canal opened in 1900, reversing the flow of the south branch of the Chicago River away from Lake Michigan and sending Chicago's sewage southwest to the Illinois River, which joins with the Mississippi.

Czarnecki said the canal "is like a revolving door when it comes to letting exotic species into the lakes. But we can also use the canal as a choke point where we can attend to the threats."

After Asian carp were found in the canal, Rasmussen wanted it closed.

"Why do we need this canal today?" he said. "It's there because it was easier for Chicago to divert its waste down the canal to the Illinois River, and because some boaters use it.

"But when you examine the boat traffic that moves on that canal, it isn't very much. I'd like to see the canal closed for a couple of years, allow it to go stagnant. That would let us treat the carp that are in there now and figure out what to do in the future."

Chicago Mayor Richard Daley wrote governors and mayors on the Great Lakes and the Illinois and Mississippi rivers, saying the exotic species problem concerns all of them and needs a regional solution.

John Rogner, who heads the U.S. Fish and Wildlife Service's Chicago office, said the idea of closing the canal "is just one of the things that have been thrown on the table for discussion. It's not our official position. Treated sewage is still sent down the canal, and that's a big issue. In addition, there are the industries along the canal and the canal shippers' association."

Tests have shown that Asian carp flee from noise and bubbles, and Rogner thinks multiple barriers should be placed in the canal, including bubble curtains and acoustic arrays.

"We should be doing everything possible to keep Asian carp and other exotics out of the Great Lakes," Rogner said. "This would be one more species competing for the limited plankton base that supports the entire food chain."

Eliminating Asian carp in the wild will be a problem, Rasmussen said.

"Asians eat them, but they want the fish kept alive until just before they are thrown in the fryer," he said. "There's a group in Illinois that's trying to develop a market for them, but it won't be easy. Maybe they can be used in the fertilizer or catfish markets."

The Arkansas Agriculture Research Services office hopes to create a domestic market, saying its testing showed that six of 10 people who tried bighead carp preferred it over tuna.

Exotic species often are a case of one person's meat being another's poison, Czarnecki said.

"We got a call from some people in Japan," he said. "They couldn't believe we were having a problem with Asian carp, because they raise them there and use them for food. But they do have a problem with another exotic species that is giving them trouble in some of their lakes — the largemouth bass."

Chapter 19

Lake St. Clair

EVERY YEAR, ANGLERS CATCH MORE THAN 1.5-MILLION FISH from Lake St. Clair, mostly smallmouth and largemouth bass, channel catfish, bullheads, yellow perch, northern pike, muskellunge, bluegills and sunfish, walleyes and white bass.

Sitting along a metropolitan area that's home to 4.5-million people, or nearly half of Michigan's population, the lake gets nearly 50 percent of all of the angling effort on Michigan's Great Lakes and their connecting waters.

Despite the heavy fishing pressure, Lake St. Clair is a far better fishery than it was 30 years ago and produces almost 40 percent of all the fish caught in the state's Great Lakes system.

You might get an argument about the quality of the fishing from veteran walleye anglers who fondly remember the days they could get five keepers for dinner in an hour or two of trolling. Today, it probably would require at least a half-day's effort.

But if you're someone like me, who likes a lot of variety in his angling and fishes more for the fun of catching the fish than eating them, Lake St. Clair is fabulous.

The abundance of game fish in Lake St. Clair is amazing. A study of the muskellunge population 10 years ago figured that there were about 30,000 of these big, toothy members of the pike family. Today, Bob Haas, head of the state Department of Natural Resources' Lake St. Clair and Lake Erie research laboratory at Mt. Clemens, says it wouldn't surprise him if a new study puts that figure at 50,000 or more.

While sturgeon in 22,000-square-mile Lake Michigan have decreased from a historical estimate of 11 million 150 years ago to perhaps 11,000 today, scientists figure that 30,000 to 50,000 of those prehistoric fish still swim in 420-square-mile Lake St. Clair.

As for smallmouth bass, studies are just beginning to try to get a handle on their numbers, but Haas thinks it has to be in the hundreds of thousands, and for perch the figure reaches the millions. That's impressive for a body of water that really isn't so much a lake as a wide spot in a big river.

And even though walleye numbers have decreased, several hundred thousand of these tasty fish still call Lake St. Clair home, and that number tops seven figures during the spring spawning season.

Lake St. Clair is only a twentieth as big as Lake Erie, to which its waters flow, and 50 times smaller than Lake Huron, from whence they come, but it is a conduit for all of the waters that pour out of the three immense Great Lakes farther upstream.

The basin of Lake Superior was formed about a billion years ago when volcanic activity laid down a thick layer of rock that sank more than 1,000 feet under its own weight. The other four Great Lakes didn't form until about a million years ago, gouged out by glaciers that drove like a spear into the heart of Michigan.

The Great Lakes are one of the youngest geological features on the North American continent, and Lake St. Clair is the youngest feature in the Great Lakes system. It formed about 9,000 years ago, when the last glacier scoured out the deep channels we call the St. Clair and Detroit rivers. What is now Lake St. Clair was then a low spot in an ancient lake bed, and waters from the melting glacier flowed down the St. Clair River channel from Lake Huron and flooded the low spot.

At the southern end, the waters were constricted again into the narrow channel of the Detroit River. Detroit is the French term for a strait, a narrow place between two large bodies of water. Though we gave the area three names, the St. Clair River-Lake St. Clair-Detroit River system is really just a long strait between lakes Huron and Erie.

Five-hundred thousand years ago, Lake St. Clair was one of several ways for water to flow out of the Great Lakes. Other rivers took Great Lakes water to the Gulf of Mexico and Hudson Bay. But the land around the lakes rose a few feet every thousand years as the weight of a mile-thick sheet of ice was removed, and it wasn't long in geological terms before the land rose so high those other exits were cut off.

A chart of Lake St. Clair and its associated rivers looks remarkably like a human heart and its surrounding blood vessels. The main body of the lake has a north-south axis of about 26 miles and east-west axis of about 24 miles.

Lake Huron supplies 98 percent of the water that flows into Lake St. Clair through the St. Clair River delta, the largest wetland of its kind left in the Great Lakes. The other two percent comes from smaller streams that enter below Lake Huron.

The water that reaches Lake St. Clair usually moves through to the Detroit River in an average of about seven days. By contrast, the retention time for water in Lake Huron is 22 years. That's not only because Lake St. Clair is so much smaller but because it's so shallow.

Lake St. Clair holds about one cubic mile of water, compared to 850 cubic miles in Lake Huron. All of the Great Lakes together contain more than 5,400

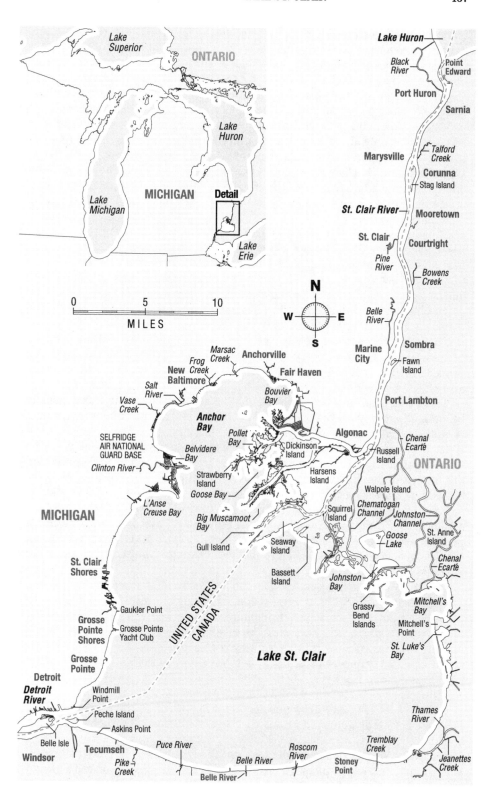

cubic miles of fresh water, 20 percent of all the fresh water in the world and enough to cover the 48 contiguous states to a depth of about nine feet.

Eventually, nearly all of that water moves through the channels and across the flats of Lake St. Clair on its way to Lake Erie, Lake Ontario, the St. Lawrence River and the northern Atlantic Ocean. The only water that doesn't finish the trip is the small percentage that evaporates or is used by people.

It's easy to understand why water doesn't linger long in Lake St. Clair. The lake averages only about 10 feet deep, and the deepest point is 21 feet (outside of a 27-foot shipping channel dredged for the St. Lawrence Seaway in 1959). Water from the St. Clair River pours in at a rate of 182,000 cubic feet per second. That's enough to flood a football field to a depth of more than three feet — in one second. So the water already in Lake St. Clair must move through quickly to make room.

Canada owns two-thirds of the lake, but because of the way the St. Clair River delta formed, half of the water pours in on the American side. Harsens Island (American) and Walpole Island (Canadian) sit in the mouth of the St. Clair River like a split cork. The main shipping channel runs between them, and two other major channels funnel water to the outsides of the islands. The north channel enters Lake St. Clair at Anchor Bay on the Michigan side, and the south channel feeds Mitchell's Bay in Ontario.

The Lake Huron water delivered by the river is very clear, and the half that pours into American territory moves swiftly down the shoreline and into the Detroit River in a couple of days. (The speed of the water through the lake is also affected by winds.)

The other half moves more slowly on the Canadian side and usually becomes cloudier with the outflow from two big rivers that cut through a part of Ontario that is intensely agricultural.

It's often easy to see the difference in the two chunks of liquid. Just go to the head of the Detroit River, where they come together again. The demarcation line between the colder, clearer American water and the warmer, cloudier Canadian water sometimes is as well defined as if it had been cut with a knife.

Lake St. Clair was named by early French fur traders for St. Claire of Assisi, a follower of St. Francis and a founder of the Poor Claires order of nuns. Some people have mistakenly identified it as the namesake of Gen. Arthur St. Clair, the first governor of the American Northwest Territory, but he came along 150 years later.

One thing that makes Lake St. Clair so interesting to me is that it is so busy. The waves on its waters are often produced not by the wind but by thousands of people enjoying themselves in fishing boats, sailboats, speedboats and jet skis. Others make a living crossing the lake on ships that move about 70-million tons of cargo across its waters every year. Most of the ships are long, narrow ore boats that never leave the sweetwater seas, but others are salties that haul cargo to and from every ocean in the world.

Most of the cargo is bound from the upper lakes in the form of iron ore, limestone and coal for steel mills and factories in the industrial East (including Detroit's auto industry), and grains that feed people and livestock around the world.

But the vast bulk of the people who use the lake travel aboard small boats, with more than 150,000 pleasure craft registered in the three counties adjacent to its waters. Tens of thousands more come from across Michigan and the

Midwest.

One of those people is Joe Belanger, a fishing nut and charter captain out of Tilbury, Ontario, who runs a boat called Up Our Alley. (He also owns a small restaurant and bowling lanes.)

On one trip with Belanger, we got into a school of enormous perch, fish so big we didn't keep any less than 12 inches. That day we caught several perch that measured an honest 14 inches and weighed 1 ¾ pounds, but Belanger said they weren't real bragging fish.

"When we get out here in November and December, we sometimes get perch that go 16 inches," he said. "They look more like walleyes. The trick is to come out every day so you can stay on the schools as they move. They usually don't move far in one day, but if you don't come out for four or five days, you can have trouble locating them again."

Perch like clear water and feed during the day, so there's no doubt the clearing waters have helped their spawning and survival.

But Haas said another important factor in perch production might be the warmer winters of the past decade. The Lake St. Clair ice has formed later and melted earlier, greatly reducing the lake's traditionally huge ice-fishing effort.

Lake St. Clair's water quality is quite good, except for a few spots where agricultural drains or combined sewage overflows concentrate contaminants. Unfortunately, those areas are inshore and often near beaches that occasionally close when rainfall flushes human sewage into the lake and raises the level of E. coli bacteria to dangerous levels.

But overall the lake is clean, with a pH level about 8.7 and saturated oxygen levels near maximum (both ideal for game fish). The water is in such good shape partly because the lake is susceptible to the formation of wind-induced gyres, huge eddies that move with the current and swirl clockwise on the American side and counterclockwise on the Canadian. The gyres help mix and oxygenate the water, dilute contaminants and distribute nutrients and zooplankton throughout the lake.

Until about 10 years ago, the Canadian and American waters were usually so different that they seemed like different lakes. That diverse habitat supported a number of species, from big northern pike, which prefer colder, clearer waters that allow for the growth of weeds where they can hide in ambush, to largemouth bass, which feed happily in water so muddy they must hunt by sound. But since most of the water was on the more turbid Canadian side, the most abundant game fish was the walleye, which evolved to hunt in dim light and found the lake an excellent refuge.

That has changed in the past decade, with the Canadian waters of Lake St. Clair starting to approach the clarity of the American side, especially at mid-lake, and the reason is a tiny creature from the Baltic Sea about the size of a pencil eraser.

Before the arrival of the zebra mussel in the mid-1980s, about 70 percent of the anglers who fished Lake St. Clair targeted walleyes, 11 percent went after bass, nine percent fished for perch and nine percent for muskellunge. A 1999 survey turned up a dramatic change, with 20 percent fishing for walleyes, 24 percent for bass, 22 percent for perch and 29 percent for muskies.

The reason for the change was an explosion in the zebra mussel population, resulting in far clearer water that favored sight-feeders like bass, muskies and perch and made it tougher for murky-water specialists like walleyes to make a living.

Walleyes once were found just about everywhere in Lake St. Clair, although the best fishing was usually on the Canadian side. But by 1995, zebra mussels had cleared the water so much that most of the walleyes were found in the deeper, dimmer waters at mid-lake or in places with a lot of aquatic vegetation.

But the changes are a lot more subtle and complex than the increased ability of a predator to see prey fish. The clearer water also let sunlight penetrate deeper and encouraged weed growth, which increased the places where fish like muskellunge could spawn, and where bait fish could find refuge.

The mussels also might be helping the one-million ducks, geese and other waterfowl that use the lake each year, either for nesting or as a refuge during spring and fall migrations. Biologists have found that scaup and other diving ducks eat mussels, and the clearer water has increased the growth of wild celery and other underwater greenery ducks eat.

Scientists also are looking at ways clearer water has brought back the fantastic mayfly populations in Lake St. Clair. Their larvae are probably one of the most important food sources for dozens of species that range from sport fish like bass, sturgeon and walleyes to bait fish like alewives, spot-tail minnows and round gobies.

When we lived in Grosse Pointe Woods nearly 30 years ago, June always brought dense hatches of the Ephemerella and Hexagenia mayfly species that most people lumped together as Canadian soldiers, or more often, "those damned bugs."

The mayflies would collect by the thousands or hundreds of thousands on windows, buildings, cars, boats and anything else that was smooth, shiny and stationary. They also were responsible for a lot of rear-end collisions at stop signs and lights. It might seem hard to believe, but the accidents occurred when cars slid on the greasy slicks formed by the crushed bodies of untold numbers of mayflies that landed on the pavement where a streetlight formed a pool of light on the road.

There were so many mayflies I once helped a manufacturer of fly-tying equipment try to come up with a way of putting scents of eau de mayfly on materials. His idea was to crush the mayflies and treat the stuff used to make fly bodies with the resulting fluids.

We spent one night driving around the Grosse Pointes, stopping at places where flies had concentrated on the road and sweeping them into paper shopping bags. There were so many insects that we could fill a bag at every stop. The project wasn't successful, and I still remember trying to explain what we were doing to some cops who stopped and shined their spotlight on a couple of apparent lunatics sweeping mounds of bugs off the street.

Mayflies like high water quality, and their numbers fell off through the 1980s as water quality in the Great Lakes reached its nadir. Then changes caused by the Clean Water Act began to take effect, and by the early 1990s the mayfly numbers began to rebound, often to the chagrin of people who had moved to lakeshore neighborhoods during the years when the flies were not much in evidence.

Today, Lake St. Clair again is covered with brown slicks a half-mile square in June, the husks of billions of mayflies that hatched out of their nymphal skins at night. (At these times the best bass bait is a tube lure the same sandy-brown as a mayfly larva.)

Every experienced bass and walleye angler can tell stories of days when the fish were so stuffed with mayflies that a brown sludge poured out of their mouths as they were brought into the boat. Scientists now think the mayfly larvae might be of much greater importance to many species of fish than was previously imagined.

There is also evidence that a mayfly migration of sorts takes place under the ice during the winter, when the larvae leave the safety of the rocks and travel about. That might explain why wigglers, the larvae of Hexagania species, are among the best perch baits for ice fishermen.

The effects of billions of zebra mussels sucking zooplankton and other suspended matter out of the water is best illustrated by the changes in Secchi disk numbers that researchers have seen in 15 years.

A Secchi disk is a 12-inch circle of plastic or metal divided into alternating quadrants of white and black. Scientists lower it on a piece of rope and record the depth at which it disappears. It's brilliant in its simplicity and effectiveness.

In the mid-1980s, Secchi disk numbers for Lake St. Clair were about three feet in Mitchell's Bay on the Canadian side, about five feet in Anchor Bay on the American side and 4.2 feet in the middle. Today, the numbers are 10 feet in Anchor Bay, 10 feet in Mitchell's Bay and 13 to 14 feet in the middle, and the lake-wide average has increased from four feet to 10.

The water clarity gave a boost to muskies, which also were helped by an increased minimum size limit to 42 inches and a decrease in the daily bag limit from two to one. (This followed a steady decrease in muskie numbers and sizes in 1977-87.)

By the late 1990s, anglers were catching three times as many muskies than they had 10 years before. Fish bigger than 25 pounds had become commonplace, and today 30-pounders aren't unusual.

Similar results were seen in bass numbers, which have increased almost threefold since the mid-1980s, and perch, which have nearly doubled. Lake St. Clair is considered one of the top five bass lakes in North America, where tournament anglers routinely land stringers of five fish that top 20 pounds. Jumbo perch of 12 inches or better also are fairly routine, especially in the fall when the big perch school for the annual feeding binge.

Fall is the time to hunt big muskies, too. In many lakes across the United States and Canada, the muskie is called "the fish of 1,000 casts," and anglers consider it a good season if they catch a half-dozen. For the trolling muskie anglers on Lake St. Clair, six fish would be a so-so day.

The clearer water in Lake St. Clair gave sight-feeders like bass, pike and muskies a competitive advantage over walleyes, which had been the primary sport fish. Walleyes evolved to feed at night or in murky water, and they couldn't compete against bigger, stronger and more aggressive species.

"We really started to see a difference by 1990," said Jody Lambert, a St. Clair Shores angler who has fished Lake St. Clair for 40 years. "The water started getting clearer, and the walleyes got harder to find.

"But at the same time, we were catching a lot more smallmouths, and instead of the 10-, 12-inchers we used to get, we were catching a lot of two- to three-pounders that went 14 to 18 inches. My father and all of his old fishing cronies were moaning about the walleyes going down, but for someone like me who loves to fish smallmouths, it couldn't have been better."

The biggest changes happened on the Ontario side, because the Michigan side had less material in the water for zebra mussels to filter out. Underwater plant life in Ontario waters increased fivefold in 1984-94, 1½ times on the Michigan side.

The number of fish and species diversity increased, but the one fish that paid the price for the success of others was the walleye.

In 1970-77, DNR biologists who sampled the lake netted about two to five walleyes at a time on an average day. In 1978-87, that figured climbed to as high as nine a day. But the netting samples started to decline when the mussels arrived and are now back at early 1970s levels.

At the same time, the average age of the walleyes has increased, a worrisome trend because it usually indicates that fewer are being born and surviving to adulthood. The average age of walleyes netted in research programs ranged from about three to five years in 1980-85. But since 1985 it has climbed steadily to nearly seven years.

There also are indications that walleyes born in Lake St. Clair are less likely to stay there than they were two or three decades ago. Biologists tagged Lake St. Clair walleyes and charted their movements after the fish were caught by anglers who returned the tags to the DNR.

Before zebra mussels, 52 percent of the tagged fish caught by anglers came from Lake St. Clair and 48 percent from the St. Clair River or Lake Huron.

After the mussels had been at work for a few years, only 31 percent of the tagged fish were caught in the lake, while 69 percent had moved upstream to the St. Clair River and Lake Huron.

One other charted trend has Haas just as worried. Until about 1987, the year-class trends among walleyes in lakes St. Clair and Erie showed strong synchronicity. In other words, if the walleyes born in Lake Erie in 1977 showed excellent survival and growth in 1982, then the walleyes born in 1977 in Lake St. Clair showed excellent survival and growth in 1982.

The synchronicity among these adjacent walleye populations made it clear that the primary factors affecting walleye spawning success and survival weren't sport fishing or commercial fishing but weather. Unseasonable cold snaps killed plankton and other small creatures the walleye fry ate, and fewer little walleyes made it to adulthood.

But by 1990, scientists saw that synchronicity broken. Walleyes in Lake St. Clair were not doing as well as the walleye in Lake Erie. Throughout the 1990s, walleyes had several good years of reproduction in Lake Erie and its tributary streams, like the Maumee in Ohio, but poor reproduction in Lake St. Clair and its tributaries.

Scientists suspect that the difference is the product of a couple of other changes. One is a drastic decrease in chlorophyll levels in the water now that zebra mussels have removed so much of the green algae. The chlorophyll reduction might have reduced the amount of food available to larval walleye moving into the lake from the Thames River in Ontario.

The other change is a puzzling die-off of walleye fry and fingerlings in the Thames. It once was the spawning ground for millions of walleyes. Now it gets a fraction of its traditional numbers.

"It's very disturbing, and we don't know what's happening there," Haas said. "Some people would like to blame it on Indian commercial netters, but that's not the cause. The netters didn't cause a decline in the days when the Lake St. Clair walleyes were doing as well as the Lake Erie fish."

But if walleyes are the losers in Lake St. Clair's game of life, the winners are not just game fish like bass and muskellunge but exotic imports like round gobies.

Round gobies were first seen in Lake St. Clair in 1993. Today, they are the most numerous fish in the lake and are crowding out native gobies and other small bottom-feeders. There are so many it sometimes seems that the bottom must have a goby every square foot.

I once took a tray of 1,000 night crawlers to a couple of professional walleye anglers who knew I was going to cover a national tournament held on the lake. They went through all of the worms in three days and said 98 percent of the crawlers were eaten by gobies that pulled them off the hooks without being caught.

The silver lining to this ecological cloud is that round gobies have become the favorite food of just about anything that eats small fish, and especially smallmouth bass.

When sturgeon researchers first put out lines a couple of years ago to catch fish for a long-term research project, they tried different baits on the 25 hooks to determine if the sturgeon had a preference. It turned out to be gobies, 5-1. The gobies have increased at such a rate that Haas said it's essential to maintain a large population of bass in Lake St. Clair as the first line of defense against them.

I fished Lake St. Clair a half-dozen times in the summer of 2002 for bass, muskellunge, walleyes and perch, but I was really looking forward to fall, when the fish go on the annual feeding binge that seems to be triggered by cooling water.

I was even looking at leasing some deer hunting land close enough to the lake that I could bow-hunt in the morning, fish Lake St. Clair at midday and be back in a tree stand in the evening.

What a fall that would be.

Chapter 20

Great Lakes

I'M SEASICK.

That's not unusual in these conditions. Lake Erie is being raked by 20-knot easterlies along its 241-mile length, and despite a lifetime spent on boats, green seas sometimes make me green around the gills.

But I suffer in silence (other than the occasional retch over the side), because with fishing as great as it is today, there's no way we're going in early.

In the past few weeks, the gang I fish with has caught trophy-sized walleyes, chinook and coho salmon, steelhead trout, smallmouth and largemouth bass, yellow perch, northern pike and white bass from these waters, which might well be the finest freshwater fishing grounds in the world.

Today, we've caught and released about 50 steelhead up to 14 pounds in less than five hours. Slumped in a corner of the cockpit, where no one is likely to step on me, I find that mind-boggling.

Michigan's 54 miles of shoreline on Lake Erie are minuscule compared to 917 miles on Lake Superior, 1,058 on Lake Michigan and 934 on Lake Huron (much of it along massive Saginaw Bay). But Erie is by far the most important of the Great Lakes to Michigan anglers because it is within an hour's drive of 50 percent of the state's population and supports a lot of the angling effort (although still far less than Lake St. Clair, the hardest-fished lake in the state).

Readers under, say, 40, might find it hard to imagine, but only four decades ago many people had written off Lake Erie as America's Dead Sea after years of pollution.

The idea that Erie would support millions of fish like these big steelhead, creatures that demand high water quality, seemed as unlikely then as, well, a president would get caught engaging in sex in the White House with an intern half his age.

Even though I've watched it happen, it's hard to believe the amazing changes in this 9,910-square-mile inland sea, bigger than the land area of Massachusetts and Rhode Island combined, and yet the second-smallest of the five Great lakes in surface area and smallest in water volume.

I'm 59. When I was twenty-something, Lake Erie was so thick with algae that the water along the beaches looked like a pot of cold spinach and smelled like a landfill. The predominant marine life, in the memory of one fisheries biologist, was "lamprey eels and alewives."

One of the first stories I wrote as a reporter for the Associated Press in 1968 was about scientists who chartered the last commercial fishing boat in Barcelona, N.Y., for a project to find out why walleyes and other valuable species had disappeared. There were so many alewives — herring-like invaders from the Atlantic — that when algae blooms peaked in the summer and used up the water's oxygen, they died by the millions. Beaches were covered with knee-high windrows of rotting, stinking fish that made the sand uninhabitable.

Not only was the smell intolerable, gases from rotting vegetation and fish stung the eyes of people who lived near the beach. I know families who still own Lake Erie waterfront cottages that are worth a lot of money only because they couldn't find anyone who would buy the place during the bad old days.

That doesn't happen now. Alewives are so well controlled by huge schools of game fish that anglers worry that alewife numbers will fall too low. Eliminating phosphates and other pollutants drastically reduced algae growth and, combined with the arrival of zebra mussels from the Baltic Sea, increased underwater visibility from inches in the 1960s to 30 to 40 feet today.

In a bizarre turnabout, water quality in Erie's eastern basin has become so high — approaching that of relatively unsullied Lake Superior — that some biologists worry it soon won't be able to support the enormous numbers of game fish. They even have suggested putting controlled amounts of phosphates into the water to increase its richness.

Despite these changes, I worry for the future of this lake, and the other Great Lakes, for that matter, because Erie is changing again, and for reasons biologists don't fully understand. And because Erie is the shallowest of the Great Lakes, what happens there happens fastest and is a portent for the entire Great Lakes watershed.

Many biologists worry that we are beginning to see the results of our arrogance in thinking that we can treat an ecosystem as huge and complex as Lake Erie as if it were a big aquarium.

"Ah, it's just another steelhead. For a minute there I thought it was a nice 'eye," said Joe Belanger, a charterboat skipper from Tilbury, Ontario.

He netted the 12-pound, silvery fish, unhooked it and dropped it over the stern of Up Our Alley, his 35-foot Magnum, without another glance. Bert Cummings, a Monroe angler who founded Bert's Custom Tackle and often fishes with his buddy Joe, was incredulous.

"You Canadians drive me nuts," said Big Bert.

Belanger grew up fishing out of Erieau, a Canadian port about 50 miles southeast of Detroit. Cummings was one of the first Americans to begin fishing there 10 years ago, when it was the world's most incredible walleye factory. That claim now is rivaled by Saginaw Bay and Little Bay de Noc in Michigan.

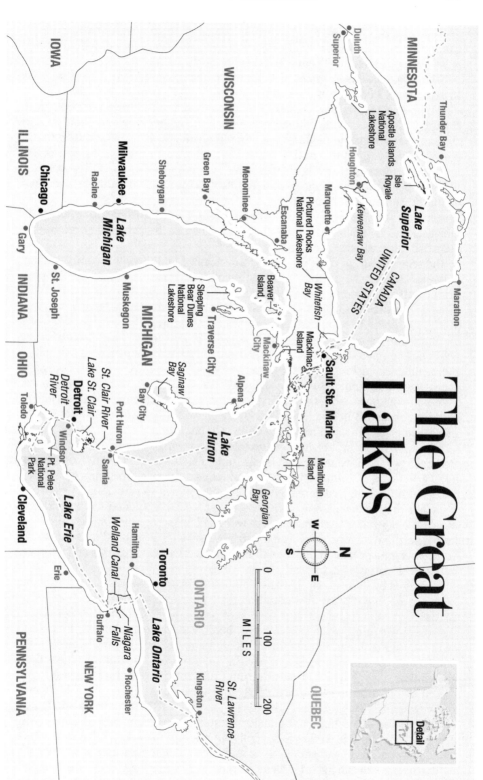

The Great Lakes

MINNESOTA

IOWA

WISCONSIN

ILLINOIS

Duluth
Superior
Thunder Bay
Marathon

Apostle Islands National Lakeshore
Isle Royale
Houghton
Keweenaw Bay

Lake Superior

UNITED STATES
CANADA

Marquette
Pictured Rocks National Lakeshore
Escanaba
Menominee
Green Bay
Sheboygan
Racine
Milwaukee
Chicago
Gary
St. Joseph

Lake Michigan

Muskegon

MICHIGAN

Beaver Island
Whitefish Bay
Mackinac Island
Sault Ste. Marie
Manitoulin Island

Sleeping Bear Dunes National Lakeshore
Traverse City
Mackinaw City
Saginaw Bay
Bay City
Alpena

Lake Huron

Georgian Bay

St. Clair River
Lake St. Clair
Detroit River
Detroit
Windsor
Port Huron
Sarnia

Pt. Pelee National Park

Lake Erie

Toledo
Cleveland

Hamilton
Welland Canal
Toronto

Lake Ontario

Buffalo
Niagara Falls
Erie
Rochester
Kingston

St. Lawrence River

INDIANA
OHIO
PENNSYLVANIA
NEW YORK
ONTARIO
QUEBEC

N
W E
S

0 100 200
MILES

Detail

"All you do is moan that 'the walleyes are gone, the walleyes are gone,'" Cummings told Belanger. "You catch more big steelhead in a day than people out West will catch in 10 years. What more do you want?"

"Walleyes," Belanger grunted as he reached over the side to lift yet another 10-pound steelhead out of the water.

Walleyes are fish our Canadian cousins insist on calling pickerel, even though it should be evident to anyone smart enough to walk and chew gum at the same time that the pickerel is a completely different fish and a member of the pike family (but I digress).

Where a bragging walleye in much of North America is three pounds, Erieau anglers 10 years ago routinely filled stringers with fish that averaged eight and sometimes topped 12.

Alewife numbers were at an all-time high, and an estimated 100- to 200-million walleyes invaded Lake Erie's western basin each spring to gorge on the prey fish all summer.

But such bounty couldn't last. The massive numbers of walleyes soon dropped the alewife numbers by a factor of four or five, and without the prey base to sustain them, walleye numbers dropped to about 30 million.

The size of the walleyes fell a bit, too, although the average of six pounds was still eye-popping to people in most parts of the country.

Then the steelhead showed up about 1995. Perhaps it was because they could out-compete the walleyes in the race for prey. Perhaps it was a result of the commercial fishing operations on the Canadian side of the lake. Or perhaps there was some subtle change in the prey base that we haven't yet recognized.

Whatever the reason, the walleye catch for sports anglers at Erieau fell off by as much as 90 percent, while the steelhead fishery exploded, along with increased numbers of chinook and coho salmon.

In the Pacific watershed where their ancestors came, the steelhead Belanger released would be fish to die for. Unlike resident stream trout, steelhead are a race of rainbow trout that are anadromous — born in a river, then going to the Pacific Ocean to feed for three years before returning to spawn.

When they were introduced to the Great Lakes, it turned out they didn't care if the big water they migrated to were salt or fresh, as long as it contained lots of bait fish to gobble up. The anadromous Pacific steelhead quickly adapted and became potadromous, fish that spawn in rivers and creeks and grow up in big freshwater lakes instead of salt water.

Damaged by dams, pollution and deforestation, most western steelhead and salmon runs have been decimated or wiped out. Anglers from California to British Columbia consider it a good day on many streams if they get a few strikes, never mind catch one. When I fish in the Detroit suburb of Flat Rock each fall for steelhead in the Huron River, a Lake Erie tributary where I have landed and released 11 steelies in one day on a fly rod, I sometimes meet fishermen who have flown to Michigan from California or Washington state.

Out of Erieau, a decent day of trolling is 20 to 40 steelhead. (One skipper I know won a bet by catching and releasing more than 70 in a 12-hour day.) But like many Canadian anglers, Belanger is upset by the change in Erieau's fishery. Lake Erie is still Walleye Central, but the numbers have declined while populations of steelhead and chinook and coho salmon have increased sharply.

The exotic salmon and steelhead introduced 35 years ago have been helped in their task of alewife control by another exotic that is far less welcome, the zebra mussel, which showed up in the mid-1980s.

Zebra mussels are filter-feeders that suck so much water through their bodies that they cleared out immense quantities of the phytoplankton that had made the lakes so murky. One dime-sized mussel can filter enough water every day to fill an oil drum. Multiply that by 1,000 to 10,000 mussels per square yard of lake bottom in a relatively shallow lake (average depth about 60 feet), and the amount of water filtered each day is staggering. It's the primary reason underwater visibility has improved so spectacularly.

That clarity gave an edge to sight-feeders like salmonids over species like walleyes, which find food in lower visibility. And it wasn't just the salmon that were helped.

On another sparkling Lake Erie day southeast of the mouth of the Detroit River, outdoors writer and charter skipper Mike Zielinski and I were telling lies and letting the 10-knot breeze push the boat across the surface. We were doing the Erie drag, allowing our plastic tube lures to bounce across the bottom as the boat drifted while we added an additional twitch every few seconds. The tip of Zielinski's spinning rod dipped, he reared back, and 50 feet from the boat a three-pound smallmouth bass burst through the surface and did a full-gainer with a half-twist before splashing in.

"It's an OK fish, but we still haven't got any of the big ones I ran into yesterday," Zielinski grumbled as he fought the bronzeback to the side of the boat. "We had over 50 fish, and 15 of them were over four pounds."

Smallmouth bass, which had been a by-catch for most Lake Erie anglers, are all over the place now, and in trophy sizes.

The tube lures we were using were a nondescript brown-green that locals refer to as "baby shit." It's an inelegant description but apt. The color matches the round gobies that showed up about 10 years ago after making the trip from the Baltic. These big-headed, bug-eyed little fish have become the preferred food of smallmouth bass in lakes Erie and St. Clair. (They also are preferred by lake sturgeon.)

Bass anglers happily adapted to the goby with mimicking lures, but biologists worry about the long-term effect from a creature that one said "can suck a fish egg out of three inches of gravel."

With all this going for Lake Erie, why do biologists and anglers worry about the future of the lake? To get an answer, look at Lake Superior, the largest of the Great Lakes, nearly 400 miles to the north. With little development on its shorelines, massive Superior is still relatively pristine, but its waters never supported the rich and diverse marine life that Erie did in the days before white settlers arrived.

A Lake Erie as clear and pure as Lake Superior would in large part be an underwater desert with far fewer game fish and the animals at the bottom of the food chain that support the game fish.

The Great Lakes hold about 20 percent of all the world's fresh water because they drain an enormous watershed at the heart of North America. They are laid out much like the decorative fountains in Italian restaurants, a series of immense bowls that spill into one other through connecting rivers.

Superior, which covers 31,700 square miles, or about the same area as Maine, is the highest, with its surface 600 feet above sea level. Michigan (22,300 square miles) and Huron (23,000) are considered separate lakes. (Each is about the size of West Virginia.) But both are 579 feet above sea level and are shaped like a pair of human lungs separated only by the trachea of the five-mile-wide Straits of Mackinac.

Lake Erie is 10 feet below Huron and receives 95 percent of its water from the three upper lakes via the St. Clair River, 420-square-mile Lake St. Clair (really an aneurysm between two rivers) and the Detroit River. From Erie, the water rushes down the Niagara River, plunges 167 feet over Niagara Falls and roars downstream through the maelstrom of the Lower Niagara Gorge to 7,300-square-mile Lake Ontario, 325 feet below Erie but still 246 feet above the sea.

Ontario is the smallest of the lakes in surface area (although not in volume), but you almost could fit New Jersey between its shores.

For millennia, only Lake Ontario had a direct connection to the ocean, and that was through the 800-mile St. Lawrence River, a difficult stretch to navigate. A landlocked form of Atlantic salmon lived in Lake Ontario, and the salmon were so plentiful that colonial farmers could use a pitchfork to fill wagons with 15- to 30-pound fish from spawning streams in a few hours. But those salmon probably hadn't run to the sea since the last ice age, and by 1900 they were extirpated by overfishing and pollution.

Erie contains less water than any of the other Great Lakes. Though Ontario is smaller in surface area, it holds more than three times as much water — 393 cubic miles for Ontario, 116 for Erie. The figures for the other Great Lakes are 2,934 cubic miles for Superior, 1,180 for Michigan and 850 for Huron.

The four lakes other than Erie range in depth from 748 feet in Lake Huron to 1,335 for Lake Superior, far beyond the range of conventional scuba gear. But more than 30 years ago some friends and I, hard-core divers with more machismo than brains, tried to find the deepest place in Lake Erie, which the charts said was a 210-foot depression off Long Point, Ontario. We did some insanely long dives on compressed air, but the most we could record on our depth meters was 203 feet.

Lake Erie averages only 62 feet in depth (compared to 194 to 489 feet for the other four). That means its waters get warmer than the other lakes in summer, although all five can freeze in winter. It takes about 191 years for all the water in Lake Superior to be replaced, 99 years for Michigan, 22 for Huron and six for Ontario. It takes only 2½ years to replace all of the water in Lake Erie.

Lake Erie probably is as clear today as when Samuel Champlain brought the first European ship, the Griffin, onto its waters in 1679. (The Griffin disappeared on its way from Green Bay to Montreal and is one of the most sought-after mystery wrecks in North America.)

When white settlers began carving farms out along Erie's 871 miles of shoreline and building cities on its rivers, there were no trout or Pacific salmon in the lake. There were enormous numbers of lake trout, lake and round whitefish (known locally as herring), sturgeon and a subspecies of walleye that was misnamed the blue pike.

Such taxonomic confusion wasn't unusual. In our day of widespread literacy, libraries, Disney nature movies and the Discovery Channel, many six-year-olds can rattle off the names of 20 species of dinosaurs. But when the Great Lakes were settled by whites, most people couldn't even read and had only the vaguest notions of exotic zoology.

Walleyes are the prime eating fish in Lake Erie today, both for sportsmen and commercial fishermen. But 150 years ago, blue pike were largely a by-catch taken by fishermen targeting the far more valuable Big Four — herring, lake whitefish, lake trout and sturgeon.

Commercial fisheries on Lake Erie shipped 103-million pounds of the Big Four species to market in 1899. Walleye and yellow perch were lumped as "rough fish" along with carp, sheepshead and suckers.

Carp were introduced from Europe about 1880, and by 1900 Lake Erie ports were shipping up to nine-million pounds of carp a year to New York and Chicago, where they were processed into the gefilte fish popular with Jewish immigrants.

Sturgeon eight to 10 feet long and bigger than 300 pounds were so common in the mid-1800s that when they made their annual spawning run out of Lake Erie and up the Detroit River, people speared them out of the rapids (long since dredged away). Then their oily carcasses were stacked on the bank like cord-wood and used as fuel for steamship boilers.

The huge numbers of cold-water species like whitefish and lake trout indicate that Lake Erie was colder in those days before logging and farmland development stripped away the trees that shaded tributary streams.

Blue pike, a subspecies of walleye, became the dominant commercial fish in the 1900s after the Big Four were largely wiped out, but not even the warm-water-tolerant blue pike could withstand the unrelenting onslaught of pollution. By the 1960s, they were extinct.

When clean-water laws began to remove phosphates and other enriching pollutants from their waters, the Great Lakes became places where big fish could make a living again.

Once the water cleanup started, extirpated native species were replaced by other species of walleyes, most introduced from hatcheries. Pacific salmon and steelhead were introduced in all of the Great Lakes in the 1960s (and Atlantic salmon in the 1990s), and the sport fisheries boomed again.

Commercial fisheries also have rebounded, mostly along the northern shore in Ontario, where the town of Wheatley boats the biggest commercial fish landings of any freshwater port in the world (mostly walleyes and perch.)

Something that continues to puzzle researchers is the decline in the perch population in all of the Great Lakes except Erie. Perch were once the most popular food and sport fish in the Great Lakes because they could be caught in large numbers by people fishing from piers or small boats just offshore.

The big question about the difference in Lake Erie is why? And the answer might lie in a tiny, freshwater crustacean, an amphipod called diporeia. This relic of the ice age lives in the deeper, colder waters of the Great Lakes, and some scientists think it's the single-most important food source for many juvenile forage fish and even some baby game species.

Research indicates that diporeia are being starved out of existence by huge numbers of zebra mussels, which can out-compete the amphipods in the daily food-sucking contest. Chunks of Lake Michigan bottom once had tens of thousands of diporeia per square yard, but now often don't have any.

The diporeia in Lake Erie (and adjacent Lake St. Clair) are a different species that evolved to live in warmer water. Not only can the diporeia compete with the mussels, they apparently can eat zebra mussel poop.

I once went fishing for lake trout in western Lake Superior with then-Interior Secretary Bruce Babbitt, whom I admire as a committed and practical environmentalist. (The two don't always go together.)

The occasion was really a dog-and-pony show put together by the U.S. Fish and Wildlife Service, which was pushing the line that lamprey numbers were so low that lake trout had achieved a self-sustaining population in that area and soon would do the same in the rest of the Great Lakes.

I couldn't figure out if the Fish and Wildlife Service were being a bit premature and optimistic, or if it simply was declaring a victory and retreating to cut its losses. But it was a chance to fish the Apostle Islands in the far western end of the lake, and I jumped at it.

Superior is huge, holding as much water as the other four Great Lakes combined. It is cold, clear, and, by the standards of the lower lakes, has a low density of fish. Lake trout, brook trout, steelhead, salmon and walleyes are caught there, but not in the same numbers as in the lower lakes.

In many ways Superior is like the waters that cover tropical reefs. To divers, it looks like a lot of fish are in the tropics, but that's because the reef congregates them and the water is clear enough to see them.

Clear waters don't have much suspended matter, and that makes it tough to support a food chain. Hunting for wrecks, I've been towed miles across a tropical flat on an underwater sled without seeing much more than a couple of six-inch goatfish.

Lake Superior isn't as debauched as the lower lakes partly because of its enormous size and location at the head of the pollution train. But the most important factor is its location north of 48 degrees latitude. There just aren't any big cities or many people on Lake Superior, at least not like Milwaukee, Chicago, Toledo, Cleveland, Buffalo and Toronto.

Those cities pour large amounts of pollutants into the water, some in liquid form and a lot more in airborne particulates from smokestacks. Even if illegal pollution sources are 99 percent controlled, the one percent still getting in is a significant figure when it's produced by 25-million people.

Lakes Michigan and Huron are the twins of the Great Lakes family, but Michigan is richer in fish life and in the number of people along its shores. That's partly because Lake Michigan has the greatest number of tributary streams that have developed natural salmon runs.

The Pere Marquette River sometimes gets runs of more than 50,000 chinooks, and the St. Joseph to the south might well be the finest steelhead river in the lower 48, with big steelies running upriver to spawn in every season of the year. Lake Michigan is also where Michigan started the Great Lakes salmon boom by stocking cohos, and the fish still return to Platte Bay every fall.

Lake Michigan anglers now can fish salmon offshore in spring and summer, along the beaches and from the piers in late summer and in the rivers from mid-August through October. The wonderful salmon runs have turned a dozen once-sleepy waterfront resorts into major charter fishing ports.

One of the most exciting fisheries in the state takes place off southwestern Michigan in May and June, when a wave of coho salmon moves past places like Grand Haven and St. Joseph as the fish migrate around the southern end of the lake to their summering grounds off Wisconsin.

Much more acrobatic than chinooks, cohos are also called silver salmon, and anyone who has seen a leaping coho flash in the sun like a chrome bumper understands why.

The southern end of Lake Michigan also is home to immense numbers of steelhead, mostly the skamania variety propagated in hatcheries in Indiana.

But while salmon get the most attention, there are a lot of other game species in Lake Michigan and great places to fish for them.

Among my favorites, largely because they're harder to reach and get much less fishing pressure, are the islands off the northwest coast of the Lower Peninsula. The Manitous, North and South Fox Island and the Beaver Island group all offer superb fishing for smallmouth bass, and I've also caught large walleyes there in spring and fall.

One of the most unusual Great Lakes fisheries is on the east and west arms of Grand Traverse Bay, usually on nights when the air is so still that lights on shore form long, shimmering streams across the water.

Boats with underwater lights move slowly along the bay with one person at the front holding a spear with a 20-foot handle. The spear man spots a white-fish swimming along ahead of the boat and guides the driver until the boat is almost directly over the fish and the spear can be thrust straight down, pinning the whitefish to the bottom.

It's about as atavistic a form of fishing as you could find, and the first time I did it I kept picturing paintings I had seen of Indians doing the same thing with torches in the bows of their canoes.

The southern shoreline of the Upper Peninsula offers some of the best fishing in Lake Michigan. Little Bay de Noc is justly famed as one of the world's top walleye grounds, but it also produces excellent numbers of splake in spring, smallmouth bass all summer and perch and whitefish from fall through winter. The ice shanty village that pops up each January has to be seen to be believed.

The Garden Peninsula, which forms the eastern shore of Big Bay de Noc, is another superb place to find walleyes and smallmouth bass, and the Summer Islands just off the tip are among my favorite places to sight-fish for big carp.

In terms of shoreline development, Lake Huron is the least spoiled of the Great Lakes after Lake Superior, especially along the Canadian side. There are no big cities on this lake, although it is a conduit for all of the pollutants that wash down from lakes Superior and Michigan.

Lake Huron is also a wonderful fishing lake, but it is still suffering the effects of the huge lamprey numbers produced in the St. Marys River.

The Upper Peninsula forms the northern shoreline of Lake Huron and used to be famous for perch fishing, centered on the village of Hessel. Perch numbers have fallen off dramatically in recent years, and locals blame the immense numbers of fish-eating cormorants, a hook-billed diving bird the size of a small goose that can eat a couple of pounds of perch-sized fish a day.

Cormorants have increased so dramatically that even the politically skittish U.S. Fish and Wildlife Service has swallowed its fears of lawsuits from animal rights groups and agreed to let states kill cormorants in areas where they are causing environmental harm. (The guano from nesting cormorants will turn a green island into a lifeless rock pile in a few years.)

Chinook salmon, steelhead and lake trout are the primary game fish north of Saginaw Bay, and there are large numbers of smallmouth bass, whitefish, brown trout and carp that get relatively little fishing pressure away from a handful of small ports.

In Saginaw Bay, walleye is king, or queen, to be exact, because all of the eight- to 12-pound fish the bay gives up in amazing numbers each year are females. At one walleye tournament in the summer of 2002, anglers who made the cut for the top 20 were bringing in six fish each day that averaged six to seven pounds, and the winner posted a four-day average of 7.2 pounds per fish.

Saginaw Bay also has some excellent smallmouth and largemouth bass fishing, but the most underused and underappreciated species is probably the channel catfish, which can be caught in large numbers by still-fishing or trolling night crawlers behind a spinner. A four- or five-pound catfish is a nice size in most of Michigan, but Saginaw Bay routinely gives up channel cats of 15 to 25 pounds.

South of Saginaw Bay, Lake Huron fishing is mostly about salmon, with a big enough mix of lake trout, brown trout and steelhead that the angler can never be sure what has grabbed a trolled lure until he sees the fish.

Ontario is the only Great Lake on which Michigan does not have a shoreline, yet what goes on in Lake Ontario has a bearing on what happens in the other four.

Cities like Rochester, N.Y., and Toronto are destinations for ocean-going vessels that bring in unwanted exotic species, both plants and animals. Ontario is also the most polluted of the Great Lakes, its waters so tainted by mercury, Mirex and other harmful chemicals that no fish is fit for human consumption. That shouldn't surprise anyone, because it sits at the bottom of the chain, and Ontario gets all of the contaminants that don't settle out in the four lakes above it.

The irony is that while Ontario is contaminated with harmful chemicals that weren't there before World War II, the lake actually looks much cleaner than it did 60 years ago.

That's because the national Clean Water Act of 1972 led to the removal of most of the nutrients that caused algae blooms. Reducing the density of these tiny plants turned Lake Ontario from a rich broth to a consomme, a change that was enhanced by the arrival of zebra mussels.

A couple of days from now I'll go on another Lake Erie fishing trip, this one with my pro bass fishing buddy Gerry Gostenik and Free Press photo editor Craig Porter, another avid angler. We'll catch some big smallmouths, one of which will grace the cover of this book, and we'll have a wonderful time.

And we'll undoubtedly talk about what the future will bring for this remarkable body of water and its sisters. Government agencies talk about managing the lakes, but the truth is that they have largely treated them as a giant aquarium, throwing in various species and then standing back to see what happens.

Management assumes that you have control over a situation, and the truth is that with the steady influx of exotic species, we really can't say what will happen next in the Great Lakes. So far, we haven't shown the will to overcome the political roadblocks that have prevented us from imposing the drastic and admittedly expensive solutions needed to keep exotics out of the lakes, or at least slow their rate of arrival.

Perhaps it will take something like the cholera epidemic that broke out in Peru in 1991 and is thought to have originated in the ballast of a ship from Asia. (Asian cholera bacteria also have been found in Mobile Bay in Alabama and in ballast samples taken from ships that entered Chesapeake Bay.)

And things like bacterial kidney disease in salmon, the drastic decline in perch in many parts of the lakes and a recurrence of the sea lamprey scourge in northern Lake Huron in the mid-1990s taught us that we often don't have as much control over the things we try to manipulate as we thought.

One thing I do know is that no matter what we do, Erie and the other Great

Lakes will adapt to whatever we throw at them and will be here long after we are gone. I only hope that if some great-great-grandchild of mine ever reads this book, he or she won't wonder how we could have been so stupid.

Chapter 21

Fishing books

T HE FIRST FISHING BOOK, AS FAR AS WE KNOW, WAS "A Treatise on Fishing With an Angle," written about 1420 and attributed to a semi-legendary English nun named Juliana Berners, or maybe Berness, or Barnes. No one is quite sure.

The truth is, we're not even sure she existed, or that the book isn't a compendium of early Renaissance fishing lore to which someone attached a well-known lady angler's name.

My guess, from the style and language, is that most of the treatise was written by one person. And the writer could well have been the abbess of a 15th Century convent, who lived in the country and had the leisure time for such pursuits as angling at a time when 99 percent of the population spent all their waking hours trying to get enough to eat.

No matter who wrote it, it's fascinating that if you tie the flies according to the patterns described by the author nearly 600 years ago and fish them on English streams at the times recommended, you will catch trout. In fact, if you tie these wet fly patterns, you can catch fish on streams and lakes almost anytime in North America, Chile, New Zealand or anywhere else trout live.

"A Treatise on Fishing With an Angle" is proof positive that you can learn a lot about fishing from a book. The key is taking the information you derive from the printed page and practicing on a lake, river or ocean until you've mastered how to put those literary lessons into practice.

Fishing has the largest bibliography in the literature of sports. Passionate devotees were divulging their secrets on paper a half-century before the printing press was invented, and once that tool arrived (my candidate for the most influential invention in history), fishing books became commonplace.

Many plagiarized the work of previous authors. (Izaak Walton appropriated some of Berners' fly dressings.) But it was an era when the idea of copyright hadn't been conceived, and there were so few books that most authors probably thought any literate person would recognize information taken from previous texts.

My library of a couple of thousand books about fishing, hunting and other outdoors subjects would have been one of the largest collections of any kind in Europe when Walton wrote "The Compleat Angler" in 1653, yet today it would fill only a few shelves of a small municipal library.

Few of my favorite fishing books are how-tos. They're mostly stories about going to fascinating and beautiful places and meeting intriguing people, which is why I love fishing so much. Fishing has taken me around the world, from rocky bays in Japan, where I caught four-inch minnows I never identified but which my host popped instantly into a shore-side frying pan, to a rocky headland in northern New Zealand, where I caught a 200-pound striper that filled my dance card for all of the world's marlin species.

Fishing has taken me from a mangrove swamp on Australia's Van Diemen's Land, where I used a fly rod to catch turbocharged snook called barramundi, to the Ile St. Louis in Paris, where the grandeur wasn't provided by the 10-inch tench we caught in the River Seine but by the gothic bulk of Notre Dame Cathedral soaring in front of us.

Fishing has taken me from the Loop in downtown Chicago to streams in the Canadian sub-Arctic, where I caught char in a horizon-to-horizon landscape with the nearest building 500 miles away. Fishing has taken me from Tierra del Fuego at the tip of South America, where I caught brook trout that measured almost as much in pounds as the native brookies measure in inches in the streams near my home in northern Michigan, to Arctic Norway, where I fished under the midnight sun.

Despite the opportunity to fish perhaps 150 days a year and travel to wonderful places, I'm still a sucker for a good fishing book and go armchair-angling four or five evenings a week. I even carry fishing books with me to read in hotels, cabins and tents while I'm on fishing trips.

The following selection includes most of my favorites, at least this week. They are books I would be happy to have on a desert island if I also could have a fishing rod, some hooks and a few other bits of tackle. A few of these books are still in print, but most would have to be found in libraries or used-book stores.

"The Compleat Angler," Izaak Walton, 1653

Born in Stafford, England, in 1593, this unrepentant bait-flinger went to London, where he became an ironmonger, a high calling for a merchant in those days. His status as far more than a lowly tradesman is evidenced by close friendships with wealthy and influential merchants and noblemen, and he gained literary acclaim as the biographer of several celebrated Englishmen.

But what we remember him for best is the wonderful book about fishing in 17th Century England that translates beautifully into a lesson on why we fish in 21st Century America. The language seems quaint, even naive, something a lot of literary critics think was the deliberate ploy of a sophisticated writer, and a lot of the biology is well-dressed superstition. But we can still learn a lot from Walton's argument that fishing should be the contemplative man's recreation.

Walton was also one of the first writers to appreciate the wonders of nature for their own sake. And when we read his instructions on making tackle, collecting hair from a horse tail and twisting and dying it to make lines, and preparing elaborate baits, we realize that this man took his fishing a lot more seriously than most of us do.

Make sure the copy you read contains the additional section on fly-fishing, added to the book by Walton's influential and worldly young friend, pupil and promoter, Charles Cotton. Cotton's addendum is to this day one of the best books written about fly-fishing, and even 350 years later we should heed his most famous admonition: "Fish fine and far off."

"A River Runs Through It," Norman McLean, 1976

If you want to learn the facts of Southern history in the first half of the 20th Century, read historian C. Van Woodward. If you want to understand what it was like to live in the South in those days, read the novels of William Faulkner.

McLean was more than 70 years old and a retired University of Chicago English professor when he sat down and did for the smaller world of trout fishing what Faulkner did for Southern history. McLean used the experiences and perspective from his long and rich life to write a novel that tells us far more about why people are the way they are than any history book could.

In McLean's case, the story is about a family and the powerful role that fly-fishing and trout and the love of wild places played in creating and maintaining the relationships among the people in it.

"A River Runs Through It" is one of three stories in the book. When director Robert Redford convinced McLean to let him make it into a movie, Redford was wise enough to recognize that this was a case where less was more, and he didn't try to jam bits of the other works into the framework of the most important one. He also did something I think was brilliant, lifting entire long lines and even paragraphs from the book and keeping them in the characters' mouths rather than trying to rewrite something that was nearly perfect.

A number of anglers curse the day the movie came out, saying it filled their previously uncrowded streams with hordes of yuppies whose only fly-fishing skill was pulling out a credit card in a tackle shop.

Most of those new fly anglers probably never went back to read "A River Runs Through It," never mind its two companion pieces. But if you love fish and fishing and wonderful writing, you should.

"Going Fishing," Negley Farson, 1943

The son of an American Civil War general, Farson was a journalist who roamed South America and Europe in the tumultuous days between World War I and World War II, when economic and social revolutions shook the fabric of civilization.

He began fishing as a kid in New Jersey, and to get through his early, lean years as a short-story and freelance writer, he moved his new bride to British Columbia, where living was cheap and he could provide much of their food with a fly rod. But even more remarkable than his passion for fishing was his ability to draw word-pictures of some disparate characters, from semi-derelict oyster dredgers on Chesapeake Bay to the fish chef on the luxury liner Olympic.

Farson was a wonderful writer, and he soon became the American correspondent for a London newspaper. Then he was hired by a wire service that recognized his talent and sense of adventure and sent him to Europe. He lived in England until his death in 1960.

A bon vivant, connoisseur of fine wines and whiskeys and a brilliant observer, Farson always carried some fishing tackle, bought tackle wherever he found himself or borrowed some from a local.

Farson's luminescent words were recognized by the publisher of "Gone Fishing" (Harcourt, Brace), who acknowledged his skills by hiring the brilliant illustrator CF Tunnicliffe to produce the superb drawings.

This is my favorite fishing book. It includes virtually no how-to information other than some casual mention of favorite lures and places, and it might be the best book about fishing for people who don't fish.

By the way, my copy was bought at a used-book store and is inscribed: "To Scott from Bob and Anne, Birthday #9, Grand Rapids, Mich., Aug. 14, 1976. When you read this, please write me telling me how to fish. Your Grandfather."

I wonder if anyone around Grand Rapids knows who Scott, Bob or Anne were?

"Trout Madness," 1960, "Trout Magic," 1974, John D. Voelker

I own first editions of each of these books by one of Michigan's most celebrated writers, printed under his pseudonym of Robert Traver. But I also own the 1992 reprints issued in his real name a year after his death, and I think it's more fitting that people read those.

Better known to the reading public for writing "Anatomy of a Murder," a best-seller that became a successful movie, Voelker had a folksy, gentlemanly style that comes off even better in the wonderful books he wrote about his first love — fly-fishing for trout.

He managed to get across — even to people who didn't fish — the reasons anglers love the sport, a passion best expressed in his eloquent "Testament of a Fisherman."

But the lines from John D. Voelker that best explain why and what we do come from the preface to "Trout Madness." While he speaks of trout anglers, the lines apply equally to all of us whom Walton called "brothers of the angle."

"The true trout fisherman is like a drug addict; he dwells in a tight little dream world all his own, and the men about him, whom he observes obliviously spending their days pursuing money and power, genuinely puzzle him, as he doubtless does them. He prides himself on being an unbribed soul. So he is by way of being a philosopher, too, and sometimes he fishes not because he regards fishing as being so terribly important but because he suspects that so many of the other concerns of men are equally unimportant."

Voelker, a former chief justice of the Michigan Supreme Court, was born and reared in the Upper Peninsula around Negaunee, where his father ran a bar in the days when logging was king and loggers were serfs. I was lucky enough to know Voelker and drink and argue with him at Frenchman's Bend, his UP fishing camp near Marquette.

When I met him, I was a hotheaded young environmental writer who wanted all the world's evils to change now, and my way, by God, and he used to infuriate me because he wouldn't use his fame to get out front in the fight for environmental causes.

Actually, "argue" isn't the right word, because arguing wasn't John's style. I would rage on while he sat there drinking his old-fashioned from a tin cup he claimed had touched the lips of actress Lee Remick. ("Anatomy" made her a star.) He would shake his head at the points in the diatribe where he disagreed, then smile and say, "That's just not what I do."

In the long run, I guess he was right, because no one can read "Trout Madness" or "Trout Magic" without learning a lot about why it's important to keep the places he wrote about alive. And I suspect John Voelker will be teaching that lesson for generations to come.

Ken Schultz's "Fishing Encyclopedia & Worldwide Angling Guide," 2000

Schultz was well into his plan to rewrite, expand and reissue the fishing encyclopedia first produced by the legendary A. J. McLane when he confessed: "If I'd known what an incredible job this was going to be, I'd never have started it."

Schultz, an editor for 26 years at Field & Stream, also said, "I don't know how A. J. did this in the days before computers. He had to keep everything on 5-by-7 file cards and in his head."

But Schultz pulled it off, and this 1,916-page, 10-pound volume contains just about everything about fishing you could possibly want to know. It's not just as good as the original, which would be saying something, but better, because it contains a lot more stuff that has come along since McLane's book was last published 20 years ago.

Want to know the best time to catch tigerfish in the Zambezi River in Africa? Page 1,705. How about instructions for tying a Bimini twist double leader for bonefish or muskellunge? Page 869.

I should tell you here that I wrote the Michigan section for the book, 12,000 words about our wonderful state. That's the equivalent of six weeks of Thursday outdoors pages in the Detroit Free Press, but it makes up only .0068 percent of the encyclopedia.

"A River Never Sleeps," Roderick Haig-Brown, 1946

Far too many fishing books, maybe most of them, are treatises on techniques that will help the angler derrick more chunks of meat out of the water and into the freezer.

If that's your reason for fishing, I would suggest that you stop wasting your time and go to the market and buy fish. But Roderick Haig-Brown knew that killing fish was the last reason to go fishing.

He was an Englishman who moved to Vancouver Island, British Columbia, where he worked at jobs ranging from logger to army officer to magistrate to chancellor of the University of Victoria. He already was a hopelessly committed angler when he moved to Canada at the age of 23, and he fell passionately in love with the trout and salmon of his new home and the stunningly beautiful landscape in which they lived.

His writing comprises a large body of work, but this one, a study of the characters of different rivers and different species in every month of the year, is probably Haig-Brown at his best.

Like most of the greatest angling writers, with the exception of Traver, Roderick Haig-Brown did not fish for a single species or with a single technique. He caught steelhead on the fly and pike with a casting rod, and he even writes of taking mackerel in the ocean with a hand-line.

He was also one of the keenest observers of nature, and his descriptions of the insects, birds and mammals that live in and around streams are as entertaining and brilliant as his descriptions of the fish.

"The Compleat McLane," A. J. McLane, 1988

The first time I ate kahawai was 20 years ago at a restaurant in West Palm Beach, Fla., where it was on the menu as Pacific cod or some such silly name, and it was delicious.

But what impressed me most was that my dinner companion, the late angling writer A. J. McLane, took one bite and said, "That's kahawai," a conclusion that was confirmed when we sent the manager to the kitchen to find out from the chef what the hell we were eating.

In a 50-year career, McLane wrote dozens of books and hundreds of magazine pieces, and his opus magnus, "McLane's Standard Fishing Encyclopedia," sold more than 750,000 copies.

"The Compleat McLane" is a superb collection of his shorter works that illustrates all facets of his writing, from simple and clear how-to treatises to an encyclopedic knowledge of ichthyology and biology to an ability to turn a phrase as colorfully as any writer in the genre.

One of my favorite examples of the latter is the beginning of a story about a trip to fish the Amazon in South America:

"I rolled over just to drain the sweat from port to starboard, and the effort woke me up."

And if you want an opening line that will guarantee that you just have to read the rest of the story, how about this one from a story about a trip to Africa:

"There is an island in the mouth of the Congo River called Ile de Pecheurs, where on any normal day you can build a fire on the beach and wait for the fish to walk out of the water."

McLane was not just one of the most prolific writers of books and magazine articles about angling and fish cookery, in my mind he was one of the two best.

The other is Zane Grey, whose third-rate western novels are still being published years after his death, while his first-rate fishing books are largely forgotten.

"The Undiscovered Zane Grey Fishing Stories," 1983

There is a varnished wall of kauri wood in a fishing club at Russell, New Zealand, where you can see a series of carefully inked lines written in a fine penmanship that has been out of style longer than the fountain pen.

That wall was found dismantled and collecting dust in a storage room about 15 years ago, and it was about to be burned with a lot of other trash when a particularly sharp teenager who had been hired to help clean the place noticed the writing and brought it to the attention of a club official.

The entries are about the marlin, yellowtail, tuna and other catches made by Zane Grey when he visited New Zealand in the 1920s while he was the most highly paid writer and most famous fisherman in the world.

Grey produced some of the worst westerns and best fishing tales ever written. But that dichotomy should only have been expected from this strange, moody and mercurial man, a dentist who couldn't make a living fixing teeth but could hit home runs for a semipro baseball team; an early conservationist and environmentalist who grew furious when Arizona refused to exempt him from new hunting laws, and a writer who could produce the dreariest and most resplendent lines not just in different books but in the same short story.

For an example of the latter, read "The Fisherman," a short story published in installments in Outdoor American magazine beginning in 1924 at the height of Grey's fame. It was to have run for years and traced the growth of Lorry Dunn from boy to man, using his deep love of fishing as the continuing centerpiece.

Writing about Lorry's early fishing lessons from an old man, Grey said, "This pond was the fisherman's place to catch the rarest bait for bass, the golden shiner. Lorry loved to go there. The walk through the rustling cornstalks, the hidden nature of the pond nestled under high-wooded banks, flower-skirted and bird-haunted, the turtles sunning themselves on logs, the water snakes gliding down through the moss and ferns, and the illusive, golden-sided, tender-mouthed shiners, so difficult to catch — these things made the place dear to Lorry."

There isn't an angler alive who can read that long, convoluted and yet crystal-clear sentence without remembering, hearing and smelling a similar secret place in his own life.

And yet later in the same story, Grey decides to have the teenaged Lorry visit a bordello, of all places, where our hero is arrested, and we encounter purple prose like this:

"Then Lorry realized that the girls had been locked in the adjoining cell. By flattening his face against the grating, Lorry could see the girl Laurie. "You're a game lad. I'm sorry. You fell in with bad company. . . . I'd like to believe you'll never go into such a house again."

"I — never will," Lorry whispered, and his thoughts flashed to the old fisherman.

"Keep away from bad women — like me," she went on. "Only ruin can come of it, for such as you. I know."

Shortly after this installment was published, "The Fisherman" disappeared from the magazine and never appeared again. Some of Grey's biographers think it's because he dared broach such taboo subjects as brothels. I suspect it was because the editors realized that much of the story was so badly written that readers were turning away in droves.

I decided a long time ago to treat Zane Grey the megalomaniac western writer and celebrity as a different person than Zane Grey the brilliant angling writer, and it has worked pretty well for me.

While Grey wrote numerous fishing books and stories, this volume is a good one for the uninitiated because it illustrates such a broad expanse of his strengths and failures, and it contains one of his most powerful pleas for conservation, "Vanishing America."

In it, Grey wrote: "Naturalists and biologists and true lovers of nature either despise or disapprove of sportsmen. There is some justice in this. Something is wrong. Our heritage of outdoor pursuits is certainly a noble and splendid thing. Manly endeavor and toil and endurance makes for the progress of the race. Nature abhors weaklings. And red-blooded pursuits operate against the appalling degeneracy of modern days. Nevertheless, sportsmen, as a mass, are hypocrites, and are blind to the handwriting on the wall."

As the French say, the more things change . . .

Epilogue

That's why it's called fishing

WHEN HE WAS EDITING EARLIER CHAPTERS OF THIS BOOK, Owen Davis, a Free Press sports editor who is an outdoors guy, said, "Don't you ever catch any big fish? All you write about is losing them." I thought you would never ask.

The best thing about being an outdoors writer is that I get to catch a lot of big fish, mostly because I go to many of the best places with the best people at the best times.

If Dan Donarski calls from Sault Ste. Marie to say there's a fantastic salmon run in the St. Marys River, I usually can drop everything and be there the next day, or even that day. If Bert Cummings calls to say that 12-inch perch are lining up to commit suicide on a hook in Lake St. Clair, he knows I might beat him to his boat.

But the average angler probably couldn't respond to those calls until the weekend, assuming other obligations don't get in the way, and a lot of things might have changed by then.

Which is why you should take newspaper and magazine stories about fantastic fishing not so much with a grain of salt as with an understanding that you might not duplicate the conditions that produced those huge catches. That said, I do have some wonderful memories of fish that could have been caught by anyone.

One June evening I wandered down to throw poppers at the bluegills rising in front of our boathouse on Lake Margrethe near Grayling. A half-dozen neighbors were sitting on the adjoining lawn, having sundowners and generally having a good time razzing me.

I was using a three-weight fly rod — seven feet, nine inches long — and when a fish rose to take a bug off the surface I dropped the popper on top of the rings and saw it disappear.

When I raised the rod to set the hook, it bent nearly double, and line started peeling off the tiny reel at a startling rate. It took nearly 15 minutes, but I caught and released a 19-inch smallmouth bass, a solid five-pounder I could be proud of landing on a three-pound tippet.

I was with Mark Orlowski on his boat Fishin' Pole, trolling for muskies on Lake St. Clair, when one of the rods started giving up line. It was sheer luck that it was my turn at bat, and the 51½-inch muskie is still my personal best (although I've had a dozen others longer than 48 inches).

I've been lucky in that I've been able to fish for dozens of species under the tutelage of some of the finest anglers in the world, and I've tried to pass on that information and encourage other people to try the same thing.

Something I want to stress is that while you can learn a lot about fishing from a book, you can't learn how to fish from one. That comes only from going out on the water and putting into practice what you learned or developing techniques of your own. And while you're learning how to fish (a process that never ends, by the way), you should follow the first commandment of fishing: Thou shalt have fun.

When we go fishing, we're not going to do much to repair the national economy, advance the cause of world peace or generally better the lot of mankind. What we can do is spend a few hours or days enjoying one of life's great pleasures — often in the company of friends.

Not long ago I packed my laptop computer, cameras and tackle and got on an airplane for another fishing trip. Three plane changes later I landed on a lake in northern Manitoba in Canada and spent five days fishing for big pike and walleyes.

Some people fished from dawn until it was time to come in for dinner. Some returned to the lake after dinner, got in the boats again and continued to fish until dark.

A few weeks ago, on another fly-in trip, I talked to a Canadian bush pilot who told me about some American anglers who enjoy a different kind of fishing experience. Each year, he flies the same four men to a remote lake in northern Ontario. They take their camping gear, a couple of canoes, some fishing tackle and 30 cases of beer.

They camp for a week in a beautiful place. They see moose, bear, deer and other wildlife, catch enough walleyes each day to make a meal, and drink beer. They don't see another human for the whole week. They don't see a television or hear a telephone. They don't see a car or hear a siren.

When the pilot picks them up, they carry out all their empties, and he said he always brings in another case of beer because they sometimes run out the day before he arrives. It's not my idea of a great fishing trip, but they're happy.

Earlier in the summer, I drove about 45 miles to join Charlie Mann and his sons, Travis, 15, and Eric, 12, fishing for bluegills on the lake at a resort where

Charlie has spent a week every summer for 36 years.

We caught a bunch of bluegills on sponge spiders and small poppers, a couple of bass on a little spinner bait, and discussed everything from the U.S. appellate court decision that banned the words "under God" from the pledge of allegiance to America's fascination with the cult of celebrity. We had a wonderful evening, and I'm looking forward to seeing them again on another little lake they fish near their home in Metamora.

The point I'm trying to make is that fishing can be a lot of things to a lot of people, and no angler or group of anglers has a corner on the right or best kind of fishing. Nor is any species of fish biologically or culturally superior to another. Only people make such distinctions, not nature.

I've been fly-fishing since I was five years old. Now I'm 59. And one thing that bothers me after 54 years of practicing this art is how it continues to be infected by snobbery.

I can assure you that fly-fishing hasn't done anything to improve my intellect, social status, looks or sex appeal. If you don't believe me, ask Susan, my wife. And from what I've seen of my fellow fly fishermen, it hasn't done any of those things for them, either.

What it has given me is a fantastic amount of enjoyment in some wonderful places and an endless amount of mental exercise in a quest to outsmart a creature that has been around a lot longer than we have.

One reason fishing is so fascinating is that it offers so many different lines of pursuit. Some people, me included, are generalists who will fish anywhere for anything. My favorite forms of fishing at the moment are with a fly rod for salmon in rivers, tarpon in salt water and big carp on the Great Lakes flats, but I'm just as happy catching crappies on a cane pole or bass on a bait-casting rig.

I'm also fascinated by the history of angling and the varied fishing techniques used by people around the world. I sometimes find myself spending more time watching how other people catch fish than I do fishing myself.

I've even been thrown out of a restaurant for casting little flies to the long-domesticated koi goldfish in a foyer fountain while our group waited for a table, just to see if the fish retained some of their wild instincts. (They took the flies, too.)

Variety is the spice of life when it comes to fishing, at least as far as I'm concerned. I get a big kick out of catching fish I've never caught before or catching familiar fish by new methods, say a catfish on a fly rod or a walleye on a hand-line.

But then I'll go out with walleye pro Mark Martin and see the delight and excitement he gets in catching a walleye by the same means he used to catch a jillion before.

I have quite a few friends who are single-species specialists, spending nearly all of their angling hours in a narrowly focused pursuit of bass or walleyes or tarpon or trout. They know far more about these species than I'll ever learn, and they soak up every new piece of information that comes out.

So who has the most fun, or gets more satisfaction out of fishing, or even learns the most? I sure as heck can't say.

Larry Nixon, one of the country's top bass pros, once came in from a day on Lake St. Clair as the leader in a tournament where first place was worth $150,000, and all he wanted to talk about was a 50-inch muskie he had landed on eight-pound spinning tackle.

"I just like any fish that will pull on my string," he said.

John Voelker, who wrote some of the best trout stories ever told under the name Robert Traver, said in his "Testament of a Fisherman" that one reason he loved trout fishing was that it took him to beautiful places.

I guess I love all kinds of fishing because it sometimes takes me to places that are beautiful, and sometimes to places that are not beautiful and yet are even more fascinating.

One of my favorite fishing memories is playing big carp on the Chicago River in the heart of one of America's biggest cities, and looking up to see office workers 10 stories above us mouthing unheard cheers of encouragement from behind the thick glass walls.

And I still laugh when I think about the time we caught big bass that were living happily in and around the rusty old cars, refrigerators, washing machines and other assorted scrap of a flooded Florida junkyard.

But what I like best about fishing is the constant challenge. It is without question the most intellectual of sports. We've been doing this for several thousand years, and yet none of us can predict with 100-percent certainty that a bass or trout or any of the hundreds of species we fish for around the world will take the same lures tomorrow that they hit so eagerly today.

Maybe that's why I get a bit nervous over the technological advances that keep coming along, things like underwater TV cameras and sonar so sophisticated we might soon be able to pick out different species without actually seeing them.

I'm such a gadget weenie that I can't help trying them. But there's usually that nagging question in the back of my mind about when do we reach the point that we give ourselves an unfair advantage, when anybody can be a success not by learning how to fish but by buying the right gear?

I guess the answer is pretty simple. I'll keep at it as long as I can continue to tell people, "That's why we call it fishing and not catching."

About the Author

E RIC SHARP, THE OUTDOORS WRITER FOR THE DETROIT FREE Press, has been a reporter for 35 years. He previously worked for the Buffalo Evening News, the Associated Press and the Miami Herald.

Sharp has covered airplane crashes, race riots in the United States, social upheaval and natural disasters in Central America and the Caribbean, a dozen manned space flights, national political conventions and environmental issues.

Covering Ronald Reagan's 1980 presidential campaign convinced him that life was far too short to waste on trivia, so he became an outdoors writer, spending 10 years at the Miami Herald and the last 12 at the Free Press.

Since then, he has opened his eyes each morning, looked around and thought, "Good. They haven't caught me yet. I have at least one more day."

Sharp, a native of Scotland, came to this country when he was 10. He has hunted and fished around the world, produced several books on outdoors issues and won numerous awards for his writing.